MW00872777

# It Is What It Is

## ...But It Wasn't A Tragedy

a sharing about life challenges, worldly living,
redemption, and new beginnings

Written by Debra Lee
with
Co-Author Frankie Valens

ISBN: 1484858840
ISBN-13: 9781484858844

Library of Congress Control Number: 2013909157
CreateSpace Independent Publishing Platform
North Charleston, South Carolina

*My soul finds rest in God alone;*

*My salvation comes from him.*

*He alone is my rock and my salvation;*

*He is my fortress, I will never be shaken.*

Psalm 62:1-2

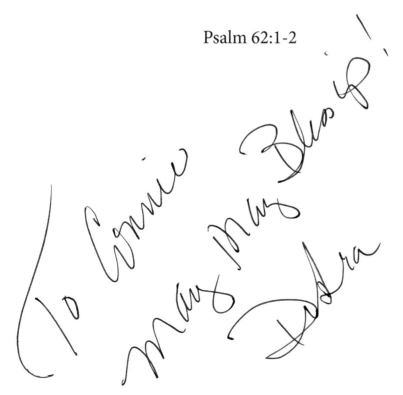

# CONTENTS

*Acknowledgments* vii

*Introduction* ix

1. A SOLID FOUNDATION 1

2. THE FISH BOWL 13

3. JAIL HOUSE ROCKS! 23

4. ABC'S…WITH A TWIST! 35

5. OFF TO THE BIG CITY! 51

6. LIFE CAN CHANGE IN AN INSTANT 65

7. BACK TO MY FUTURE 77

8. THE PRIVATE GIRL'S COLLEGE 99

9. MY SLOW DESCENT 107

10. MY MR. X 117

11. THE ROOT OF ALL EVIL? 131

12. MR. X'S SHENANIGANS 167

13. THE FIREMAN WAS A GENTLEMAN 179

14. A LIFE GIVEN, NOT TAKEN 197

15. WAS I BEING TESTED? 211

16. REDIRECTING MY LIFE 229

17. BRINGIN' HOME THE BACON 237

18. FAMILY HOMECOMINGS 247

19. CHILDREN ARE A GIFT FROM ABOVE! 261

20. AN ATTITUDE OF GRATITUDE 273

21. LESSONS LEARNED 279

Amusing Bonus Stories 311

# ACKNOWLEDGMENTS

### To My Dearest Husband:
**Thank you** *for simply loving me. I haven't always been the easiest to love! You've been with me through thick and thin, and you have seen the good, bad, and the ugly in me. I know I'm a roller coaster ride, but you are my anchor and you keep me grounded;*
*Yet, you let me take flight and soar!*
*I love you deeply!*


### To My Dear Friends
### Frankie & Phyllis Valens:
**Thank you** *for your encouragement, invested time, and help in writing this book. Without you, this project would still be just a thought in my head.*


**To All of My** *friends and acquaintances who have encouraged me over the years to write my life's story because you felt it was interesting enough to minister to others through a book.*
*Thank You!*


### Thank you Mom and Dad
### for everything!

# INTRODUCTION

This book is an unapologetic story about my life and has been written from my perspective. It just seems to be that if five people witness an accident you may end up with five different points of view, and such could be my story. So I've written this book only from my point of view and from what I felt as each event unfolded. You may have to read this book at your own risk because I have revealed myself very openly and candidly on every page.

You will see throughout my story where bad decisions resulted in bad circumstances which in turn resulted in some hard consequences to deal with. Sometimes things just happened that were not within my control, but through it all I gained an inner strength that could only come from God.

My story is about my having to face many trials that life threw at me and how I learned to keep my faith and stay encouraged and positive when I really didn't want to. My story will reveal how I thought I could do it all on my own without God's help and the problems that arose because of that choice. This is a sharing about my faith walk and how God was ever real and present in my life and through it all He revealed his saving grace that has made me extremely appreciative.

As I have grown older it has become apparent that I have been known for using a couple of phrases: "*It is what it is*" and "*Put your big girl panties on and deal*!"

The first phrase initially means that things just happen to us that are out of our control and they didn't happen because we necessarily made a bad decision or because we weren't living our life well. There was absolutely nothing within our power that could have changed what happened! As I peal open each layer of my soul you will see that sometimes my life could simply be described as *it is what it is*!

The second phrase *"Put your big girl panties on and deal"* simply means that we can choose to become a victimized, martyred, helpless soul, or we can pick ourselves up and deal with what happened, process it and move on whether it was from our fault or by default.

Many people have weaved in and out of my life over the years and some have told me that I should write a book, but for most of my life I have tried to remain private because of the circumstances under which I was raised. As you read my story you will start to understand why.

Over the years I have shared some of my testimony in public forums, but because of time limitations and the venue settings I do not always have the time to share details or the whole story. Many people have stopped to talk with me after my speaking engagements and want to know the rest of the story, so here it is!

This book no doubt may spark some people into gossip sessions and if that might be you then you simply have missed the point.

The point of this book is to share a story that I have been given. To share about a God that is always patient, loving, caring, and protective and a story of how He waited for his child to return to the faith. It's about my faith walk and how I grew in that faith with Him by my side. It's a story that I pray will offer hope and encouragement to those who are struggling with many of the same issues and circumstances that I have lived through.

I am not someone who just wants to take up space on this earth, so I hope that this book will reveal that I want to make a positive difference wherever I am, wherever I go, while sharing my story.

Again, read at your own risk. Sometimes the *real* may jump out at you and rip at your heart, the *real* at other times may leave you shaking your head and then again the *real* may have you laughing out loud, because after all, *it is what it is*!

# ONE

# A Solid Foundation

*But as for me and my household, we will serve the Lord.*
**Joshua 24:15**

### Roots of Faith

All during my growing up years I have to admit that a great part of my attitude and my walk of faith came from my family who honored the Lord. I cannot remember a time in my life that I hadn't heard about Jesus. Even though we didn't go to church regularly when I was young, I always knew about God's love. My immediate family and extended family members all helped to ground me in the faith. It all began with them…

### My Father's Family

I remember my dad's parents as Christian people and even though my grandpa passed away when I was six years of age I can still remember grandpa as being a very big tall man; a very gentle giant. He had gotten up one morning and suddenly died of a heart attack. Grandpa was a very good writer and knew how to articulate his letters well and they were always filled with love. With his gift of carpentry he made his grandchildren pieces of furniture or toys that they could cherish forever. He had made me a small dresser with a mirror that was just my size and I kept it for years. I have since passed the dresser on to my niece and told her that it was a special gift from her great-grandfather whom she never knew.

When grandpa was a single man he served in the armed forces in France during the war. He had promised God that if he was brought home safe and sound from the war he and his family would serve the Lord. Grandpa held true to his word because when he returned home he was able to get his siblings to attend church again. He also wanted to attend college but the family had other plans for him and wanted him to stay on the farm and work. He ended up leaving the family farm near Argonia, Kansas, and *walked* to Hutchinson, Kansas, to attend college to earn a business degree. I know where some of my stubbornness comes from!

My grandpa's parents were Christian folks and raised their children the same. My Grandpa had a great start in life as well. His mother was a very colorful lady and most kids were afraid of her. She was a tall German woman who ruled the roost. She insisted that all of her family be with her every Sunday for dinner. In her house the adults always ate before the children did. Grandpa's father was a short German man and was the quiet type. Hmmmm...I wonder why?!

My grandparents met in Hutchinson while grandpa was still in college and while my grandma was living at a boarding house. When they married grandma was not exactly welcomed into grandpa's family with open arms mainly because she had come from a divorced family, and back then there was quite a stigma placed on divorced people.

My grandparents had five children. How many generations were affected by grandpa's decision to follow the Lord? All five of their children became believers and a great legacy was left for all of their grandchildren and great-grandchildren to come.

My dad and his younger brother were the youngest of the five kids. They always seemed to be into mischief and full of orneriness while they were growing up. Grandma had to use her broom a lot on those two boys! I can only imagine what that might have looked like; grandma chasing those boys around as she swatted them with her broom!

My grandmother outlived grandpa and unfortunately the last few years of her life was spent in a nursing home as she was unable to care for herself. I will always remember my grandma for her flower gardens and large vegetable garden. She canned vegetables, made sweet beets, sweet tea, and made homemade apple butter. She loved to quilt and even taught me how to knit.

There was a time when we lived only a few blocks from grandmother and I would see her walk past our house on her way to the grocery store pulling her two wheeled wire grocery cart behind her. Grandmother was lost when grandpa passed away. She didn't drive and she hadn't even written a check on her own. When she would walk by our house she always looked so lonely. I knew it must have been difficult for her without grandpa. I felt so sorry for her and would run out to greet her on the dirt walk path and she would always give me a hug and a smile.

## My Mama's Family

My mother's parents were both Christians. My grandma became a Christian when she was quite young but my grandpa became a Christian after he had met my grandma. After they married they decided to live near grandma's family in Arkansas.

My grandparent's first daughter, Betty Josephine, died at birth. I could always see the hurt in grandma's eyes when she would talk about her. Before they laid their daughter to rest they took many pictures of her. She was a beautifully formed baby girl.

Soon the war and the depression made everything really rough and there weren't any jobs around. It was then that my grandparents move up north to Dayton, Ohio, to be near my grandpa's side of the family where there seemed to be more jobs available. Defense work during WW II was the trade at that time and that was what my grandparents did for a living. My mother was born in Dayton.

Mother was eight years of age when her family decided to move to Wichita. Grandma went to work at a defense plant until the war ended and then she started working at a meat packing plant and packaged wieners.

Grandpa went to work for a defense plant as well. After the war he and a brother-in-law went into business and started an auto repair shop. The business was located next to my grandparent's home. They worked that business together until it caught fire and burned to the ground. The flames came extremely close to their family home and grandma stood outside with her garden hose hosing down the house to protect it. Grandpa then went to work managing a drive-in theatre for several years and later became a security guard until he retired.

There was a time during my grandparent's younger years of marriage that their spiritual life had taken a turn to the left and they had fallen into social drinking with all of the silliness that that involved. Grandmother finally put a stop to it and they got back into attending church. My mother was about eleven years of age at the time.

I knew my mother's parents the longest and have the fondest memories of them. We had lived next door to them for several years. Grandma was a very hard worker. She, after all, was raised on a farm and was used to working like a man! (She would always remind us of that!) She would work all day at the plant, come home and tend to her gardens, and then made sure that the inside of her home was spotless! Grandma's home was quite modern and very nice. She was quite a super woman!

Grandma would give anyone the shirt from off her back. She was quite a business woman and she amassed a good sized fortune. She had put away funds and invested well. It was not out of the ordinary at all for family members to come to her and ask for a loan. I don't recall her ever turning anyone away. She was such a giving person especially to her church and family.

If you showed up at grandma's unannounced, no *biggy*! She would always put on a big spread and she was a great cook! No one ever left her home hungry! She was also a great hostess as well and invited not only family and friends but also her preacher and his family over for Sunday dinners after church. Most big family get-togethers were held at her house and what great times we had! The house was usually full of relatives, good food galore, and those who knew how to play an instrument (mostly all by ear mind you), would pick up an instrument and play. We would all sing hymns or just have fun singing folk songs.

Grandma was a beautiful strong woman who dressed very fashionably and up-to-date! She was quite a lady. We used to call her our swingin' granny! She exuded confidence and had a fight within her like none other. However, she really was insecure about a lot of things and felt inadequate most of the time. She just never saw herself the same way as others saw her.

On the other hand, grandpa was a quiet gentle soul and not very outgoing at all, but a good decent man. He and my mother were best friends. They were pretty tight while mom was growing up. He would spoil her, in his own way. She was definitely daddy's little girl!

He could do magic tricks and loved to keep us kids entertained and amazed by his talent. He also loved to collect coins. I will always remember the times he spent looking at his prized coin collection. He would hum a tune while he examined his coins or when grandmother was getting on his case about something! I always thought that it was so funny how grandpa controlled his temper by humming. Kudos to grandpa!

I remember my grandparents were very active in their church. Grandpa served as a deacon and as the church secretary while grandma served as the Sunday school teacher for the teen group.

When we were quite young my family moved out of town and away from my grandparents. My brother and I would look forward to their visits as they would always bring us gifts! The minute they pulled up into our driveway my brother and I would run out to meet them with excitement.

"What did you bring us?" we would ask.

We would quickly open the gift that they brought us and we'd jump for joy! Holidays were just as special with them. Grandma would always go all out for us two kids! She always treated my brother and me like we were her own kids. Yes, she was awesome!

I lost my grandfather to cancer when I was in my mid-twenties and I lost my grandmother to Alzheimer's when I was in my early forties. I have such treasured memories of my grandparents for them being in my life. Memories that are forever etched into my heart!

My grandma's parents, my great-grandparents, were simply good hard-working farmers. My great-grandmother was a very, very sweet Christian woman. She never cursed and never had a temper. On the other hand, my grandma's father, my great-grandfather, was overly strict with his children. He had lost his first wife in child birth and came into the marriage with three children. My great-grandmother was a divorced woman who came into the new marriage with three children of her own. The stigma of divorce left her not being treated well by some of my great-grandfather's family. Together they had five more children! I could kind of see how great-grandfather might have been out of sorts with the kiddos! That was definitely a house full! In *their* household the children and the adults ate together.

My great-grandfather was a pretty good business man who owned property and amassed a large sum of money from his farming skills. He didn't trust banks and he never told anyone where he had hid all of his money. He passed away from the results of a stroke and never had a chance to tell anyone. Rumor was that he had buried his small fortune on his property. He only had one trusted long-time friend and some speculated that possibly the friend had taken it. There was a lot of property to search but no one ever found it, which left my great-grandmother penniless!

My great-grandmother eventually came to live with my grandparents and my mom. She spent a lot of time with my mother while my grandma worked. Mom told me all kinds of wonderful stories about her grandmother and about all of the fun they had together. Towards the end of my great-grandma's life her children took turns taking her in to live with them. She eventually died from injuries that she received from a car accident.

My grandpa's parents, my great-grandparents, were quite colorful I might say! While they lived in Dayton, Ohio, they had divorced. My great-grandfather was a traveling preacher man and traveled the country. Not much else was known about him except for what state he was buried in. On the other hand, my great-grandmother was quite something else!

Even though I was quite young I can still remember my great-grandmother. In fact I was afraid of her! It seemed like she just didn't like children and I think I had sensed that. She was into spiritualism, the Ouija Board, talking to the dead and levitating tables! Yes, my mother was a witness to that. Pretty creepy stuff!

My great-grandmother had a twin sister, my great-aunt, but I didn't think that they looked much alike at all. I met her only once when she came for a visit and all I can remember about her was that she was so nice and liked children!

## Mom and Dad

My parents seemed to me to be the best looking people on this planet earth! They simply looked good together. Even when I was in grade school and a classmate would ask me what my dad looked like, I would always tell them that he looked like Elvis Presley!

My parents had the usual courtship and became engaged in 1952. My mother had become a Christian when she was about twelve years of age and dad became a Christian during the time of their engagement. They married in 1953.

Dad had been attending WSU, played football, and was also a part of their music program playing the violin and playing it very well!! After mom and dad were married he didn't finish college and joined the Marines after being drafted and was stationed in California. Mom had been working at the county courthouse as a secretary and after dad had finished boot camp, mother was able to be with her husband in California. When dad left the Marine Corps they returned to Kansas and I was born in 1956 and my brother was born in 1958.

My dad was a larger-than-life kind of a person! When he walked into a room and smiled, the party began! My dad's career determined where we would live like most families in those days. Dad was a very outgoing, hardworking, a little rough around the edges sometimes, and wasn't afraid of anything which was good considering he chose law enforcement for his career!

Dad was also an inventor and he liked to make board games that we as a family could enjoy. The games that he created were fun and entertaining. Even some of my parents' friends would enjoy playing the games. Dad actually had applied for a patent for one of the games, but he forgot to follow up on some paperwork and the game was taken by a well-known company who produced it! He kicked himself over that one! Another time, he and some of his friends invented the first keyless entry pushbutton lock for vehicles back in the 60's. They had applied for the patent, but the idea was stolen by a large motor company and we see that system still being used to this day. Bummer!

In my dad's later years he became very involved in the church serving as a deacon and singing in the church choir. On occasion he would play violin solos. He was never afraid to witness to anyone and often would go downtown early on Sunday mornings and bang on the train cars to wake up the people who had spent the night there and ask them to come to church. He also visited the homeless shelters and did the same. I only wish I had his bravery! The church would provide breakfast for them and dad learned early on to be sure that none of the people had been drinking. A fight broke out in church one Sunday…oops!!

One time my dad knocked on the door of a prostitute who lived across the street from my parents and asked her if he could take all of her children to church on Sundays. She didn't mind at all and the kids loved my dad. I can remember those kids running through the church halls after Sunday school waving their color pages.

"Mr. Hanna, Mr. Hanna!" they would scream.

They were so excited to show him their art work and would tell him what they had learned in Sunday school. Eventually they moved away but just to think that those kids will probably never forget Mr. Hanna. He took the time to be with them and gave them attention regardless of what their family situation at home was all about.

My dad made a positive influence on many people while he was on this earth. If a prisoner asked him faith questions it was nothing for him to witness to them as he drove them off to the state pen. When he retired from law enforcement he tried his hand at several kinds of sales jobs and security guard positions but eventually started his own business. He worked very hard at his business molding it and shaping it and in doing so he learned a new trade that he practiced till the end of his life. He in fact had paid off his business a month before he passed away!

Several years after my dad had passed, my mother received a phone call from a woman who had tried to get a hold of my dad through the police station but was told that he had died. She was so insistent upon talking to one of his family members so the police station gave her my mother's phone number. The woman had been watching a television show about camps for troubled youth where they could go to and get help and it had reminded her of her younger days and how she had had a run-in with my dad when she had visited the town where he was the Police Chief. She said that she had been selling sweepers door-to-door in the community and my dad was called out to have a visit with her because there was a city ordinance that did not allow for door-to-door sales. He had given her a verbal warning.

My dad received yet another call a little bit later stating that the young woman was still out there selling door-to-door! My dad went to meet her again, and once again he gave her a verbal warning. She was so gutsy that she continued to go door-to-door and my dad had no choice but to arrest her. That could have been a very bad experience for her except for the fact that within the short amount of time that she was in his custody, his said something to her that literally changed her life.

She said that while she was watching the television show she had come to the realization that if my dad had not arrested her, her life would have gone down the wrong path and she could have very easily become one of those troubled youth shown on that television screen in one of those camps! The woman simply wanted to tell my dad how thankful she was and that because of him her life had changed! Yes, my dad was larger than life!

My mother was a stay-at-home mom who raised us kids basically on her own because of my dad's work. My brother and I were very close in age so my mother had her hands full most of the time. I always felt that she was a very stern willed woman and very beautiful. She always had on her make-up, her hair was always well kept, and she was always in a dress. Even to this day she always looks all gussied up and I'm proud of her!

My mother has an operatic singing voice and she plays the piano. One Sunday, when I was quite young, mother sang a solo in church, "The Lord's Prayer." It was like hearing an angel sing. She has served in the church choirs wherever she has attended and has taught piano lessons over the years and still gives lessons to this day.

She is also quite an artist and has done many drawings and paintings. She loves all kinds of crafts and does each one very well. When we were in grade school she enjoyed teaching Bible lessons to the neighborhood kids once a week.

Mother was always involved in genealogy and traced both sides of our family's history. She has compiled two books over the years that took many hours of research. I remember as a small child we would travel from cemetery to cemetery looking for head stones with certain names. Most were very old cemeteries and were overgrown. I remember one time I had gotten up really close to a head stone that was all over grown with brush. I was getting ready to clear away the debris when a rabbit jumped out of the grave! I tripped as I scrambled backwards and let out a loud scream…and about wet my pants! Silly *wabbit*!

When we kids were about to graduate from high school mom took up a new career and started working at a nursing home as an aide. Soon afterwards, my dad convinced her to become an Emergency Medical Technician. Because of all of the gore that was involved in that one I was really shocked that she was doing that! The next thing I knew she had started studying to become a Physical Therapist Assistant. She remained a P.T.A. until she retired.

Yep, my mom and dad were meant for each other. Their different personalities and strengths complemented each other and family was very important to them. They raised their two children to have good values, good work ethics, and to love the Lord with all of their hearts.

"We come from a background of stubborn, hard-headed, hard-working people!" my mother states.

My parents really did do it right, not always perfectly, but right! They gave us a solid foundation to build our lives upon.

# TWO
# The Fish Bowl

*In everything set them an example by doing what is good.*
*In your teaching show integrity, seriousness and soundness*
*of speech that cannot be condemned, so that those*
*who oppose you may be ashamed because they have*
*nothing bad to say about us.*
**Titus 2:7-8**

### My Childhood Home

I personally do not remember my early childhood home in Wichita. Our first home was the home that my mother grew up in. My grandparents had purchased the property when they had moved to Wichita along with several lots around their home. My mother and my grandma described the property as having several different varieties of fruit and nut trees and a large vegetable garden that produced every year. The house had been painted light grey with pink trim and had decorative window shutters all around. There was also a small detached garage that matched. It was a very cute well-manicured home, at least from the pictures that I've seen.

In the early 1950's my grandparents built their new home right next to that small house. The new home was quite modern for its time and was beautiful but not overstated. My parents even held their wedding reception in the new house.

After both of us kids were born, my dad joined the Sedgwick County Sheriff's Department and it was required of him to move to the small town of Clearwater, Kansas, in order for him to hold that position. I don't remember the move because I was only about three years of age at the time.

During the move, according to my mother, she had packed the medicine cabinet in the back seat of the car and apparently I had taken some of her diet pills. Yes, they caused me to be wired for a bit. My eyes were as big as saucers and I was pretty jittery! The doctor told my mother that there was nothing to do but to let the diet pills wear off! This could explain a lot of "*things*" about me, right?

Clearwater, Kansas, is where I have my earliest recollections of a childhood home and it was called the Carter house. I am assuming that was the family name of the folks who owned the house. It was a white bungalow house with a basement, an attic, and a detached garage. On one side of the house were pear trees while the other side of the house had stickers!!! My little brother was still in a crib and we shared the same bedroom. When my parents first brought him home from the hospital apparently I told them that he was *my* baby! Mom told me that she never had to watch him much because I was always watching and taking care of him for her.

One day while we both were playing in the back yard my brother accidentally flipped some dirt into his eyes. So being the little mommy that I seemed to think that I was, washing his eyes out was the most logical thing to do, so I took him inside to our bathroom and proceeded to wash his eyes out…with *Borax Soap*!!! Mom had been outside working in the side yard and my little brother's bloodcurdling screams coming from the bathroom caused her to rush into the house to see what was going on. By the way…she took over for me.

With my brother and I being so very close in age people sometimes thought that we were twins. We were very close to each other and I am sure that we gave mom a run for her money most of the time. There was a family that lived across the street from us who had a rather large family and I am guessing that they had fifteen children. There were a few times that our mother had to get the experienced-neighbor-lady-mom to help get us out of a fix, especially with my little brother!

I can still remember the time when my brother had gotten a dry cleaner clip stuck on his tongue. It was one of those clips that you couldn't tell if you were to squeeze it to open it up or pull it to open it up. With the wrong move my brother could have ended up with a pierced tongue and that was way before piercing the tongue was an in-thing! Mom of course had to go get the neighbor lady to help and of course she knew just what to do. With the right motion she freed my brother's tongue!

My brother was not alone when it came to silliness and getting into mischief. I too, yes me, caused a little chaos as well. My dad had brought home a retired German shepherd police dog to live with us. I didn't like the dog because he scared me. He would bark all of the time and was a little mean and I did not like it when he would jump up on me. We mainly kept him chained to the side of the house. (Back in those days that was still acceptable.) To avoid him, I would walk on the other side of the house, the sticker side, to get to the backyard and take my chances with the stickers.

One morning, while my dad was trying to eat his breakfast, he became very annoyed that our dog was barking so he told me to go shut the dog up. I did. Being the obedient child that I was I wouldn't want to refuse a direct order. Now mind you, I do not remember this incident but was told about what had happened. I am sure that I have blocked it from my memory banks. Anyway, that's my story and I'm sticking to it! I went out to the garage and picked up a crowbar. I proceeded to walk over to the dog and whacked him over the head, and yes, knocked him out…

job done! Needless to say, dad later ended up getting rid of the dog. That dog just wasn't a good fit for us.

My mother's parents purchased a swing set for us kids while we lived in that house. It was a very well-made colorful swing set that was placed on the side of the house where the pears trees were. It was very sturdy and it lasted for many years. We had so much fun playing on that set! My grandma was also into home videos and she had recorded in living color some of the times that she had watched us play on that swing set. It was always fun to watch the reel to reel tapes as we grew up. Those old home movies were a wonderful reminder of the fun that we had when we were quite little.

A scary incident happened at that house that left quite an impression on me. My mother was pregnant with her third child. Mom didn't have easy pregnancies and that one went awry in the early stages. All I can remember was that my mother had gone to my brother's crib and tried to lift him up when something didn't seem right. Mom quickly put him back down in the crib and ran to the bathroom! My brother was secure in his crib and after quite a while I went into the bathroom to check on mom. When I opened the bathroom door I saw blood everywhere. At that point I was truly scared!

Mom told me to close the door and to please go sit down in the living room. I can remember her making her way slowly to the telephone and watched as she almost passed out. The next thing that I remember was the ambulance arriving and the attendants bringing in a little bed; I watched as they placed my nearly lifeless mother on it. Quickly the ambulance disappeared with our mommy. The experienced-nice-neighbor-mom from across the street stayed with us and kept us calm until my dad could arrive to take us to stay with my grandparents in Wichita.

My mother barely made it to the hospital in time. She accredits the ambulance driver, who wasted no time at all, for driving her quickly to a hospital in Wichita. He literally saved her life because of his fast driving skills.

We sure missed mom a lot while she was in the hospital and our grandma had realized that, so she made a plan to surprise us kids. When mother was released from the hospital grandma kept us occupied in her kitchen while mom was being snuck into the house. Once mom was seated in the living room grandma told us that she had a surprise for us. It was mommy!!! I will never forget how she looked. She was so beautiful with her makeup on and her hair so perfect, and all dressed up in a pretty light blue dress. We were so happy to see her! We both ran to her and hugged her as she kissed all over us.

For many years after that incident and well into my grade school years I would often have the same reoccurring dream. Mom would be driving down a dark dirt road at night. While I peered through the windshield all I could see was dust all lit up by the headlights. We were moving along at a pretty good speed. My brother and I were sitting in the back seat when all of a sudden mom would disappear and the car was driving its self! I always woke up startled and totally scared. I suffered with that reoccurring dream for a long time until I finally had the nerve to tell my parents about it. My father simply explained to me that after what I had witnessed with my mother's miscarriage, I was afraid of losing my mom. Dad's words made sense and were comforting and the dreams eventually stopped.

### Living in a Fishbowl

I can barely remember our move from Clearwater, Kansas, to Kingman, Kansas. I just remember mom driving our car following a truck that carried all of our belongings. Someone must not have packed the boxes very well because I can remember that some clothing had flown out of the back of the truck as we traveled down the highway.

The home that we moved to in Kingman, Kansas, was in the same building as the sheriff's office and the county jail. *Yes, I grew up in a jail house!* The entire building was made of cement, steel, and cinder blocks for obvious reasons. The outside of the building was of red brick and it had a bright blue trim all around the top of the roof line. On the inside of the building were the sheriff's office, a waiting room, a public restroom, and jail cells. The only thing separating our living quarters from the jail was our kitchen door. The jail itself had a smell all of its own that I will never forget! To best describe the eau de toilette to you, I would have to say that it consisted of a mix of disinfectant with a high note of body odor while adding a rich woodsy tone of sleeping off a drunken night!

Our back porch was 'U' shaped with my bedroom window on one side, the kitchen window and a door in the middle, and jail windows on the other side. We had an attached garage that had a door that also led into the jail. The sheriff's office had its own front entrance and we had our own front entrance as well.

As a little girl I thought the home was large but my mom referred to it as an apartment. The home was fairly new and quite modern but there was no carpet, just cement floors covered with linoleum tile. We had two bedrooms, one bathroom, a nice large living room, a dining room, and a kitchen. All of the walls were painted cinder blocks.

We had a nice large basement with simple wooden stairs leading down to the cement floor. We used the basement for storage and a play area and eventually dad turned a part of the basement into a gun range to practice target shooting. Yep, that could get pretty loud at times! Then there was THE FURNACE; a very large furnace. It looked mean and when it kicked on it looked like a dragon with fiery teeth. Yes, that was the one thing that I was afraid of in the basement!

Our yard was huge with many tall trees. Everything was very neatly manicured and was kept up by a gentleman who was responsible for the upkeep of the county property that we lived on. A creek ran through our backyard that branched from the Ninnescah River. I remember the fresh mint that grew wild along the creek and I played in the creek whether the sandy creek bed was dry or whether it had water flowing through it.

The mint smell filled the air with its good fragrance, but the snakes… not so good!

The back yard had a long clothes line and a large incinerator to burn trash in. Our swing set had been set up in the back yard where we spent many playful hours. My dad taught me to ride a bike in our long drive-way and I had lots of fun making mud pies on the back porch.

We lived next door to the county courthouse. The building was made of beautiful old brick and limestone and it had a grand limestone stair-case entrance. It was huge with many floors. Inside of the courthouse were wooden staircases and old ornate architect pieces from the era in which it had been built. I thought that it was a really cool courthouse! I even pretended that it was a palace and that a princess lived at the very top! We kids were never allowed to play in the courthouse for obvious reasons but once in a while we would sneak over and check it out before mom would discover us missing and have to come and retrieve us.

Between the sheriff's office and the county courthouse was a large parking lot that visitors could use for either building. We kids would use the parking lot when it was empty to ride our bikes in. It was graveled so you didn't want to crash on it!

Across the street to the south of us was a train station. At times it got pretty noisy as trains came through. I remember waking up during the night when a train blew its whistle and I would look out of my bedroom window and watch the trains quickly move through our area. I often made up stories in my head about who was riding on the trains and wondered where they were headed. These trains were sometimes mostly cargo trains but that didn't matter to me; my imagination would still play the game. During the day I would watch the train cars back up and connect to other cars. I found the whole activity very interesting!

Across the street to the west of us was a funeral home. I tried not to think about that one too much! I didn't want to creep myself out by thinking about the dead bodies in there. There was a lot next to the funeral home where mangled vehicles were towed to. That was pretty creepy too, especially if someone had died in a crash. Out of morbid curiosity we would sometimes walk by the locked chain link fence to see the smashed cars wondering if we would be able to see any blood.

The downtown area of Kingman was a block away from our home. Since we only had one car and my dad would have to use it as a patrol car most of the time, we usually ended up walking wherever we wanted to go. Downtown was a typical old Kansas small town scene with brick paved streets, a few stop lights, and cross walks. The buildings were from the original era of long ago. We had a grocery store, a theatre, banks, and many businesses. School was about five blocks away from our home and that trip was made on foot as well. And yes, to my little self it seemed like a mile uphill both coming and going!

Kingman was a quaint little town where neighbors were friendly and everyone helped each other out during the hard times. Some of the homes had the white picket fences and all! To all appearances it would be a really good place to raise children. Most who lived there only saw the good in the community and cherished it for all of their lives. However, our family got to see the dark side that lived in that small town. We saw how cruel people could be to each other. We knew of the darkness that lived in some of the homes. Yes, we sometimes got to look evil right in the eyes!

The move to Kingman put our family in a fish bowl for the whole community and county to watch. Dad had originally taken the position as undersheriff and at the next election he ran for sheriff and won. He won future elections as well. It was hard growing up with every move that we made being watched, every speculation about us being made, with gossip and malice heard here and there. Our lives were no longer our own. We lived in the public eye to be scrutinized by friends and foes.

We did not ask for that kind of a life. We loved dad and supported him fully but mom and us kids, well, I just don't think that we were ready for all of that. We kids were very young in the beginning of the fish bowl experience so we only had basic understandings about what was going on. We came to a more subtle awakening when we started attending school.

All I know is that we all had to learn how to deal with life in the *fish bowl,* and very quickly.

## THREE
# Jail House Rocks!

*Blessed is the man who perseveres under trial, because when he has stood the test, he will receive the crown of life that God has promised to those who love him.*
**James 1:12**

### Family Dynamics

I was only four years of age when we moved to Kingman, Kansas. One memory that I have of that moving day occurred right after we had just arrived at our new home and it left quite an impression on me. A local sheriff's officer snuck up behind me and hollered as he lifted me high into the air. It caught me so off guard that it scared me to death! The officer ended up being one of my dad's good friends and co-worker.

My parents had been raised in homes where affection was just not shown much. Everyone just *knew* that everyone loved one another. Love was shown by what one person did for the other, how they treated each other, how each other was provided for, standing by each other, and the love put into that good old home cooking spoke volumes and provided great comfort! There was not much affection shown, if any, in our home as well. I did witness my dad sneaking up and giving mom some affection with a quick kiss on the cheek or a quick slap on her behind. Those slaps made her yelp and caused us kids to giggle! I always like watching them together as they shared such rare moments like those displayed in front of us.

I think that living in a fish bowl really affected our family dynamics on several different levels and we always had to be careful with how we acted in public. I learned those lessons pretty early on.

One example of learning how to live in a fish bowl was a time when my dad had brought some high ranking men home to meet our family. Apparently they had first stopped in at the sheriff's office for a visit. We hardly ever had a chance to see dad because it seemed like he was always working. So when we had a rare occasion such as that one, we jumped on it. I innocently ran to my dad and grabbed him around his legs and hugged him as hard as I could, but mom quickly grabbed me and pulled me away. She then pulled me aside and told me to never hug my father in front of other people ever again! I was totally perplexed and asked her why.

"Because it doesn't look good," she said

I have never forgotten how strange I felt and how hurt I was at the time, but then again, it was all just part of living in a fish bowl.

My family didn't show much affection at home and they especially did not show emotions or affections in front of other people or in public. I do remember my dad holding me a few times when we were watching television together. I would run and hug him when he came home from work and he would grin ear to ear and then raise me high to the sky. I can only remember dad spanking me once and boy was that a spanking! The next time I actually remember dad ever hugging me was when I was a twenty-eight year old adult!

Please don't get me wrong my parents loved us kids unconditionally and we loved our parents the same. It did take me many years to figure out a few things about my personality type though; I do like to hug people and I also love touching people when I talk to them. It was just something that I had to suppress as long as we lived in the fish bowl.

Because of the way that I am wired affection was something that I really needed, craved, and missed as I was growing up.

I remember that it was really hard for us to go out in public as a family like going to a movie, eating out, or for any other occasion for that matter. Even going to church as a family proved to have the same crazy effect, so we didn't go to church together on a regular basis. People would *always* approach dad with problems that they were having with a neighbor or with land issues, public issues or a crises in their lives, instead of letting us simply enjoy our time together as a family. Many times we would just go to another county to have family time.

My dad was on call 24/7, so when he could get time off we would get away by going camping and fishing. We had some pretty fun times with our camping excursions. Mom would always pack fun food for our trips, or in other words, junk food! I always looked forward to those special sweet cakes that she would pack!!

Invariably we would always get a storm when we would go to one lake in particular and one time we even encountered a tornado! We had just gotten camp set up with our tent pitched and all was good with the world when out of nowhere came a tornado! It quickly grew dark but we could see the tornado between lightning strikes out on the lake. We immediately took shelter in our car and slept in the car all night long while the storm passed by and rocked us kids to sleep.

The next morning we noticed that the camp sites were all mixed together with camping gear and debris everywhere. We decided to pack it up and head for home…a total bust! We kids were very disappointed to have to return home with all of the fun food still packed away and never opened. Mom joyfully declared to us that we could have those tasty treats anyway!!! Yippee!! By the way…we never attempted to camp at that lake again.

There were times when my grandparents would go camping with us as well. One time we had a camp site set up at Fall River Lake, Kansas, and it was our first time to visit there. It was a different type of place than what we were used to. The Fall River Dam is located on Fall River, a tributary of the Verdigris River in Greenwood County. The scene was beautiful with lots of wildlife and plants and it was a perfect place to camp and fish. There were a lot of sharp rocks and different types of creatures to watch. After we had pitched our tent we retired for the evening. We had a large tent which slept all of us. Everything was very, very quiet, except for a few occasional bugs calling. Then out of nowhere, in the midst of the silence, my grandmother started screaming.

"Bear, bear, bear!" she hollered.

It woke all of us up with such a startle! We were all scrambling in the dark and the next thing we heard was my dad's very annoyed voice.

"Oh good grief, it's just the dog!" he growled.

Apparently our dog was outside of the tent and my grandmother's fingers were sticking out a bit under the bottom of the tent and the dog started licking her fingers. Grandma had grown up in an area where there were bears and in her unconscious sleep she thought she was being attacked! What a hoot!

I had an aunt and uncle who owned a vacation spot on a lake in Oklahoma where we would spend time together as a family. To me it was like taking an explorers adventure. It was wooded and the entire atmosphere offered up a lot of fun. What I didn't like was the outhouse with all of its smells and bugs, but staying in the homey trailer made up for it! Sometimes our aunt, uncle, and cousins would be there as well. The older cousins had their own small trailer that they stayed in and it was of course a privilege to be invited into *their* hangout!

I remember my dad taking us on boat rides to the marina in the mornings where we would get bottled chocolate milk! I loved it!! I also remember a couple of funny stories from when we took those Oklahoma trips.

We always took our family dog with us and he was quite a protector for a Dachshund! He would take on any creature like possums, cats, and a SKUNK!!! Oh yes, he took on a skunk and the skunk won the fight!

That poor dog was so sick…and so were we as we had to deal with the skunk stinking dog. We did everything we could to get that smell out of the dog which included throwing him into the lake! He was just so miserable and had developed white rings around his poor little eyes. It took a bit of time for that awful smell to wear off.

I also remember one time when I had gotten something in my eye and it was hurting. My dad tried to take a closer look at my eye by lighting a match and holding up my eyelid. It was evening and the lighting was not all that great in the trailer. He would have me roll my eyes up and down while he tried to find the object. Then all of a sudden we both started smelling something…oh my! It was my hair! Dad had caught my bangs on fire!!! What a smell!! I think my burning hair smelled worse than the skunked dog! Yes, I had funny looking charred black short little bangs for a while.

In spite of our strange family dynamics that we were living in, we still managed to have fun and created memories that would be cherished forever.

## The Jailhouse

Our growing up in the jailhouse proved to be quite rocky at times and the venue created its own dynamics for the family. All of a sudden my mom was thrown into being the jail matron and cooking for all of the prisoners when they arrived. She was paid fifty cents per plate for the food and her labor. That doesn't seem like a very good deal to me! It just seemed like she was always in the kitchen cooking three meals a day for several prisoners on a regular basis as well as cooking for her own family. Then she had all of those pots, pans, and dishes to clean up and without an electric dishwasher in our home! Mom taught me how to wash the dishes for our own family but she didn't think that it was fair for me to also have to wash the dishes for the jail. Those she did herself.

The grocery shopping for our family and for the jail was yet another challenge. Trying to make ends meet with her being paid just fifty cents per plate...well let's just say that mom had to be very creative and she made it work. When she prepared the meals she would load up the jail trays and deliver them to each prisoner. Often the sheriff's office would receive a letter from a past inmate thanking my mom for the great food that she had prepared for them.

Since there were no police women around at that time, mom had to be in attendance for the body searches done on women prisoners. She would also have to sit in on women's or girl's depositions regardless of how ugly the situations or crimes were. And mind you, some of the stories that she sat in on were the descriptions of horrible sexual violations that the women and children had endured.

The sheriff's office was where everyone would come who had issues and most didn't care if the office *was* closed. They were going to show up and voice their opinions about something regardless of the time of day, or night.

I remember one night when a drunken man came knocking on our back door and it was late. Of course, as luck would have it, dad was out on duty and mom had to deal with that man. I woke up from a deep sleep and listened to a conversation that my mother was having with that drunken man as she tried to get him to leave. He simply didn't understand that my dad was not at home for him to talk to. She finally convinced him to leave. Soon I heard a crunching sound. Low and behold the man had crashed into one of our trees while backing his car out of our driveway! Where is a cop when you need one?

When we had moved to the jailhouse my brother and I were very young and we didn't understand the total picture of living with prisoners and the constant danger that we were in. We could hear the prisoners talking whenever we played on our back porch. Sometimes they would holler out at us and talk to us. In our orneriness we thought it was pretty funny to go around to the other side of the house where mom could not see us and we'd taunt and harass the prisoners through their bared windows that were open. Sometimes we would get a response from one of them. But, as it would be, we finally got caught by one of the officers and got into some big time trouble for doing that!

Through all of that unconventional life that we were living my parents had to be very protective of us kids. Not like normal parents who only had to worry about bicycle wrecks, crossing the streets safely, or childhood illnesses. My parents had to teach us on a level that we could understand about the dangers and threats that were always lurking around the corner for our family. But they didn't want us to be scared, fearful, or nervous, so they were very careful on how they instructed us about those dangers. They were adamant that we were to always come straight home after school and they wouldn't let us go to anyone's house until the families were basically checked out. We were never told about any of the crimes going on in the community or any of the cases that my dad was working on in order to protect us. My parents had to constantly know where we were at all times.

I remember one repeat prisoner in particular. He stayed in our jail so often that we kids even knew his name! Mom and dad had warned us about him and told us to report it to them immediately if we were to ever see him hanging around. Apparently he had threatened to harm us kids. He showed up one day while we were outside playing on our swing set. He stood near the corner of the house where dad and mom couldn't see him and watched us play for some time until I got nervous enough to run into the house to tell mom. Of course he had disappeared before dad could get outside.

We also had two jailbreaks that happen while we lived there. We're talking pretty scary stuff! The first jail break happened when two prisoners were able to break out of the outside bared windows. The windows and bars looked like they had been blasted out. Their escape was done only by their hands, a saw, and with some sure determination; that was what got it done!

They somehow got into our home probably with the hopes of finding money to help with their getaway. As fate would have it mom was sound asleep on the sofa while we kids were asleep in our beds. They left when they came across mom *and she never even knew that they were in the house!* She didn't find out about it until later. I can only imagine how creepy she felt as she realized how horribly wrong that all could have turned out!

The second jailbreak involved the same two men that were involved in the first jail break and that one happened a few months later! The two were caught pretty quickly after the first jailbreak and were brought back into custody at our jail. That time their plan was to break out of jail while we were at church. Somehow they knew that our family would be attending the evening Christmas program that my brother and I were performing in. One of the prisoners had starved himself for quite some time so he could eventually squeeze through the bars located at the point of the ceiling. Apparently there was a little bit larger gap at the top. Once he got through he was then able to let his partner in crime out.

When we returned home from our church program dad had opened our kitchen door that led into the jail to check on the prisoners. There in front of him on the floor was glass scattered everywhere from where one of the doors had been broken out. Dad went all white and looked like he had seen a ghost! We were all just a little frightened by the whole event unfolding before our eyes. Dad immediately searched our home just in case they were still in the building, but they had already gone. However, we knew that they had been in our home. I found where one of them had been in my closet because I had found some blood on one of my shoes that was stored on the floor. He probably had gotten cut on the glass from the broken door.

There was one lonely prisoner who stayed behind and he was just sitting there in the jail. He could have left but he didn't. My dad asked him why he didn't run too. Apparently he was smarter than the others because he knew that his jail time would be much longer if he had escaped.

While my dad was serving as an undersheriff he had to use our family vehicle as a patrol car. The county didn't have a budget for each officer to have the use of a patrol car not until sometime later. Because of that, our car was equipped with a siren and a red light that sat on top of our car. Pretty cool stuff I thought. The control for the siren was on the floor of the car. Back in those days you had buttons on the floor board to dim or brighten your headlights and a second floor button was added to our car for the siren. I just have to say that it took mom a few times to remember which was which. She faced total embarrassment a few times when she got the switches mixed up! We kids thought it was pretty funny when she hit the wrong button and she jumped from the surprise of the siren going off!

Dad not only had to deal with law, order, and crimes. He also had to work some horrific car accidents. I didn't learn about most of these things until I was much older. Yes, he had worked some gruesome accidents.

One day mom needed to go to the grocery store and we kids went everywhere with her so we proceeded to get into the back seat of our car as usual. It was winter and dad had left his parka coat in the back seat when he returned from his work the night before. As I went to move his coat out of the way I saw that it was splattered and covered with blood. I asked mom what had happened as she immediately tried to move the coat away from my sight. My first thought was that dad had been hurt but she proceeded to tell me that he had worked a car accident case the night before trying to save a woman's life, but she didn't make it. Apparently, he had covered her with his coat. It made me wonder about whom she was and how horribly she must have died. I felt sad. I think I may have learned about the finality and sometimes the horror of some deaths sooner than most.

My dad learned a lot in his early career in Kingman, Kansas. His life had been threatened, he had been shot at, and his family had been threatened as well. With dad being in a public office there were lawsuits brought against him also. All that to say that for all of the risks, I don't think he even made four hundred dollars a month in his early career!

Dad was quite a story teller and I remember one funny story he told me about his early days in law enforcement. He told me that he had learned a lesson the hard way one day; and the lesson was to make sure that the suspect's vehicle was turned off before you yanked them out of their vehicles. Apparently dad was on a car chase one day and as he told it (with exaggeration I might add) they were racing around fences, under clothes lines, through fields, and finally the suspect was stopped. Dad got out of his patrol car and ran up to the suspect and yanked him out of his vehicle by his shirt collar to place him under arrest. Uh oh!!! The vehicle was still running and still in drive!!!! Yes, the vehicle took off on its own down the road!!! Pretty funny and pretty Barney Fife-ish!!!

He was a great story teller and he shared many other stories with me many, many years after the facts. One such story was about how one of the lawsuits was brought against him. He was called out to a home to work a suicide case. The deceased was still in the home and dad was there by himself to process the scene. One window was open in the room where he was working. Officers have to have coping mechanisms to help them through such scenes and for other ugly horrific circumstances that they handle throughout their careers. While dad was walking around the body taking notes he was softly whistling a tune. A neighbor had snuck over to the house and was peeping through the open window. A law suit was brought against dad for showing disrespect to the dead by whistling! Really?

Another story he told me was kind of morbid and had happened many years later when he was the Police Chief. He was called out to a car accident that had happened on the highway. Highway crashes are the worst to work. They are ugly. In that particular case a person had died.

Dad arrived upon the scene that was already being processed by several officials. In fairness it was late at night and very dark. Remember that I had previously told you that dad could be a little rough around the edges sometimes. Well here's a perfect example of that. He had walked up to one of the officers to gather information about the case. The officer looked down at my dad's feet with raised eyebrows.

"Uhhhh…Chief…you are standing in…his brains," he slowly and quietly stated. (He made his statement with no meaning of disrespect to the deceased.)

Ah yes, growing up in the jailhouse always had its moments! It seemed like there was always something happening or something strange going on that mom had to explain to us kids. I would have to say that even though we were protected a lot, we still saw a bit of life's realities that most young children would never have gotten to see or experience, especially from our advantaged point, *the jailhouse*.

FOUR

# ABC's...With a Twist!

*The heart of the discerning acquires knowledge; for the ears of the wise seek it out.*
**Proverbs 18:15**

### My Early School Years

As a young girl I was very shy and I didn't have a lot of confidence in myself. As a matter-of-fact, I felt painfully inadequate in a lot of ways. Even though I had honey blonde hair with golden flecks that sparkled in the sunlight and bright blue eyes that my uncle told me you could swim in, I was a head taller than most of all of my classmates which left me vulnerable to kidding and snide remarks!

### Kindergarten

I had a wonderful kindergarten teacher and I loved her. She was such a kind patient person and she had actually discovered why I was failing in that grade. One day she was standing behind me and said my name but I didn't respond. She then contacted my mother and told her what had happened and suggested that I get my hearing tested. The results of the tests showed that I had a pretty good ear infection going on. But there was a funny story behind this; my mom felt really bad when she found out that I wasn't really ignoring her on purpose at home! She would spank me for not answering her or coming to her when she asked me to...young mother ooopsies!!!

As I had mentioned earlier, my dad had taken the position of undersheriff when we first moved to Kingman and had decided to run for public office when the sheriff position became available. That took place the summer after my kindergarten year. The current sheriff was retiring and dad decided to throw his hat into the ring. We kids were quite young and didn't quite understand what running for office meant but we really thought it was so cool that dad's pictures were posted up and down the highways, on light poles, and on electrical poles. There were posters of dad everywhere! I remember grinning from ear to ear when I saw those posters as we were flying down the highway and would ask mom why dad's pictures were all over the place!

Dad did win the election and became the Kingman County Sheriff. He later ran for sheriff two more times and won as well. Recently someone mentioned to me that everyone liked my dad. However, I discovered very young that some people didn't care for him at all and unfortunately a lot of the ridicule and attitudes came from my teachers and classmates.

## First Grade

I always liked getting ready for my first day of school. My parents would get us new clothes, new crayons, and various other school supplies. What I can remember so well was that everything smelled so *new*! When I started first grade it was so much fun, at least for the most part. Unlike kindergarten we had full days of school, no naps, and extra playground time.

The matter of *who* I was started to become a reality during my first grade school year. I learned how hard it was to make friends and I also learned to be very careful of others motives when they wanted to become my friend.

I kept noticing a girl who walked past our house on her way to school so one day I purposely looked for her and joined her on the sidewalk in front of our home. I asked her if we could walk together and that started a very special friendship. We didn't always have the same classrooms but we remained pretty close friends regardless.

She was different and I noticed it right away. I think we both had an immediate connection because we both had endured a lot of ridicule and harassments from our classmates. You see she had been born with a birth defect that took her hearing. She wore a hearing aid and the box that she wore strapped about her chest was the size of a cigarette pack. It had two wires that led up to her unshaped ears. Because of her hearing loss her speech was hindered a bit. The sounds she made for words sounded just a little bit different. I would try to always protect her when the other kids would gang up on her and made fun of her and she would also stand up for me when they were ridiculing me for who my dad was. That bond we shared together taught me to have a heart for the underdogs of life. Sometimes people just need someone to be on their side to help them to get through the tough stuff!

What really made it hard on me that year was that my first grade teacher didn't seem to know how to separate her teaching from her politics. I remember being sent to stand in the coat closet as a way of punishment and I'm not sure what I really did to deserve that. Apparently my classmates caught on about her attitude towards me as well. I have always thought it to be very strange with how grownups can take their frustrations out on an innocent child. I definitely learned early on what it meant to be the sheriff's kid!

One day I wore a brand new petticoat to school that had pretty flowers on it. I had told one of my classmates about my new under garment in the restroom and she wanted to see it. So innocently, while standing in one of the stalls, I lifted up my dress to show her my pretty new petticoat. It seemed very harmless, right? Wrong! When I got back into the classroom the girl had told our teacher in front of the whole class that

I was showing off my new petticoat. My teacher shamed me in front of everyone which also included the boys! I just could not understand the reason for the public ridicule and it only added more to my insecurities.

One day my dad took my brother and me across the street from our home past the train depot and to the banks of the Ninnescah River. What an adventure we had exploring through the brush and looking at the river! Then we came upon a snake...a BIG snake in my eyes! Of course at my age all snakes were big! We discovered that it was a Copperhead snake and not exactly the kind of snake that you want to be friends with. Dad quickly picked up some stones and pummeled it to death. Wow! What a story I had for show-and-tell at school!!!

At our next show-and-tell time I bravely raised my hand so I could stand in front of the class and tell the story of how my dad killed a *helicopter* snake!!! Well that sounded like what my dad called it! Copperhead? Helicopter? Of course my teacher used that as another weapon against me in front of the whole class as well.

On one occasion my teacher stood me up in front of the class and proclaimed that I was *stupid*! THAT DID IT! When mom heard about how the teacher was treating me she came unglued. Of course mom in all of her gutsy ness came to school and sat with me in the classroom for a whole week! I had a feeling that she probably had already had a verbal confrontation with my teacher.

Hmmmmmmmmm...I didn't have any more problems with my teacher after that!

It was during my first grade in school that I lost my grandfather. I remember his funeral very well. At the funeral home my family sat to one side of the chapel behind the bereavement curtain and I sat right next to my dad. That was the first time that I had ever seen my dad cry as he mourned for his father. When I saw his tears fall I quickly looked down. After the service, it was time for the family to walk past grandpa's coffin and the curtain was pulled back. His coffin was draped with an

American flag and beautiful flowers were placed everywhere. I quickly peaked into the coffin and turned away.

As we were being seated again my grandmother fell apart! Her sobs turned into bellows and her tears streamed down her face as her cries became louder and louder. No one seemed to be able to console her. Her uncontrollable grief had such an effect on me and I felt so sad for her. It was that episode, for some reason, that caused my young self to make a vow to always have full control over my emotions regardless of the situation. I started training myself to never cry publicly and to remain cool, calm, and collected at all times. Mom would get very frustrated with me at times when she would try to punish me because I just wouldn't cry when she spanked me. I would just look at her and of course that made her even madder and the spankings harder. It didn't matter to me because I would just look at her.

My grandfather's sister died a couple of years later and I was quite proud of myself in the fact that I managed not to cry. It had taken me several years to master my newfound control issue. I would even get frustrated with myself if I couldn't keep it together. I don't think that it was a good thing or even a healthy thing to train myself to do but it certainly has come in handy a few times when faced with some real dangers or some of life's tests. I do think that it bred a bit of stubbornness in me or maybe a bit of determination as I like to call it. I think that the trait has also caused me to be viewed as someone who is always as *hard as a rock;* which is not always true. I've also have learned that some folks don't always view this trait of mine as being very feminine either.

## Second Grade

When I started second grade it wasn't so bad. I did always manage to get placed with my desk facing the wall for punishment because my teacher always claimed that I was cheating! I wasn't cheating so when I was placed facing the wall I would tear up.

That was also the same year that President Kennedy was assassinated. I remember that day well because the principal interrupted our class and announced over the intercom what had just happened and school was let out early that day. I came home to find my dad seated in the living room glued to the television set. It was such a rarity for me to see him at home during the day anyway, let alone seeing him in front of the television set. He had such a sad face!

For the most part I always felt like I was too protected. There were things that I was just never told about; things that would have been very helpful to have known about. When I went to school one day I noticed a lot of the girls in my class were all dressed alike! They all were dressed in brown dresses, a brown cap, and white socks with an emblem on them. I did not know what was going on and I felt a little left out. Towards the end of the day I had enough courage to ask one of the girls what was going on. Of course everyone giggled out loud at my naiveté. Again, I felt like I was left out in the dark. They told me that they were Brownies.

"What's a Brownie?" I asked.

The giggles went on and on. When I got home after school that day I announced to mom that I wanted to be a Brownie. And that was the start of my career in the Girl Scouts!

It was also during that time that I started to learn how to play the piano. My grandmother had bought us kids a very nice piano so that we could learn to play. I had had several piano teachers but I kept losing them for one reason or another! Finally my mom decided that she would teach me. She taught me as far as her knowledge would take her but that was enough for me to get a good start and to eventually end up playing at church on occasions during my teen years.

Most lessons that my dad taught us were lessons that no school could teach us. Some of my family members had told me how dad used to play with me like I was a boy when I was little. He tossed me about and rough and tumbled with me. My family members told dad to be careful because he might turn me into a tomboy! One lesson that he taught me as a child was priceless. He took me across the street from our home to the train station one sunny day. He had me stand on top of the dock. The dock was a sturdy wooden structure that slanted at one end so that trucks could drive up onto the dock to load or unload the train cars. I can't say how tall it was but for my small body it sure could have been a story high! It was then that dad, still standing on the ground, looked up at me and told me to jump. I froze. I couldn't move. I have to say that it took him quite a while to get me to jump.

He kept promising me over and over again that he would catch me. After much coaxing I finally overcame my fear and jumped right into his arms. He caught me and I learned that day that I could always trust him. I am sure that he had no idea what that small exercise did for me as I gained a bit of confidence that day.

Second grade was when my classmates started teasing me for being so tall. It was so irritating to my mother because I would never talk about what was really bothering me. She instinctively knew when something was wrong and she would almost have to beat it out of me in order for me to say something. The reason I didn't want to talk about what was going on at school most of the time was because I didn't want my dad to know what the other kids were saying about him.

Well, mom finally got it out of me about my being teased for my height. When mom told dad about it he had a chat with me. I will never forget what he told me because it was one of the most brilliant confidence boosters I could have ever had and it has stuck with me my entire life. Dad sat down and looked at me on eye level.

"Tall is beautiful, and don't you *ever* forget it," he stated.

Dads if you have never told your daughters that they are beautiful you are missing out!

The next story I'm about to tell you is kind of funny but it is also a dangerous one about jumping. It comes with a warning: **Do not try this at home**!

We kids loved Halloween and mom would sometimes make our outfits. We would hit the neighborhoods trying to fill up our sacks with candy! One year my brother dressed up as Superman in a store bought costume that was red and blue with a cape and it had the big red letter 'S' stamped on the chest. He kept that outfit after Halloween and would wear it around the house and play in it from time to time. Our playroom was in the basement and one day he stood at the top of the wooden stairs in all of his Superman powers because, after all, he had on *the suit*. He asked me if I thought he could fly. I was at the bottom of the stairs playing on the cement floor.

"Of course you can, you are Superman!" I replied flippantly.

So away he went by launching himself into mid-air but hit all of the wooden stairs, thump, thump, and thump all the way down to the cement floor below and splattered. Mom came running when she heard the scream...uh, I was in my mid-thirties before I ever admitted to mom what had really happened that day.

### Third Grade

My third grade in school was a very eventful year, I must say. That year I had a great teacher but my classmates were quite a challenge and to top it all off there was a boy that was madly in love with me! Oh brother!! That boy sat right behind me and would often write me love notes and chase me around the playground asking me to marry him. I didn't want anything to do with him but he just didn't get it!

One day when I had gotten home from school my dad proudly announced that he had just hired a new police officer. The new officer was standing next to dad in our kitchen as the announcement was made and he was introduced to our family...uh, *he was that boy's father!* I was so upset and I couldn't believe that my dad would do such a thing to me! I'm sure my face showed my shock and horror. Of course mom and dad had no idea about the boy's behavior at school; the kid thought that he had an easy *in*! *That did not help the matter any in my opinion.* But as young puppy love and romance usually ends up the boy eventually *got over it and moved on*! Whew!!

It was also in third grade that I started hearing things from the other kids that were just plain mean.

"You think you are so much better than everyone else because your dad is the sheriff," they would chant. "You just think you are so much smarter than us because your dad is the sheriff," they would snidely remark.

Sometimes they would surround me and get me cornered to make their rude remarks about my dad, which I knew probably originated from their parents. I learned that school year how to stand up for myself that was for sure!

Do you remember my telling you about a spanking that my dad had given me; the only spanking that I ever received from him? Well, that was the year of the spanking! Yes, it was a goody and with a belt. My dear friend that I walked home from school with would also receive a spanking from her dad as well. Okay so what could two little innocent girls do that was so horrible to receive such a punishment you ask? Let me tell you!

My friend and I walked past a church on our way home from school that had the most adorable small round cedar bushes and they were all lined up in a row, so they made perfect hurdles! That day we jumped and jumped and jumped over them; over and over again. We were trying to see who could jump the best and the highest and we simply lost track of the time. It was starting to get dusk and you know how protective parents can be. Well our tardiness did not fly well with them at all. When we finally had our fill of jumping we started walking home. A block away from my home we could see my mom standing out on the sidewalk right next to my friend's father. We knew right then and there that there was going to be a *whippin'*. We cautiously continued our walk home fearing what was to come. Her father had a belt in his hand and my mom was going to let my dad deal with me, which he did. I was never late again!

There was an incident that happened to me that school year that allowed me to look evil right in the eyes for the very first time and I will never forget it! I learned how important it was to be home on time from school and why my parents were so strict. I had a close encounter with someone who wanted to get even with my dad!

I was walking home from school during one of my lunch breaks and yes I walked up hill both ways to and from school for my lunches as well! Unbeknownst to me a young man was lying in wait! I was walking all by myself and was about half a block from my home when the young man came out of an alley entrance and confronted me! He said he had something to show me. I knew the young man from school. He was older than me and had these cold dark eyes. I have always described them as "Manson" eyes and no I am not talking about Marilyn Manson the singer. I am talking about the famed murderer Charles Manson! To me it just seemed as though the guy's soul was dark and empty. I later found out why!

He had me accompany him down the alley and I soon found myself at knife point. He took me down into a dry creek bed where I observed a pile of bloody entrails. I'm guessing that he had already slaughtered a small animal to make his point. As we stood there looking at those innards he told me that when he got through with me I would look just like the slaughtered mess that I was staring at. He had some newspapers already wadded up and he stuffed them into my mouth. Then he continued to describe to me how my death was going to happen.

I guess I was already becoming a tough cookie by the third grade and was very cool and didn't panic. I never even cried during the ordeal. Like I said earlier, I had already trained myself to not show my emotions in certain situations. I did manage to get the wadded newspaper out of my mouth and I started talking to him. For the life of me I cannot tell you what negotiations I had made with him but it caused him to lose eye contact with me for just a flinch of a second and I took off running. I ran for my life all the way home. The minute I hit the kitchen door I fell apart! I was crying loudly and hysterically as I tried to tell mom what had just happened. She immediately went to dad's office and brought him into the kitchen where they both questioned me further.

I know that my dad had gone to visit with the young man's mother. I never knew what was exchanged between the two of them and that would not the last time that we would have to deal with the person. I never told anyone at school what had happened, ever! That was one of those episodes that thankfully did not make it into the newspapers.

Many years later I found out the rest of the story about the boy's family. Horrible, horrible things took place in their home. The young man had both parents living at home and he was the youngest of several siblings with him being the only boy. What I found out was that the father used to make his family perform sexual acts with each other and that went on for years! Back in those days those kinds of things were not talked about nor was there much help for mothers or children who tried to get away from such abusers. Finally the abuse was stopped when the father of the family was arrested by my dad. He went on trial was found guilty and was sent to the state pen to reside there for many years.

We understand more so today than in the past that victims who have been abused by a parent struggle with the fact that no matter what the abuse was that was heaped upon them, they still can love their parent and such was the case with that young man. He hated my dad fiercely for sending his father away and vowed to get even! He was such a troubled young man and the hate and anger that had built up inside of him eventually took over his soul. As he grew up he continued with a life of crime with heinous acts that were unspeakable. You will read of him again later in my story.

## Fourth Grade

When I entered fourth grade my teacher was a bit of a challenge for me. She was an older woman with the patience of…well, not exactly of a saint! My teacher would sit my desk side right next to the daughter of the school superintendent! She was a *brainiac* of course and I was the… *not brainiac*! She would compare the two of us in front of the whole class. Swell! And then she would never pick me to help with things in the classroom like she did with the others.

One day she finally did pick me to water the classroom plants and I was so excited to finally get to do something! Of course in my clumsiness and insecurities I splattered some of the water. I thought she was going to come unglued and splatter all over the walls herself! Really, was this all about some spilled water?

The summer between my fourth and fifth grades was when I became a Christ follower. Of course we all use different terms for this but I accepted Jesus into my heart and became a Christian. I prayed the prayer of thankfulness and asked for forgiveness and experienced a life changing event to walk in the Lord's way.

My parents had sent us to Vacation Bible School during the summer and we kids loved it. I especially loved the teachers and the stories that they told. I loved the crafts we did, and of course the Kool-Aid and cookies that were served to us. That particular week of VBS turned out to be especially different.

Each day as the Bible stories were told I felt a stirring going on within me. It was like a conviction in my soul or something like that. I knew that some of the other kids in my class were accepting Christ for the very first time but I was too shy and didn't know what to do. It was Friday the final and last day of VBS. I waited after class until everyone had gone and I was alone with the teacher. I expressed to her my interest in making a decision for Christ and my teacher got so excited. She walked me over to the lady who was the leader of VBS. I was familiar with the leader because she worked at my eye doctor's office. She was so nice and so pretty. Her own daughters were several years older than me and they were absolutely gorgeous and equally as kind to me as their mother.

She took me by the hand and led me into the church office. Then she started asking me questions and prayed the prayer with me to thank the Lord for saving me from my sins and had me ask Jesus into my heart. It was such a simple prayer and a very tearful experience for me, but wow, I felt like a heavy weight had been lifted off of me! She then handed me a Bible after she had written the date in it. Then she kindly walked me outside to meet up with my mother explaining to her why it was taking me so long to come out of the church. On our walk home I was so excited to tell mom all about my experience!

For many years I thought that I had lost that Bible but found it again, and I still have it. I never knew what had happened to the Bible and when I was cleaning out my grandparent's home I found it! My grandfather had used it for years and had written full rich notes in it. The binding was gone but he had taped it together. I cherish it even more so now.

## Fifth Grade

My fifth grade teacher was a very good looking man and as I can remember it, all of us girls thought he was the greatest! One day he had our classroom do a free art project, which was sort of a science fair. Even the local newspaper came out to visit our class and wrote an article about our inventions. The article featured a picture of several students and their projects including mine! I had created a rainbow making machine! Okay it really didn't do anything, but it sure was fun to make! That was the first clue that one of my life's calls was that of an eternal optimist; I created a rainbow machine! Of course! I think I have always had it in me to see the bright and sunny side of everything and in everyone and in every situation. Of course, a rainbow machine, it was a symbol of God's love and new beginnings!

That was the year that one of my classmate's families faced a very difficult tragedy. Late one night my classmate's father had stabbed and killed a family friend at their home and the victim died in their front yard. Of course the newspaper covered the whole sordid story in the morning edition. That next day after the murder my classmate was not at school, nor for the next several days. My parents told me nothing about it.

I remember that the playground at school did not hold that good-time-to-be-had-by-all atmosphere that day. When the kids starting talking about what had happened the night before I was stunned! I really didn't know about anything at all about the case as I didn't even know that it had happened! That was when a gang situation occurred when the kids had me surrounded calling me a liar because they didn't believe that I couldn't tell them anything about the murder. I was quite scared and no one came to my defense. But I had faced nothing compared to my poor classmate who witnessed the whole tragedy unfolding at her family home and then had to eventually face the unkindness of her classmates as well.

My classmate's dad was charged with the murder and the story about his trial was captured by the local newspaper with all of the details displayed for all to read. But then he was found not guilty because the murder was ruled as a self-defense. My classmate and I, though not close friends, always remained friendly to each other. While justice was being served I think her family appreciated the way my father showed them respect throughout their whole situation.

## Sixth Grade – Part One

Sixth grade in Kingman was considered junior high at that time. That was the year that I remember wearing fish-net stockings because it was all the rage! I also remember being worried that I might not remember where my locker was located and if I could get to the different classrooms on time. It was just the usual dreams and nightmares that all kids have when going through the transition to junior high. The transition period didn't last long though because my dad decided to resign as sheriff and move our family right in the middle of the school year to Wichita, Kansas.

I remembered that I was so excited about leaving Kingman and the town that had caused us so much grief. I hated leaving my friends behind but I felt that life had to be much easier for all of us by moving. Our living in Wichita meant that we would be living closer to my grandparents and we would have our dad back full time!

Remember I had mentioned earlier that my fourth grade teacher was not very patient? I had her husband as my math teacher in the sixth grade. He was so very kind to me and very patient. I really liked him a lot. The day I found out that we were moving I approached him after class and told him about it. *Of course* he already knew about it because it had been announced in the local newspaper...*silly me, always behind in the news!* He had tears in his eyes as he told me that he really liked my dad and was saddened that we were leaving town and that we would be greatly missed. I do believe that his response was actually genuine and sincere. I will never forget him and his kindness.

FIVE

# Off to the Big City!

*Therefore go and make disciples of all nations, baptizing them in the name of the Father and of the Son and of the Holy Spirit.*
**Matthew 28:19**

### Wichita

As I had mentioned in the last chapter my dad had resigned as the sheriff of Kingman County, Kansas, when I was mid-way through my sixth grade to accept a position with Sedgwick County in the Office of Corrections as a parole officer. It was mid-winter and it was very, very cold with snow on the ground. Regardless of the weather the move and transition to Wichita seemed to go pretty smoothly.

My grandparents still owned the house next door to their home but they had leased it out. It was the house that my mother had grown up in, the first house that my parents lived in after they were married, and the first house my brother and I lived in when we were just babies. Since that house was not readily available for us to move into we had to move to a rental house a few miles away.

The rental house we moved to was a much older house. The all white house featured a bay window in the living room and it had three bedrooms! That was the first time ever that my brother and I had our own bedrooms! We were both very excited about that!

## Sixth Grade – Part Two

When I resumed my sixth grade in Wichita it was at grade school level. At the time I didn't think it was fair that I had come from a junior high school and ended up back in a grade school in a matter of minutes!!! That could be hard on a child but my teacher, the grandma type, happened to be the best! She knew who I was because we just couldn't keep dad's transition and position from being published in the local Wichita paper. Although she knew, the rest of my class didn't and I thought that was great. I was finally known by my name Debra and no longer known as the sheriff's daughter.

My teacher doted over me and gave me so much attention! I sensed that she must have known how hard it was for me to move in the middle of a school year and she did her best to make me feel comfortable. I flourished in her classroom and started for the first time ever making A's! She cared for me and the time that she spent with me really helped me to build up my confidence level. I also discovered that I was great at spelling and loved the spelling bees that she held quite frequently.

That teacher of mine was the perfect teacher for me and I have thought of her quite often. I don't know if she ever knew how much she had helped me especially during that transition period. I just feel that many of today's teachers could learn a lot from her example. She was one who genuinely cared for the children in her classroom and she wanted to help them all succeed.

I even made a few friends that year. One particular friend lived in our neighborhood about a block away and we would play together whenever we could. We would walk home together at least to the point to where we had to split to go our own ways.

One particular time my friend held a birthday party at her house and of course my parents made sure that her parents would be home during the party. Her parents ended up leaving for a while in the evening and left a house full of young girls running amuck! It was dusk outside and all of us girls decided that we wanted to go out into the front yard to play. All of a sudden one of the girls screamed and said that she thought that she saw a strange man in the house walking past a window! We all freaked out! A neighbor must have heard the commotion and called the police. The next thing we knew the police had arrived and did a thorough search of the house. Her parents returned home to quite a scene.

Of course all of our parents were notified and my friend's parents ended up apologizing to the police and to all of the parents for leaving us alone. Uh…no strangers were found in the house! Maybe it was just one of the girl's vivid imaginations?

Early spring that year I remember walking home from school with a group of girls when they started asking me where I had moved from and asked me questions about my family. I innocently told them that my dad had been the sheriff of the town where we had lived. Of course they didn't believe me and I just shrugged it off. When I told my grandmother about that conversation and how they didn't believe me she immediately told me to never tell anyone about my dad being a sheriff. When I asked her why, she told me that information might cause some problems. Again as I think back, I didn't understand all the implications at the time but it basically was about the safety of our family.

The days began to warm as the school year was coming to an end. It was on one of those warm days while I was on my way home from school that some kids ran up to me to tell me that my brother was in a fight!

"Come quickly!" they yelled.

So I took off running to see what the fight was all about and discovered that my brother and another boy were rolling all over the sidewalk fighting. My brother was receiving some awful punches so I, as the elder, was not going to stand for that! I went over to that mean boy and picked him up by his belt and threw him several feet away into the grass! I kind of surprised myself at how strong I really was! Oh well, I thought to myself, a job well done and the fight was over and I'd done a good thing, right? Wrong! My brother was furious with me and I just didn't get it! By the time my brother and I had walked home he was all worked up and madder than a wet hen! He even told mom all about what I had done the minute he hit the door. After she got him all calmed down she took me into another room to have a stern talk with me.

"Debra," she said, "let your brother fight his own fights."

I just hadn't understood the whole male macho thing yet, but I never interfered again!

During the summer the family home next to my grandparents became available to us. It only had two bedrooms but my parents turned an enclosed back porch into a bedroom for my brother. The house was an older house and had a floor furnace for heat but there wasn't any air-conditioning except for one window unit in my parent's bedroom. A lot of work had to be done to make the house more livable after having had renters. It was a small house but we made it work for us.

We had a huge back yard with lots of room to play. We also had two nut trees that had survived from when our back yard had been plentiful with fruit trees. A large lilac bush and honeysuckle vines filled the back yard with a lovely fragrance. There were large elm trees that helped shade part of the back yard and then we had a sunny spot where we had a vegetable garden. Later on we added a go-cart track where we could race around in a figure eight pattern.

In our front yard we had beautiful bushy Spirea shrubs. These bushes are also known as Bridal Wreath and their beautiful full draping flowers lined our driveway. These bushes are of the rose family with dense clusters of small white flowers. Our Spirea bushes yielded these beautiful flowers every year. On the south side of our house we also had these same shrubs that lined the full length of the property. They provided privacy from the neighbors and from the businesses that were on that side of our house. Additionally we had three Catalpa trees that lined the walking path in front of our house. These Catalpa trees had heart-shaped leaves and often had showy clusters of white trumpet-shaped flowers and the trees also had long slender beanlike pods that hung down from the branches. These trees provided a lot of shade for our front yard.

The neighborhood was the place where my mom grew up and the neighborhood in which my dad lived as a teenager. They knew most of the neighbors and their children so it made it easier for us as we had instant friends. My grandparents lived right next door to us and on the other side of their house lived our cousins and next door to them were some very good friends of my parents who had several children. There were other neighbors with children that my parents knew as well. It really felt like we were *finally* home!

## Our Neighborhood Baptist Church

My family started attending the neighborhood church where my parents were married and the one that they were members of. It was the church that my grandparents and other extended family members attended as well. It was just a small neighborhood Missionary Baptist church that was filled with lots of friends and family with whom I was familiar with. Everyone would get all dressed up for church and that included getting their cars all washed up and cleaned. And of course they would put on their best Sunday attitudes as well. I started to realize that some people acted a little bit different in church than they acted outside of church during the week!

The pastor usually got pretty up close and serious when he started preaching. He made his points during his sermons by pounding the pulpit with his fist and speaking pretty loudly and with great authority. He always seemed to be able to capture everyone's attention. There were not too many people who slept through his sermons because they were real toe-stompers!

For some reason my dad quit attending church for a while when we moved back to Wichita. I never asked him why but I always felt that after his being a sheriff for so long and all the "stuff" that he had witnessed he probably had much sorting out to do about his faith.

During an altar call one Sunday morning I felt that it was time for me to be baptized. I was twelve years of age when I walked forward to express my wishes to the pastor. Following right behind me was my brother! We were all so excited. He ended up accepting the Lord that day as well. When we arrived home from church we found our dad sitting in the back yard under a shade tree and we ran up to him to let him know what had just happened in church. That turned out to be a deal-breaker for him and he soon started back to church again! A few weeks later both my brother and I were baptized together in the church's baptistery.

## Junior High

When I started junior high school I was listening to popular musical groups like The Monkees, The Rolling Stones, Herman's Hermits, and singer Elvis Presley and my good friend Frankie Valens. And of course, there was the ever popular Tom Jones and The Beatles! The Viet Nam war was raging on with no end in sight and even though I had observed the war in the news ever since I had been a small child the reality of the war was just starting to sink in. There were frequent protests because of the war and some were shown on the evening news as well. Becoming a *hippie* was all the rage with free lifestyle living, long hair, VW vans, drug use, and tie-dyed clothing! The phrases "Free Love," "Peace," "Flower Power," "Sex, Drugs, and Rock n' Roll," and "Love Ins" were coined. By then the fashion industry had introduced such fashion items as the mini-skirt, go-go boots, hot pants, bell-bottom low-cut jeans, bikinis and baby-doll tops. Television producers had stepped out of their comfort zones and we started to see shows and movies that we had never witnessed on TV before! One program was the Rowan & Martin's "Laugh-In" show and it had become all of the rage. There were a lot of different influences being presented to our world that started tugging at all of us baby-boomers shaping us into what we would eventually become.

I made many friends during my junior high school days. I found out that the principal at my school had known my dad from when both of them were in law enforcement. The school building was so much larger than the schools in which I had attended in the past so I worried a bit about being late for classes. I also worried about placing a lock on my locker. I didn't have to have a lock for my locker in Kingman and I feared that I would somehow forget the combination! Even with all the needless worrying it didn't take long for me to feel comfortable with my new surroundings.

I loved almost every class I took except for physical education. I just hated having to change clothes in front of the others and then having to take showers as well. You might say that I was not too comfortable with some of the sports that they had us participate in as well. I didn't like the hurdle jumps, rope climbing, and soccer. However I did like baseball, running, basketball, volleyball, and the high jump. When I played baseball it just seemed like I always broke something; a few pairs of glasses, a finger, cracked nose, and some pride! I loved the game but it just didn't like me. The school had no air-conditioning and the gym became a sweat factory on warm days. Since we girls were required to wear dresses for school, getting back into a dress and hose and trying to make your hair look good after gym class was futile, uncomfortable, and so ridiculous!

One of my most favorite classes was my choral class. My teacher was the famed movie actress Vera Miles' sister and she was so pretty and so kind. It was in that class that I discovered that I loved to sing solos. For one of our assignments the teacher had us choose a song that we could sing in front of the class. I chose the song "Moon River", which at that time had been made popular by the singer Andy Williams. I thought that I did a fairly good job. I also liked preparing for our yearly concerts that we would put on for our family and friends. All of us girls had to make our choral dresses so that we would all look alike for our performances.

I also participated in the school musical play called "South Pacific" by playing an island girl. I actually tried out for one of the lead rolls that required a tall, round girl. I so wanted that part and I had the voice for it but I was as skinny as a rail. The part ended up being given to another girl whom I might say was…much rounder.

It was not until about the eighth grade that us girls finally put up a big protest about having to wear only dresses to school. It was no small uprising, it was BIG. Finally the principal caved in and decided that we girls could wear slacks, not shorts or jeans. At least we felt there was *some* progress no matter how small, but progress…sigh!

By my ninth grade I had grown to five feet and eleven inches tall. I was much taller than most of the boys in my class and I was also turning into a girly girl and I liked wearing makeup and playing with new hair styles. I started to grow long fingernails and painted them. I also took sewing and cooking classes and discovered that I really liked sewing. I was also good at typing and could type really fast.

I loved my art class and discovered that even though I had been pretty good in my younger years as a sketch artist my art classes helped to open up a whole new world of creative experiences for me. My confidence level started growing and growing and I wasn't feeling so inadequate like I had felt when I was younger.

It was also during the beginning of my ninth grade in school that cross-bussing started. The government had mandated that black children be taken from their neighborhood schools and bussed to white schools and vice versa. Most of the black children did not want to be bused to our schools and there were some of those redneck-white-folks that didn't want them in our schools either, and the fights began. As you might very well imagine my first days of school that year were awful. Riots broke out with fighting, pipe bombs were going off, and knives were being pulled. The school went into lock-down many times and as the news was hitting the airwaves, the police showed up and tried to get the riots under control.

The school wouldn't let the students leave until their parents showed up. My own mom was at our school so fast that it made The Road Runner look like he was traveling in reverse! No matter what the school authorities said she took control of a dangerous situation to protect her own children at whatever cost and took us out of the building, permission or not! It was just so scary during those times and all a person could do was to try to get out safely and try to avoid the mob situations. That kind of activity continued off and on all throughout the rest of the school year. After a while things did start to settle down but a person always had to watch their backs.

That was also the year when I was allowed to attend my first boy-girl birthday party. One of my classmates, a tall blonde who had that Marilyn Monroe look, had invited me to her birthday party and I was quite surprised that my parents would even let me go to it. She had invited quite a few of her guy friends to her party as well.

When mom dropped me off that evening at the party I went inside the house to find that it was full of people, both upstairs and downstairs. It was quite a blowout! It was a typical birthday party with gifts, a cake and some treats, until…the boys decided to roam the neighborhood. We girls hadn't realized that the boys had left the party. When we did take notice that they were no longer around we went to the streets to try to find them. We could hear some noises and voices coming from afar so we took off in the direction of the commotion to find them.

We girls came upon a construction site where a new apartment complex was being built. The complex was still in its early stages of construction. We girls ducked down behind some bushes and peered through them to observe the site; we discovered that the boys were trying to totally destroy that construction site. They had already gotten into the bags of cement mix and were throwing it everywhere! Some of the boys had even gotten into the heavy operating equipment and had started up the engines. The place was a total mess! All of a sudden the site was surrounded by police cars arriving from all directions. The police did not notice us girls behind the bushes and we were able to escape the scene without notice and we were not caught. Kids scattered everywhere! We ran as fast as we could back to the house while the rest of the kids that were left behind had to deal with the police. I was so petrified! First of all I could not believe what I had just witnessed and secondly I knew that if my parents found out about it, I would face sure death!

I knew from past experiences in dealing with a small town press that it was bound to be on the evening news or in the next morning's newspaper edition for sure, but my only reference up to that point was just small towns. I decided to wait it out and not tell my parents unless I really had to. I waited and waited, but nothing was being reported in the news either on TV or in the newspapers. I was sure that it was a huge crime! I got an awful sick feeling the longer I waited and knew that I was going to have to tell about the incident. Silly me, in *big* towns and cities, they just don't report everything that happens!!...and, I never told!

## Work Ethics Taught

My dad had regular work hours with his weekends off and it was so great having him around. He had much more time to teach us some things and how to work more with our hands. After a while I started resenting those few years because of all the hard work we had to do before we could go out to play. It wasn't until I got older and was out in the work force that I came to appreciate what my parents had taught us. I eventually realized that I knew more about how to do things and had developed a greater work ethic than most other young women that were my age.

Some of the work was home-improvement projects that had to be done and there *always* seemed to be some kind of a project going on. We kids would help mom with the cleaning; doing dishes, and other household chores. But dad had a fit when he found out that my brother was doing the dishes!

"That's woman's work!" he growled at my mom.

That created a fight between mom and dad, and of course, simply put, mom won that one!

Dad taught us how to shingle a roof, how to trim our large elm trees, how to take care of our yard, and taught us how to build things. Mom was in charge of our vegetable garden and taught us how to plant and grow things from seeds. She also showed us how to pull the weeds…I hated to pull the weeds!!!

We were always kept busy with remodeling or improving something around the house. When our friends would come over to see if we could come out to play the answer was usually no, not until our work was done.

I did hear rumors from some of our cousins that they thought that our parents were abusing us with all of the work they were having us do. My parents' children were never idle nor did they end up in big trouble or in jail…and I will leave it at that!

Dad had us help him build two boats and those projects were perfect for family time together! The first boat was a small pontoon fishing boat and it was so much fun watching the creation come to life. I didn't like working with the fiberglass much but it was ours to enjoy when we had finished building it. That first boat took its maiden launch on the Little Arkansas River in downtown Wichita. It actually floated!

Later we built a much larger pontoon boat. Dad had purchased the large pontoons for that boat and the rest of the structure was up to us to build! Both boats served us well for several years to come. We usually took them out to Cheney Lake to enjoy some fishing. A lot of fond memories happened on those two boats.

### We Changed Churches

I do not remember exactly what happened but I do remember a lot of discussion between the adults about what was going on at the church. Some people were very upset and some people were talking about their dissatisfaction. The next thing I knew the church had a major split. It was so sad because I really had enjoyed going to that church and worshiping with all of our extended family members. Unfortunately the split caused our extended family members to go in different directions as well.

My immediate family started attending a Southern Baptist Church. My dad's parents had attended the church so we were somewhat familiar with it. I will never forget our first Sunday in attendance. The church was much larger than our small neighborhood church that we had been attending and it had more programs for children. Their music sounded very professional and they had a wonderful pastor.

When we walked in the door that first Sunday we were immediately greeted by the pastor and his wife. They seemed so kind. The pastor's wife took me by the hand and walked me to my Sunday school class. She was dressed in a beautiful white dress that had a colorful embroidered hand-stitched paisley design. I could not remember ever seeing such beautiful fabric in my entire life! She took an immediate interest in me and asked me if I liked singing because the church had a youth choir!

All four of us became very involved in the church and dad even became a deacon. My parents sang in the adult choir and my brother and I sang in the youth choir. We were all at church at the same time and I loved it!! Every Sunday we would go to church and Sunday school in the morning and late afternoon my brother and I would go to youth choir practice. We went to Sunday evening services which was when the youth choir performed. Wednesday nights we met with our youth pastor for mid-week services and Thursday evenings I would practice with the church band that I was in. I played piano for the group. Friday or Saturday evenings were times that the youth would get together for fun events.

I had a great respect for our youth pastor and I thought a great deal of him. He had lived through a rough spell of drugs and alcohol and could preach and teach about the perils of that lifestyle that he had found himself in. He had already experienced what most kids had just started to get involved with and was a perfect teacher for being able to warn the youth about those kinds of choices. I thought he was just awesome!

He had made up hundreds of invitations for us to hand out at school so we could invite our friends to our youth group meetings. I was so excited about the Lord that I handed those invitations out everywhere!

My faith had really started to come alive and I was no longer living my parents' faith. It was my faith that I was walking in!

I loved to study my Bible and I still have the Bible that I had used from that time. It's all marked up with all kinds of notes from the sermons to the teachings that I had received. I love looking at that Bible from time to time because it reminds me of such a *wondermous* time in my life when my faith walk was the most glorious for me. I was truly on fire for the Lord and I was ready to go and take on the great commission!

## SIX

# Life Can Change In An Instant

*Even though I walk through the valley of the shadow of death, I will fear no evil, for you are with me; your rod and your staff, they comfort me.*
**Psalm 23:4**

### Summer

I somehow made it through my junior high years and was greatly anticipating high school. I was also looking forward to our church choir trip that had been scheduled for that summer. Our church youth choir had performed a couple of musicals titled "Now Hear It Again!" and "Tell It Like It Is" and one of the performances had been recorded.

We had been invited to share our musical testimony by performing at a church in Texas. The trip would also include a day of fun at Six Flags Over Texas, a popular amusement park located in Arlington, Texas.

### Our Trip

I could hardly sleep the night before our trip to Texas because I was so excited. When morning finally came, my brother and I had gotten up early so that we could go to the church and join up with the choir for our trip. I remember that it was a warm sunny day and mom was the one who drove us to the church parking lot.

When we arrived at the parking lot it was full of kids who were moving their suitcases to their assigned cars. I remember developing a sick fearful feeling that just seemed to engulf me and I just couldn't shake it off, even with so much excitement in the air. And that feeling came over me before I had even gotten out of mom's car! As much as I tried to ignore it, it lingered all around me. Mind you it was not a physical sickness, just a mental downer! I knew something was wrong, but what was it? I felt very hesitant.

There were several personal vehicles being used for the trip to transport us, our suitcases, and our musical instruments. Soon I was assigned to ride in a car with several friends of mine. Our driver was a very sweet mom who was the mother of one of my friends. One of the girls riding in our car was a beautiful gifted young lady who played the piano for our choir. She was just a couple of years older than me but she had accomplished the piano in a major way! I always seemed to envy her and looked up to her in awe! The rest of us girls were all in the same Sunday school class and had known each other for some time.

It didn't take us long before we were all packed and headed down the highway and it didn't take us long before we were bored! Our conversations went from catching up with each other to playing a few road games to help keep us occupied. Of course we had to make a couple of restroom stops along the way as you could imagine with a car full of girls, but that uneasy feeling just kept bugging me and lingering in my thoughts. I just didn't want to say anything.

A jug of water was provided for us along with some Styrofoam cups so we decided to write our names on each cup so we wouldn't get them mixed up. One of the girls found a red marker and we started writing our names on each cup.

"This looks so familiar to me," said the pianist. "I can remember us writing our names on these cups in a dream I had last night."

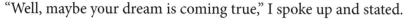

"Well, maybe your dream is coming true," I spoke up and stated.

"I hope not, the trip didn't end well," she sadly stated.

I finally told the girls that I too had a bad feeling about the trip and couldn't shake it off.

We traveled several more miles into Oklahoma when all of a sudden and with no reason our driver insisted that we stop at the next rest area. None of us girls had to use the restroom nor were we lacking anything, and as far as we all knew we had plenty of gas. As it turned out our driver didn't even know why we had to stop *either*. She said that she was *told* to stop! We didn't question the decision and decided to enjoy our short stay by glancing through all of the souvenirs and gift items until our driver was ready to get back on the road again.

We had been one of the last few cars to leave the church parking lot that day and because of our many stops we had long lost the rest of the caravan of cars that was ahead of us.

Heading south into Oklahoma the four-lane highway was divided by a wide median and I remember enjoying the scenic landscape as we traveled. There was one particular area along the highway that had high rocky hills on both sides of the highway. I pondered with wonderment with how the highway construction crew was able to slice through those solid rocks.

## The Horrific Accident

While traveling further down the highway into Oklahoma we came upon a mangled upside down station wagon in the wide median. We slowed to a crawl as we neared the huge scene because there was so much chaos. An ambulance, fire and rescue responders, and many other travelers were parked on both sides of the highway. The area was covered with car debris, clothing from torn open suitcases, and the grass and ground was all churned up from the accident. Everywhere I looked I saw hurt bodies with folks trying to help.

As we crept closer to the accident we were staring at the unrecognizable station wagon when all of a sudden and at the same time we all recognized one of the kids from our group that had been traveling in that upside down car. They must have been just a few miles ahead of us! Our driver immediately pulled over and stopped. She told us to stay in the car and she took off to go investigate.

We all watched in horror as one ambulance pulled away and then another ambulance pulled up. We could see from our vantage point that the kids were badly injured. One of the injured boys from the wreck found his way to our car but he was in severe shock, speechless, and dazed. He had cuts all over and someone had tied his broken arm up in a make-shift sling. We noticed also that his jaw was broken. We told him to please go back to the ambulance so they could help him.

Our driver finally came back to our car and informed us that she had been told what hospital our friends were being taken to. We quickly headed to the hospital but she was silent the whole trip and did not answer any of our questions. We soon found out why.

When we arrived at the hospital our driver and us girls immediately went to the emergency room and waited anxiously to hear any word on the condition of our friends. Finally a nurse came out to talk with our driver and invited her into the trauma area for a chat while we waited patiently for her to return.

A little while later our driver came back to join us and started asking us some generic questions about one of the girls that was in the wreck. When we answered all of her questions, she took off running back into the trauma area.

"Oh no, oh no!" she was shouting.

The station wagon that had crashed was owned by a young married couple and one of the boys in that car was the wife's brother. Two of the girls were sisters that looked very much alike and there was one girl and one more boy in that car which added up to seven. The kids were in the same small musical group who had been performing together for several years. They were all very gifted vocally and instrumentally and had been using their gifts to witness for the Lord.

The husband of the married couple had started out driving the car but had stopped to trade off to let his wife drive. She hadn't been driving for very long at all at highway speed when the station wagon suddenly flipped end over end several times landing in the median upside down!

Several weeks later, after the investigation, it was revealed that something had locked up underneath the car and it had caused the vehicle to flip!

The husband of the couple died instantly at the scene after he had gone through the windshield and his throat was severed. One of the girls who had also gone through the windshield had severe injuries and had lost a good part of her face. She was conscious and talking with the ambulance attendants. We discovered that she had died after arriving at the hospital. A few of the other kids had broken bones and had severe cuts but the wife who was driving the car escaped without any serious physical injuries.

Our driver was called upon to help identify the deceased at the hospital. What an awful horrific task and mental picture that she will no doubt carry around with her for the rest of her life. During her identifying of the bodies she accidentally confused the two sisters because they looked so much alike and had identified the wrong one as being deceased. That was why she was upset and ran away from us so she could fix her mistake. When she had finished correctly identifying the deceased she came back to join us and told us about the loss of our friends and the many injuries that the others had. Did a couple of us girls have a premonition of what was going to happen? Maybe the Lord was trying to warn us in advance of what was about to happen? In any case, it was a really bad day for all of us.

Remember this had happened before there were cell phones. We had no way of connecting to the rest of our team. However our driver was able to contact our church to let them know of the tragedy. We were also able to contact our folks who had already arrived at the church in Texas. They told us that most of the team had arrived already but not everyone. Some of the group was still traveling and had no idea about the accident.

I don't know how she did it but our driver was able to keep everything under control by consoling us girls and making all the necessary contacts. We were all in shock. She also was able to make contact with a local church that was able to provide us with overnight housing; all the while she was dealing with her own grief. We started to realize that it must have been the Lord who had us stop at the rest area because if we had not stopped when we did, we could have witnessed the whole tragic scene first hand or at least shortly afterwards because we were the next car traveling in our caravan behind the car that flipped over. To think that we *could have* been a witness to the horror of that wreck and be the first on the scene! It was bad enough just seeing what we did see afterwards.

When evening came we spent the night at the local church that offered us shelter. Most of us slept on the floor in one of the rooms at the church while some were able to sleep on a few cots that were available. One of the girls that had been injured in the wreck had been patched up and later release from the hospital that same night and came to stay with us at the church. When she arrived most of us had already cried ourselves to sleep but then, in the silence of the night, we listened to her cry her heart out too.

The next day our team returned to Wichita except for a few of the injured who had to stay in the Oklahoma hospital because they were not stable enough to make the trip home. We were greeted with hugs and kisses at our church by the many worried and bereaved parents. I know that many lives were changed that awful day as well as our entire church family.

Over the next few days we were able to attend the two funeral services for our friends that perished on that trip. The families of the lost ones were strong but they were just going through the motions. It was a horrible week but we were able to find solace and peace in knowing that our loved ones were in heaven. The next few months proved to be very challenging for our church as everyone tried dealing with what had happened. There were just so many questions that could not be answered like…why?

The experience did help us to become a stronger and better people and the church eventually developed a bus program so that the youth could travel wherever they wanted to go making travel much safer. The bus program eventually became a great outreach tool for the church. The church also decided to name one of the rooms at the church after the young girl who had died. A bronze plaque of her likeness had been made in her honor and was hung in that special room. The young man who had died in the accident was memorialized at his own church home. The special room that was dedicated to our lost friend was the room that we used for our Wednesday evening youth group meetings. We would never forget her.

## Our High School Busing Issue

A few weeks later it was time for me to start school again but I knew I had been forever changed by the event that took place over the summer. I started school with a whole new and different outlook on life.

That was the first year that I would have to ride a school bus to school and that meant that I would have to be getting up pretty early to catch the bus. Lucky for me the bus picked me up right at our corner!

I met a new friend while riding the school bus. She was new to the area and a bit shy but we befriended each other and right away we became the best of friends and are still friends to this day!

We were both just a little nervous about the possibility of missing the bus after school, at least until we figured out the schedules. The really cool thing was that I had an uncle who worked as a custodian at our school and I knew that he would look out for us, and he did. We missed the bus a few times!

Occasionally we would still experience a riot breakout because of the cross-busing issue. The school would go into lock-down and we would get locked into our classrooms until we got the all clear. In high school the kids were a lot bigger and meaner and oftentimes carried more dangerous weapons. The lockdowns, however, didn't stop us from leaving! We would just crawl out of the class room windows to escape!

Many problems came about because of the busing issue. We learned very quickly to never go to the restrooms alone because that was one of the easiest places to be attacked. Needless to say the restrooms became a nasty place of defecation created by the ones who did not want to be there! It was just not a good situation most of the time. One day, after school, one of the school buses was attacked with pipe bombs. Luckily our bus barely escaped the attack as we ducked our heads down during a fast exit.

One morning after I had gotten off of the bus three black girls started to pick a fight with me in the school hall. I reared back and created what I called the *stink eye*. It worked and they backed off. I'd have to say that the *stink eye* look that I had created was intimidating and with my height on my side I could be quite intimidating if I needed to be. Hey, it worked and I don't remember ever having to throw a punch to protect myself!

### Lightning Strikes!

My uncle who was working at our high school as a custodian was a really neat guy. He was married to my grandmother's sister. He was retired, survived a bad bout with cancer, and later went to work part-time at the school. I so enjoyed having a nice familiar face at school especially during those first few weeks when fights would break out or the occasional we-missed-the-bus-again *doodahs*!

Back then, and during the month of September, my mom's side of our family held family reunions in Arkansas. That particular year my grandparents attended the reunion but our immediate family did not.

The reunion was held over a weekend and was finished by Sunday afternoon. Folks had said their goodbyes and were headed out on the road to return home. From what we were told by some of our relatives a huge storm came up quite quickly in Oklahoma and it had become very difficult to see the road because of the heavy rain and bright lightening. My uncle decided to take an exit to get off of the highway and as he did, lightning struck his camper and it had a propane tank on board. The vehicle exploded! Both my aunt and uncle were burned alive in the truck because they were unable to escape. One of their daughters had been working at her job only a few miles away from the explosion and she saw the plume of smoke that arose, not knowing that it was her parents that had perished in that fire!

I will never forget the phone call that we received shortly after that accident. We were enjoying the sunny day together as a family in our backyard when we heard the phone ring. Mom went inside to answer the phone and when she returned she had an awful sick look on her face. When she told us what had happened we could not believe it. We just sat there and stared at each other in disbelief.

A double funeral was held that week so we could say our goodbyes to a wonderful Christian couple who like the others earlier that summer, had died way too young.

## My First Date

It was hard for me to return to school because I would remember where my uncle would often stand in the school hallways as he waited to greet me with a smile. The rest of the school year would have to continue without his presence.

I was fifteen when I wanted to go out on a date with my girlfriend's brother but the house rules were that I could not date until I was sixteen! Somehow my girlfriend and I had convinced my parents to let us go on a double date. Afterwards, I wished that they would have just said no!

Here we were, my girlfriend and her boyfriend, my girlfriend's brother and I, on a double date. Her brother and I sat in the back seat. Oh *peachy*, was that a mistake! We were not even out of the driveway and within two seconds my date was all over me like jelly on a peanut butter sandwich! I could not believe how presumptuous he was! In fact my girlfriend was so embarrassed by her own brother's actions that she told him to behave himself.

"Cool it!" she scolded him.

We decided to go bowling. Needless to say I had never been bowling before and I wore the wrong attire, a mini skirt. It was a little bit difficult to bowl in that skirt but I did my best. Well sort of. I accidentally threw the ball backwards and I watched in horror as the ball flew out of my hand and dropped to the floor with a loud thud and then it rolled all of the way to the concession stand! My date was chasing the ball as I stood there with my hands on my face dying of embarrassment! Everyone was laughing!

As if that wasn't enough, after bowling the boys wanted to go driving around and we found ourselves in a park…*grand*! *Here we go again*! I found myself constantly slapping my date's hands and pulling him off of me…*really*!!!!! Are dates always going to be like this? I was so mortified as well as mad! I certainly did not need that in my life! I decided to *move on*.

## My Re-occurring Dream!

My school year was coming to an end and that was when my dad decided to resign as a parole officer stating to us that there were just too many politics to deal with. He didn't really know what he was going to do for work but soon was encouraged by a friend at church to become a cross-country truck driver. His friend owned his own truck and taught my dad the trade.

There for a while dad would be gone for weeks as he and his friend traveled together, but dad always managed to stay in touch with us at his stops. Oftentimes dad would call us to pick him up at night at a local truck stop where they had parked their rig and then he'd wait for the next job. But traveling all the time also had its downside as well. Dad had gotten food poisoning once and ended up with a stay in a hospital while he was out of state. He missed us tremendously as we were missing him. It didn't look like the job was going to be a fit.

For many years after we had left Kingman, Kansas, I had a re-occurring dream and it was quite bothersome to me. I never told anyone about the dream because I feared that it might just come true. I had dreamed that we had moved back to Kingman and each time that I had the dream it would bring such a dreadful feeling over me and it gave me a bit of anxiety. What a silly dream, right? *After all, it was just a dream!*

My summer break was just around the corner and it was decided that I would take a driver's education class during June and July. We also found out that dad was offered the position of Police Chief…IN KINGMAN, KANSAS! We'll just put it this way…that job offer created a family crisis. He had accepted the position and mom in her frustration stated that she was going to divorce dad. She was crying every day! We kids were also ticked off and speaking loudly with disapproval! *How could he do this to us??!!!!!*

Dad ended up moving to Kingman without his family and started his new job with the understanding that we would come join him as soon as I had finished my driver's education class. He was invited to stay with his aunt who lived in Kingman until we could arrive. Mom was still undecided as to what she was going to do at that point because she was still hurt by his decision and was crying a lot. After all, this was sprung on us so suddenly that I think she just needed some time to wrap her mind around it and accept it. Dad also made it clear that one of the stipulations of his position was the requirement that his family had to live in the community with him.

Yes, life can change in an *instant*, whether it's a car accident or some unexpected upheaval. Some of our greatest fears can actually come true. It's not always easy and it's not always fair. We definitely didn't ask for *it* but we still have to deal with *it*.

We can choose to hide from *it* or we can choose to face *it* head on. Gather your strength from the Lord and face *it* together with him. *It* just becomes a little bit easier to deal with.

## SEVEN
# Back To My Future

*"For I know the plans I have for you," declares the Lord,*
*"plans to prosper you and not to harm you, plans to give*
*you a hope and a future."*
**Jeremiah 29:11**

### Driver's Ed

It had been decided that I would take a driver's education class during the summer months in Wichita. The driver's education class at least helped me to place the impending move to Kingman out of my mind for the few hours that I was in class. I really liked taking driver's education as it was moving me just one more step towards new responsibilities, independence, and freedom! What I didn't like was the part of the curriculum that required us to watch movies of car wreck scenes with pictures of accident victims. They were awful to look at because they were a reminder to me of what had happened the summer before with my church choir and my aunt and uncle. The real fun finally began once our driver's education group was allowed to get behind the wheel of the car; there were some pretty scary car rides!

I recall specifically one evening when my parents had let me drive them around town for a while. I had made a left turn and ended up taking up two other lanes with my very fast turn. My parents were just a little bit shaken up by it and at the time I hadn't even realized what I had done until they explained it to me. Silly beginner!

Several years later, dad and I had a *real special teaching moment together* when he tried to teach me how to drive a stick-shift! (Can you feel my sarcasm?) It was a good thing that we were on the side streets because when I started out driving all I could do was jerked the car up and down each street. Jerking, jerking, and jerking! Yes, *I knew that wasn't how it was supposed to work* but I just wasn't catching onto it. UNTIL, my dad had had enough. While I was still driving, and in who knows what gear, he yelled at me.

"Pull this car *over!*" he loudly and gruffly stated.

I, of course, immediately pulled over and stopped because I was more scared of him than God at that moment.

"*Now you are going to stop this nonsense, quit jerking this car and drive it the right way!*" he sternly and emphatically stated.

I don't know what happened but suddenly I knew how to drive a stick and I never jerked the car again!

### Back to Kingman

The decision was made and we would move back to Kingman. The reality of the move started to sink in as I helped mom box up household items for our move. The return to Kingman was quiet, uneventful, and bitter sweet. It was good to see some of my old friends again from when I had attended school there before, but I didn't really want to be there.

My dad had found a cool old bungalow house to rent that probably was built in the 1900 era and it had some really neat features. The house had three bedrooms, one bathroom, and a small room at the back of the house that mom had turned into a sewing room. There was also a spacious living room with large wood sliding doors that opened to reveal a wonderful large dining room. My room was large and was painted a light lavender color. The kitchen was good sized and featured a swinging butler door that opened to the dining room. The house was heated by wall registers that were located in every room. Beautiful wood moldings trimmed the walls and high ceilings. The covered front porch of the house was nice sized and overlooked a small yard that was shaded by very large trees. The side yard had a covered porch stoop for loading and unloading the car. The back porch was all enclosed. We spent the rest of the summer getting settled in.

## Church Homeless

Regardless of our move to Kingman I was determined to keep attending church. I sure missed my church home back in Wichita and especially all of my friends. I started attending the same church that I had attended as a child when I was going to Vacation Bible School. It was there that I had made my first profession of faith. Dad was no longer attending church and mom could have cared less because the move had really set her back. My brother had quit going altogether so I went alone.

Without the support of my family it was hard for me to keep attending. I was a bit older and was developing a different understanding about some of the church attendees; definitely not the same memories that I once had as a child.

With my being the police chief's daughter I oftentimes overheard conversations about various people and their shady dealings. One Sunday morning I was totally taken back when I looked up and saw one of the deacons speaking from the pulpit. I knew that he wasn't a well-respected man in the town because of some of his business dealings. I didn't quite understand how the church would allow such a person to hold that position in the church! Needless to say, in my act of hasty *judgementalness* I decided to never go back to that church. I then became *church homeless*!

## My Junior Year

The Kingman High School was the newest of the schools in the area and it had a very modern architectural look. Many of the classrooms had glass windows for walls including the library. The art department classroom overlooked a garden area with a sculpture in its midst. Even the glass walls in the business department were arranged so that you could see into every classroom from wherever you were in that department.

Our lockers were so much different than those that we had back in Wichita. These lockers were just big enough to place our books in. Our coats had to hang on a hook below the locker and out in the open. That setup really got a few of the kids in trouble, especially when some of the older bigger kids would hang some of the younger shorter ones by their belt loops on those hooks!

As I remember back to my first week of school I was just trying to find my place amongst all of the other kids. Several times there were those who would come up to me to tell me how we used to be friends back in grade school and that we had played together. Most of the time I really did not remember them and I sometimes wondered if maybe they were just trying to get on my good side by telling me that. Here I was, once again having to be very cautious with who was trying to be my friend and to what their motives were.

A former best friend from grade school and I made connections right away but it didn't take me long to figure out that I was not going to be able to hang out with her. For me it was very heart breaking, but she had chosen another path, one in which I could not follow her in. She in turn also took it pretty hard that our friendship had to be at arm's length and even resorted to sticking her tongue out at me on several occasions in the lunch room when she would look my direction. Because I didn't want to hurt her feelings even more I never offered a good explanation to her as to why. I just couldn't continue being friends with her.

Do you remember reading earlier where I had written about a boy who had held me at knife point? Even though he was no longer in school and was traveling in and out of town he began hanging around with her group of friends! I had never told anyone about what had happened to me with that boy years earlier and I still wasn't going to tell anyone. He was still up to his same old tricks and had taken advantage of some of the girls in that group.

Unfortunately my dad had to deal with that young man as he was wreaking havoc. The young man's mother had to call the police on many occasions because of her own son. I remember one time when my dad had had enough of the guy when he had come into town and raped his own mother, again! My dad was called in on the ordeal and he arrested him. When the guy lipped off to my dad at the police station, dad slammed him up against the wall and stated that that was for the time that he had pulled a knife on his daughter many years ago. There was a time when a policeman could get away with some of these types of situations and that was one of those times. When dad confessed to my mother what he had done to the guy, she was scared. She thought for sure that the guy would come after me again. Unfortunately, you will read about him yet again.

It took me several weeks to make new friends but one day a girl sitting in front of me in one of my classes turned around and introduced herself to me. She had noticed that I was pretty much a loner at school and we became instant friends. She in turn introduced me to her circle of friends. These were the *good* girls and we had so much clean fun together. Without hesitation I was welcomed into that group and it didn't matter *who* I was. A few of those girls are still very good friends of mine to this day!

Our group of girls sometimes acted so crazy and we always seemed to be laughing at all of our own silliness. We would do all kinds of things out of the ordinary just for entertainment. One of the things we loved doing was dragging Main Street after school, in the evenings, and over the week-ends. There were even times that we would put our windshield wipers on, even though it wasn't raining, and just for fun we'd watch the old people look up at the sky! We got a good laugh out of that one!

There was a time when one of the girls had been rejected by one of her guy friends but that was not the end of the story! Some of the girls from our group became accomplices in watching that girl place a dead woodpecker in a shoebox and then place that box on his front porch. She then rang his doorbell and ran away and hid. The thing that wasn't cool is that the guy lived right across the street from me and I definitely didn't want him to figure out who did it!

That same girl became the town's E. Bunny! She would select deserving people in our community who she thought should be the recipients of a surprise Easter basket. The people that were usually selected were teachers, someone elderly, or even an outstanding person who was known for their good works in the community. I had even helped her deliver several of the special baskets one time and I found it to be fun. The gift card attached was always signed by E. Bunny. One of us would place the basket on a porch, ring the doorbell, and run and hide so we wouldn't get caught. I only wish that we could have seen their faces after receiving those wonderful baskets of goodies! As far as I know, no one ever figured out who the mystery E. Bunny was.

One time after a football game we girls decided to go tee-pee the coach's house. We could have been called the Mission Impossible Girls! We were all dressed in dark clothes and I parked my car down the street a ways from the coach's house. We proceeded to crawl on our bellies using our elbows up the large inclined front yard with our trusty toilet paper in hand. Just as we were into position to start our dastardly deed a patrol car came around the corner with a spotlight no less! REALLY? With us all dressed in dark clothes and hiding in the bushes we were hoping that we were not spotted. When I looked over at the patrol car I noticed that it was my dad! *Of course*! But he kept driving on by slowly as we stayed in those bushes being as quiet as a bunch of church mice. Whew! We didn't get caught and we were able to tee-pee the coach's house. At least I didn't think that we had gotten caught. The next day at breakfast my dad mentioned that the coach's house had been tee-peed the night before. I just kept eating trying to ignore his statement. He then sternly looked across the table right at me.

"By the way, I spotted your car parked a ways down the street from his house last night," he firmly stated.

I was BUSTED!!

### Prom Night Escapade

My junior year of high school was such a fun year. Despite the fact of *who* I was, I finally felt like I was being accepted as just one of the girls. One of the junior class student's projects was to plan and put together the prom for the senior class. It was a lot of fun to plan the event and I even designed the front cover for the prom program. It turned out to be such a beautiful evening and everyone was all dressed up in seventies style prom dresses and tuxes. My mom had helped me make my prom dress. All the girls were dressed very elegantly and appropriately for their age and not as provocative as what the girls often wear to today's proms.

We had decorated the gym elegantly and everyone that came had a great time. Sometimes our crazy group of girls would get out on the dance floor and dance in a circle. As for dancing with the boys, well they could be so *shy* at times! After the prom we all went home and changed our clothes and met up later at one of our friend's house where we planned to have a slumber party. Before retiring for the night we had fun driving up and down Main Street waving to all of our friends as we passed each other by. It was a perfect spring evening and everyone was having so much fun!

After the evening of fun and laughter we returned to our friend's house and decided to call it a night. My friend had a really cool bedroom on the second floor of their home and of course we didn't go to sleep right away. We kept talking and sharing about our experiences that had happened earlier in the evening and rehashed all of the fun that we had had. We were just a bunch of giggly girls, what can I say?

After a while we started hearing pebbles being thrown at the bedroom window. When we went to the window to investigate, we looked down to the front yard and saw a couple of guys standing there who asked us go for a ride around town with them. Since my friend's parents were sound asleep by then, we decided to carefully sneak down the wooden staircase from the second floor and join the guys. We sure didn't want to wake her parents. As I think about it, we were ESCAPEES!!!

All of us girls joined the guys in one of the boy's car and took a spin around town. You need to remember that we were the good kids. There was no drinking or taking drugs, just good old clean giggly fun. We were only gone for about an hour or so when we decided to return back to the house. Again we girls found ourselves sneaking back up that creaky wooden staircase trying not to wake the guardians. Whew! We did it!

After a small amount of time had lapsed and none of us girls had fallen asleep yet we began hearing pebbles hitting the bedroom window again. We realized that the guys had come back and we found ourselves sneaking down those wooden stairs again and still not getting caught!

This time we drove all over town and even to the outskirts of town where we came to the cliffs, a very fun and dangerous place to ride around at night, *because there were cliffs!* There was even a large hill that everyone wanted to drive down very fast. At the bottom of the hill was a very huge old tree. The trick was to drive as fast as you could down that hill and not hit the tree!!! What were we teenagers thinking, really!! *We did that*? YES! The car was packed with nine or more of us kids but who was counting! There were just too many kids in that car! Somehow we were able to accomplish the trick without incident but when we drove back into town we noticed that some road blocks had been set up.

## A Murder Happened on Prom Night

I told the driver of the car how to get around the road blocks. I knew if I got caught by one of the officers it was sure punishment for me. It was way past my curfew! And I knew that we could very well get pulled over for having way too many kids in one car so when we passed close to a police car some of us would duck down. As we drove close to the hospital clinic area we saw all kinds of red lights flashing and a lot of commotion going on. We drove around the area several times always being careful not to drive too close. I mentioned to the group that maybe the place had gotten broken into again. The clinic sat on the main highway that went through town and it was always being targeted for drugs. With the clinic being located on the main highway it made for a quick get-a-way for any thieves.

We continued driving around town and we were able to elude all the road blocks that had been set up. We were having so much fun that we didn't realize that it was five-thirty a.m. in the morning!!! We quickly returned to the home where we were staying and snuck back up those wooden stairs just one more time. That time we were all exhausted and we were close to falling asleep.

At six thirty a.m. the phone started ringing off the hook. The ringing awoke my friend's mother and she answered the phone.

"Debra, it's your mother on the phone!" she hollered up the stairs.

All I could think about was that we had almost gotten caught! The girls started razzing me about my mom calling. I picked up the extension phone in the bedroom and I could not have been prepared for what my mom was about to tell me.

"You need to come home right away," she said.

She proceeded to tell me that my dad's best friend and fellow officer had been murdered!

"Come right away," she said. "I need to go sit with his wife and children."

Things got real serious real fast. The days that followed were horrible as we realized the details of a senseless murder that had taken the life of a young officer who left behind a wife and two very young children.

The funeral for a very good Christian man was attended by many and was held at his church home in Wichita. With the brotherhood came a sea of officers from all over the country to be in attendance. They were in full official dress uniforms. My mother and we kids drove to the funeral together while dad followed later behind us as he was still in investigative mode.

After returning home from the services the phone rang. It was dad calling to speak to our mother. Somehow my dad had found out about my prom night escapade. We girls apparently did not get away with our all-night prom outing after all. The look on my mother's face after she put the phone receiver down was that of horror and before she even said anything, I knew what she had just been told. I KNEW THAT I WAS IN BIG-TIME TROUBLE!!!

Mom had me tell her everything that we did. I told mom that we were just riding around and we weren't out causing any trouble. We weren't out drinking or doing drugs. We did nothing at all that was immoral. I just wasn't sure if she was buying all it or what her thoughts were. The only crime I committed was not being at my friend's house all night. Mom expressed in no uncertain terms how sick it made her feel and knowing that we could have come upon that murder scene innocently and could have very well become one of the victims ourselves. And yes we did drive many times by that clinic before the road blocks had been set up. We could have, yes we could have been victims. I was grounded and sent to my room.

When dad returned home later in the evening he came and stood at my bedroom door. His face was drawn with a sad look displayed all over his face. He lifted his head up and looked at me with tears in his eyes.

"Why did you do it?" he asked.

I knew that he was dealing with the horrible death of his very dear friend and was spending many hours on the investigation, the last thing he needed was to have to deal with me too. I felt so awful. I had never seen him so distraught like that before. He stood there for a few brief moments and then he turned and walked away. I felt that I had hurt him so badly and I wept.

### I Got Nailed!

The news and details of how the murder came about was horrifying and frightening. Apparently dad and his friend had switched places at the last minute that fateful evening. Even the dispatcher did not even know immediately of the last minute switch. My dad was exhausted and, at the request of his friend the captain, he went home to rest while his friend took the foot patrol for that evening. Foot patrol meant that that officer had to walk up and down Main Street checking each business to make sure that all of the doors were locked and that all the buildings were safe and secure. Foot patrol was a positive deterrent for the number of incidences that had occurred around the core area of town. The clinic just happened to be a part of that foot patrol beat. Apparently the captain had surprised someone breaking into the clinic and they had shot him execution style. Neighbors heard the gun shots but didn't see anything. Some time had passed and when the captain didn't check in or answer his calls the search began for him.

Because it was also prom night and all of us kids had been out driving up and down the streets all night, the high school students were targeted by the investigators for questioning. Surely one or more of the students may have seen something and could provide a possible lead?

The questioning of the students was over until one evening when my dad asked me if I had been questioned yet. I had never been called up for questioning even though I had watched each student getting called into the office one by one. The next day I was called in for questioning too. I was basically placed under oath and had to answer all of the questions truthfully. I knew that my dad would be reading my statement and he would have all the gory details of that night to do with, uh, I wasn't sure!

How did my dad find out about my prom night outing? At first I was a bit perplexed about that. I began to question the girls with the thought that one of them had said something even though I thought for sure that no one would say anything. Come to find out one of the boys in the car did not know who I was! He didn't know that I was the police chief's daughter! Because he had stayed out all night his mother locked him out of their house and he slept in his car in their driveway the rest of the night. The next morning the news of the murder was all over town and his mother insisted that he go to the police station and tell what he did and saw the night of the murder just in case he might have some valuable information to share.

As fate would have it, my dad had interviewed him. I could see it all playing out in my mind as that kid was innocently telling his story of staying out all night, naming names and telling what we all did and where we had gone. My dad was recognizing some of the names that the guy was mentioning and stopped him in mid-sentence.

"Was one of those girls tall?" he asked.

"Yes sir," he replied.

"Was her name Debra?" he asked.

"Yes, I do believe so, sir," he innocently replied back.

I WAS NAILED!!!

## Was It A Hit Intended For My Dad?

"How did you get all around town and avoid all of the road blocks?" my dad inquired. It was several weeks after the murder before he could ask me that question. I was sure that it had bugged him. If a teenage girl could figure out how to do these kinds of things, hmmmmmmm…just sayin'!

Dad worked very hard on that murder case and it became pretty much a part of his being for the next whole year and longer. I am not sure how the murderer was caught, but with dad's collaboration with other agencies he was able to bring the killer back to Kingman for trial. The trial itself was a very hard one for everyone having to recall all of the specific events that happened that evening. The newspaper covered the trial and it was all laid out in full print for the community to stay abreast of. Because of a typographical error in the recording of a serial number and even with overwhelming evidence, the jury found the person not guilty. It was a devastating blow. Dad knew that they had the right man. The criminal had warrants all over the state for his crimes. He even bragged to one of his cell mates about how he had murdered a cop in Kingman and that the crazy people had let him off. Because of his many other crimes, he did spend the rest of his life in prison.

The next mystery and rumors to arise from the murder case was that the murder could have been an intended hit for my dad. Remember I had mentioned earlier about the last minute switch between the two men that no one knew about immediately. Even ten years later, long after the murder had taken place and long after my dad had retired, he was still approached by some investigators showing an interest in re-investigating the case to see if the rumors were true. Dad became very agitated with them and even told them to please drop it! I myself was approached twenty five years later by an officer wanting to know where the files were stored at for that case because there were still people wanting to re-investigate the case. Since the case is still considered open because of the not guilty verdict, there are still people out there who have different theories as to what really happened that fateful night.

My dad always cherished the memories he had of his friend and helped plan the building of the city's rifle range that was named after the fallen hero, memorializing him forever in that community.

### I Was a Feisty One!

The summer between my junior and senior year went pretty fast. I started working at a local restaurant on Main Street as a waitress. The reason I went to work was so that I could buy my first car. I took out a loan at the local bank in the amount of five-hundred dollars and my parents co-signed for me. Between my wages of $1.10 per hour and the tips that I received, I was able to pay off the loan very quickly.

Working at the restaurant became an eye-opener for me to say the least. It was located right next to the local bar so dealing with some occasional drunks was quite an experience! It was a family owned restaurant that offered some good old home-style cooking from a menu of hamburgers to steaks. I caught on to my job pretty quickly and discovered for the first time that I really enjoyed serving people! I even got to know some of the regulars including one young man in particular. I'd say he was in his mid to late twenties and he had some mental challenges. He would ride his bike everywhere in town and wherever he wanted to go. His bike was equipped with a very tall pole sporting a bright orange flag to let drivers know to be alert and to be cautious as they approached him. Even though he had mental challenges he was a really nice person. He did however, become smitten with me. I didn't do anything to cause that to happen; he did that all on his own. I was just being my friendly self!

One day he showed up at the restaurant with a ring and he wanted me to wear it. I soon realized that he also wanted to marry me and that the ring he was carrying was from the local jewelers! I being so young really didn't take it seriously and didn't know what to do so I put the ring on anyway to save him some embarrassment. Of course I didn't give him an answer to his proposal! Later that evening he brought his father in to eat with him. I could tell by his father's expression that he was embarrassed for me and he tried to smooth things out a bit with me and his son. I offered to give the ring back to him but he told me that I could keep it. I kept that ring for over thirty years to help remind me of a very special genuine person who had many challenges to face in his life. Through all of the teasing he had endured and all of the daily ridicule he had to face from others he always had a great smiley attitude. I would always be honored to call him my friend.

At the restaurant I also had to deal with many not-so-nice people as well. One time I had a person tell me that I would be cute if I just didn't smile! It was a good thing that I was a feisty gal and didn't take much offense to his remark, so every time I served him, I gave him a *great big* smile! The way some of the other patrons acted you'd think that I was a waitress at some bar. I learned early on to be pretty quick witted with some of the real jerks and put them in their places!

I had a male co-worker who was pretty mean to me at times and he was the cook. One of his tricks was to throw hamburger patties up on the ceiling so they would stick, then he would jump up to grab them and throw them back down on the grill. Okay, this is not going to be one of those horror stories about eating out at a restaurant. Not really. Read on!

I had to always be aware of where that guy was and what he was doing. I didn't like him much at all as his innuendoes were awfully raw! He tried to scare me one time by locking me in the freezer after the restaurant had closed for the evening. I really didn't know if he was going to let me out or not. I knew that eventually my dad would come looking for me, but would it be before I froze to death? The guy did eventually come back and let me out. I think that he was just trying to scare me into some kind of submission or something. He didn't know that he was dealing with a feisty bear cat!

At yet another time he cornered me in the back room. He was so much bigger than me and I didn't know how I was going to get out of that one. I knew that I was totally cornered. Luckily the boss started shouting something to him and he had to let me go. When I told my dad about these events his officers started watching what was going on there, especially after dark in the back alley where I had to park my car.

Because of that watch, they discovered a few *"things"* that were going on there.

On many other occasions I had to deal with a drunken boss and she was a mess. She would get to drinking at the restaurant and make a total fool out of herself. One night after work we had an employee holiday party. My dad just happened to be on foot patrol and accidentally opened the front door of the restaurant but quickly closed it when he realized that we were having a party. My drunken boss was totally out of line when she made fun of me and made rude statements about how my dad was checking up on me. She went on and on about my dad and in a very bad way! For a while I tolerated her outbursts; I didn't do so well, however, on another evening when she got drunk and went off on my dad again.

It was closing time and my boss was already tanked up from drinking all evening. She was sitting at the front of the restaurant counting the cash for the day and I was back in the kitchen cleaning up. I could hear her loud and clear as she made fun of my dad and she knew that I could hear. I simply put down my cleaning gloves and walked out the back door quitting my job. I didn't even say goodbye. I went directly home and told my parents what I had done. They totally understood and they both thought that I didn't need to be subjected to that kind of treatment any longer. I knew then that I wasn't in trouble with my parents for walking out. Believe it or not my boss had the nerve to have a co-worker approach me and ask me if I would come back to work!!!

## My Senior Year

Finally I was a senior!! It was a very exciting year just knowing that graduation from high school was just around the corner. I spent most of my senior year in the business department as I took every business course that was offered. Many times I would stay after school with some of my friends to work on class projects or to use some of the office equipment.

I sure liked my business teacher even though she was a no-frills kind of person. I learned a lot from her and appreciated her so much for her professional teachings.

One day I had spent several hours after school to work on some papers. When I went out to the parking lot I found that some poor guy had waited for me all that time. He was parked right in front of my car with his trunk next to my front end. After school he had decided to show off to his friends a little by hitting the gas to peel out of his parking space. The trouble was, he had it in reverse!! Yep, he smashed the front end of my car! He was so scared of what he had done because I was the police chief's daughter. Poor guy! We did exchange information and he told me that his insurance would fix my car.

A week later I was on the highway that went through town and I was getting ready to make a left hand turn. I had stopped for a semi traveling towards me to pass. A car smacked me from behind sending me out in front of that semi and across the road landing me in front of a tree! Of course the trunk was all bent up. Okay, I thought to myself, I could see the good in this; I wasn't hurt in either case, except for a whiplash, and the car only had to go to the shop once to get both ends fixed!!!

I did not like my government class and that government teacher took the cake in all categories! I remember that I sat in the very back of his class room.

One day, and I believe it was on a Monday, he made a remark that I will never forget! Before he started teaching, he stood up and very grimly, and through clenched teeth made a startling statement.

"Guess whose dad busted the beer party Saturday night?" he smirked.

Everyone in the class turned around and looked at me. I was just mortified! First of all I didn't even know that there was even a beer party and secondly, I certainly didn't know that my dad had busted it!! Yes, we had teachers in the high school who were providing beer for the kids. Big surprise!

Not everyone at school knew who I was, especially if they were new to the area. I remember one such boy who sat in front of me in one of my classes. He had turned around and showed me his bag of weed and offered to sell me some. I started laughing so hard *inside*! Another boy sitting in front of him saw what was going on and he started waving his arms trying to get the kids attention so he would shut up. I just couldn't contain myself any longer.

"*What's wrong*?" I asked in my sheepish laughing voice to the kid waving his arms.

He finally spoke up and shouted, "Her dad's the police chief!"

The look on that seller's face was priceless!

"You are not going to tell on me are you?" he asked in a panic.

I told him that I didn't need to tell my dad anything because he already knew everything. The kid was literally shaking in his boots!!!

### Black, Oozy Stuff!

Our family moved once again to a home that my parents had purchased. It was a more modern structure and smaller than the bungalow we had just moved from. It was shortly after that move that my mother started working outside of the home. She took a job at a nursing home and worked second shift as an aide.

Mom would get home from work around eleven p.m. every night. Since mom was no longer at home when we kids got home from school there was a bit of foolishness that happened around the house. I tried picking up the slack by helping out with the chores, cooking dinner, ironing dad's police uniforms, and many other things that mom used to do. I must tell you that cooking dinner proved to be a quite an experience for me as well as for my family. Mom would leave instructions for me on how to cook the food as well as gather up all of the ingredients that I would need and placed them on the counter top before she left for work.

I remember the first time that I tried cutting up a whole chicken! I thought for sure that I was going to be sick. First I couldn't stand the way that the loose skin felt in my hands and secondly I had to cut through the joints…oh my! We were lucky to even have had dinner that night!

On another occasion mom left instructions for me to cook some steaks in the pressure cooker. I was a bit scared of the pressure cooker because I had heard how they could explode, but I seemed to get the steamer to rock okay. Shortly after I got the meat started one of my friends called me to see if I would go with her to get new tires for her car. She was a very experienced farm girl who had been cooking for her family since she was very young and she assured me that we had plenty of time to get the tires for her car and still be back in time to finish the supper.

Okay! This is my version of the story and I am sticking to it! In all fairness I didn't know how to cook. It was simply a shot-in-the-dark every time I tried cooking and getting new tires on my friend's car took just a bit longer than anticipated. When the mechanic finished we quickly drove back to my house but when we pulled up into the driveway we could smell IT! And IT was not smelling that good! We immediately ran into the house only to discover that the house was filled with smoke! We were able to get the cooker off of the stove and hurriedly opened up all of the windows and doors to let out the dark smelly smoke. A closer examination of the cooker showed black oozy stuff pouring out on all sides. The house stunk so we tried spraying air freshener all over the place to try to cover up that awful smell.

To make matters worse my dad would *have* to show up just at that time for his supper! We watched him walk around the house to the back kitchen door. We were paralyzed with anticipation of what he was going to say to us!

"What are we going to do?" we asked each other as we were freaking out.

"Quick, open the lid and we will just scrape off the burnt stuff and throw the meat in with some potatoes," my friend said.

Just as I had opened the cooker dad had arrived at the back door. When I glanced inside the pot I was struck with horror at the sight, there wasn't any meat in the bottom! It had disintegrated into a small round black blob!

Dad walked in the back door and asked us what was going on because he had noticed that the house smelled like it was on fire! My girlfriend apologized and said that it was all her fault. I was apologizing because I knew how hard it was for my family to provide groceries. Dad said that it was no big deal and that accidents do happen. Still I knew that I had to face my mother when she got home, because I not only ruined dinner, I had ruined her cooker! No matter what I did the black stuff was not coming off of the cooker and I couldn't even get the burnt smell out of the house.

Several hours later and while I was ironing one of dad's uniforms mom arrived home. Immediately when she walked in the door she made comment about the house smelling like smoke. When she saw me ironing she just assumed that I had burnt dad's uniform. I was so terrified to tell her what had actually happened.

"Accidents happen!" she exclaimed after I told her.

I asked myself if I was really off the hook that easily. I think that they had seen how frightened I was as my actions almost burned down the house; they weren't that hard on me. That day I learned a valuable lesson to never leave the stove unattended while I cooked!

## A Froggy Good Time!

One evening my brother found a frog in our back yard and he wanted to make it his house pet. I tried to tell him that mom was not going to be too happy with a frog in the house. I also told him that he better make sure that the frog made it back outside when he got through playing with it and before mom got home from work.

When it was about time for our mother to arrive home I asked him if he had gotten that frog out of the house.

"Uh…I lost the frog and it's somewhere in the house." he answered very slowly.

"You did what!?" I screamed.

So here we were turning the house upside down trying to find that silly green frog. We never did find it before mom got home!

When mom finally arrived home from work she needed to iron a couple of things for the next day so she set up the ironing board in the kitchen. I was in my room and told myself that I was not going to tell her about the loose frog in the house. My brother was in his room too and I knew for certain that he wasn't going to tell her either. All of a sudden and with great commotion we heard mom screaming! I came running out of my room just in time to see that silly frog jumping up and down mom's legs going up under her dress and then back down again to the floor. It was quite a sight! Mom and the frog were both jumping up and down with mom flapping her arms up and down and screaming. I really did not know how I could help her!

The next few words out of my mother's mouth were my brother's first, middle, and last name, which meant that she knew he was behind that ordeal and the one who was going to be in big trouble. She was expecting him to rescue her from that frog! What a sight and what a commotion. I think both the frog and mom were very thankful to be rescued from each other.

## Creating Lasting Memories

The rest of my senior year was a total blast as we were all creating lasting memories that we would cherish forever. Memories of going to our homecomings, getting ready for prom and graduation, and making plans for the future were all memories that would last a lifetime. DID I SAY THE FUTURE? I hadn't quite figured out where I was going to college yet or what I wanted to be when I grew up! Yikes!!! I made an appointment with the school counselor to see what suggested fields of study would be great fits for me. I had my choice of Interior Design, Graphic Arts, and Fashion Merchandising all of which were a match for me. Great! I had choices and I liked all of them! I was finally able to narrow down the choices and I chose Fashion Merchandising. The hunt for a college was on.

My graduation day came and went and I had chosen a college in Wichita. I was looking forward to the summer and spending what time I could with my friends before we had to all go our separate ways. I felt that I had come a long ways from that shy introverted little girl that I had been all those years before. I still wasn't that outgoing but I had finally come into my own or so it seemed.

I kind of grew into a very out-spoken opinionated young lady, especially around the house. My dad and I started rubbing each other the wrong way and it became very upsetting to him.

Because of my attitude my mom had asked me to please move out of the house earlier than what I had planned to do. So I moved back to Wichita ahead of schedule to begin my future. You might say that I was going *back to my future.*

I said all my goodbyes to my friends and moved away never to return to live there ever again.

Over the years I would oftentimes be asked why I never returned.

"I didn't *lose* anything there!" I would emphatically state.

## EIGHT
# The Private Girl's College

*Instruct a wise man and he will be wiser still; teach a righteous man and he will add to his learning.*
**Proverbs 9:9**

### Out of the Small Town Spotlight

As I look back I could see why I was asked to leave my family earlier than planned. Mom was genuinely concerned for my dad because he had so many pressures placed on him and the last thing he needed was to deal with an unruly daughter and all the drama she was creating at home. Having to leave my friends earlier than planned was very hard for me though, but I knew that a few of them would also be moving to the Wichita area soon to continue their education as well.

Everything I owned I packed into my car and moved from Kingman to Wichita. My grandparents were gracious and let me move into their very pretty guest bedroom which I basically took over. My grandmother had placed a very pretty light blue sheer fabric bedspread that had a lot of ruffles on the bed. The windows were trimmed with curtains made out of the same ruffles and were framed with dark blue brocade drapes. The matching bedroom furniture was made of the popular blonde wood that had been fashionable during the sixties. On the walls hung many family pictures including pictures of my grandparents when they were very young as well as some older pictures of our ancestors. After I moved in I remember mom having a conversation with my grandmother.

"If you smell something weird coming from Debra's room, it's just incense!" my mom told her.

It really *was* just incense.

I liked living with my grandparents even though my grandmother liked to meddle too much in my life. My grandmother was still employed at a meat-packing plant and had to be up very early in the morning for the first shift. She spent a lot of time on her hair and makeup as she had to look just right! I always thought that she was so pretty even though she never thought that of herself. Despite her wonderful smelling perfume that she wore all of the time, I still remember how she smelled of smoky wieners when she came home from work!

Grandfather was retired and was a laid-back kind of a guy and he could be pretty funny at times. He would sing old folklore tunes that had funny verses and he often quoted crazy funny poems. His two best friends were his Chihuahua dogs. It seemed like grandfather was always holding his two dogs and would let both of them sleep on his tummy when he was taking a nap on the sofa.

I became reacquainted with my cousins who lived next door to my grandparents. Their mother was a real lifesaver for me and I found myself talking with her for hours. She was a very experienced mother who had raised five children two of which were twins. She was a stay-at-home mom who proved to be very helpful to me when I was sad, frustrated, or if I just needed to get away from my grandparents for a bit. I liked not living in the spotlight of a small town again. Getting adjusted to my new life away from home took no time at all. I finally felt free!

## A College with Very High Standards

I had decided earlier in the spring of my senior year to attend a private girl's college that was located on the east side of Wichita. I felt that with my passion for creativity it would be a good fit for me. The college was very strict and the dean required that my parents participate in the initial interviewing process. The college building itself was two-storied with a white colonial façade entrance with neatly trimmed spiral evergreens located outside the front door. The interior of the building featured a large beautiful crystal chandelier that hung in the foyer with champagne colored plush carpet throughout. There was a marvelous curved wooden banister staircase that led up to the second floor. That place was so beautiful!

We met with the dean in his handsomely decorated office who gave us information about the college. He asked my parents some serious questions about me which included questions about my high school grades, which by the way, almost kept me from getting in. The dean decided to give me a chance anyway. The school held very high standards for its students and only wanted to graduate the very best. The college was known for graduating well-polished knowledgeable students and their reputation was on the line. The students were asked not to work while attending school because the course study was very fast paced and rigorous. It was like taking two years of college in nine months!

Several girls attending the school that year were not making the grade and were asked to leave the school. There simply was no tolerance for tardiness, skipping classes, bad grades, and definitely no tolerance for not acting like a lady!

I remember one time when I had a nose bleed for three days and had to miss school. That nose bleed was a doozy! I had even visited the emergency room at the hospital over three times to get my nose packed and I was even given shots to try to help stop the bleeding but nothing worked. I had lost a lot of blood and had to sleep sitting up. One time I almost strangled on the packing when it started coming out in the back of my throat but thanks to my grandmother's quick actions she saved me! I informed the school what was happening and was told that I needed to speak to the dean when I was able to return to school.

I was a bit scared my first day back at school because I had to go to the dean's office and I didn't know what to expect. After I shared my story with him he believed me and all was good. I was allowed to return to school.

My classes were scheduled for every morning until noon Monday through Friday. Although there were several different career classes being taught we students had one thing in common, we all had to attend the required finishing and modeling classes a couple of afternoons a week. And believe it or not, we all were required to wear panty girdles because proper girls did not wiggle!!! Every so often they would test us randomly to make sure we were wearing them!!! *A little too personal if you ask me.*

I repeat, the college wanted to graduate only the very best so the required finishing classes did help us to accomplish the confidence needed to do so as well as gain the grace and composure that most of us needed to have. To help with posture and balance we took fencing, ballet, and modeling. Included was a breathing class too. Yep, I thought that was kind of strange! Believe it or not, most of us do not breathe correctly. I just figured that if I was still standing, I was still breathing!!! Not so!

We also took public speaking classes which really scared the *bejeebies* out of me!! Who knew that many years later I would have to rely on the training that I received from those classes!

Of course we learned how to properly apply our makeup, learn important beauty secrets, and learn how to get in and out of a car! *Yes, we even walked down the stairs with a book on our heads.* We learned proper manners and how to act like proper ladies.

I took classes that taught retail math, marketing, graphic ad design, the study of fabrics, mercantile, and the list went on and on! When we finished one course we started another course which was sometimes even harder than the class before. I had originally chosen that college to become a fashion buyer but the information that I gained from that school really helped spur my career in to other and more fascinating directions.

When we took our winter break it was a month long and it ended up not being a break at all. My assignment for that month was to design a store from the ground up and that meant blueprints, store design, types of fixtures, logo designs, how many dollars of merchandise needed per square foot, marketing, the type of merchandise that would be carried, and basically the whole business plan for a new store. That was a lot of work and it had to be done in a month, but I aced it!!!! I truly had found my niche!

I often stayed up late into the middle of the night many times typing papers, organizing folders, and notebooks while working on assignments. It truly was a very hard year of study for me. Several times I remember sitting on the bedroom floor with my door closed with the typewriter in my lap (we didn't have computers back then) so tired and sobbing! But I was totally dedicated and delivered only the best that I had to give and did whatever it took to make it happen.

Several of my high school friends had also attended that college. It was so good to see some of them occasionally at school. But there wasn't much time for a social life because it was pretty much taken up with homework. I could see why the school didn't want their students to have jobs.

Sometimes my friends and I would take a break on weekend evenings and drive up and down Douglas Avenue, which was the main drag at that time in Wichita, flirting with the guys and having a grand time. We were never brave enough to meet up with any of the guys that wanted us to pull over and talk with them. We would drive on! Silly small town girls!

## Should I Try Attending Church Again?

I tried attending my former church home again in Wichita. It was so great seeing my friends again but I soon discovered that most of them were headed off in different directions. Some were leaving for college while others had gotten married and were moving away with their new husbands.

I remember my first Sunday back at the church. The youth pastor that I had held up in such high esteem had asked if he could come up and speak to the congregation right after the service. His request was honored. Apparently he had fallen from grace and it had destroyed his marriage and it had ruined any chances of him ever being a youth pastor again and to the point that he was excommunicated from the church! That was his first Sunday back and he wanted to apologize and ask for forgiveness from the congregation because he wanted to come back to the church; the church agreed.

I tried connecting with the church several times but it just wasn't the same for me. I eventually quit attending. I would visit my grandparent's church when they would push the issue with me but it just wasn't the same either. I ended up becoming a holiday Christian and only attended church on the important holidays.

## My Convention Center Graduation

Yes it was a lot of hard work but it was worth it. I did it! I loved that college and I graduated! It sure stretched me and I grew so much and in so many ways. The studies not only gave me some confidence but also gave me a sense of pride for my accomplishments. Our graduation was held at the Century II Convention Center in Wichita but I can barely remember anything that happened that day!

One thing I do remember was that the college staff was afraid that they would experience the uninvited *streaker* that had often appeared at the previous years' graduation ceremonies. The streaker apparently would run across the stage during the ceremony with all of his glory shining!!! Our ceremony was *not* that exciting.

One of the reasons that I had chosen that school was because I wanted to learn what I needed to know quickly so that I could get my career started right away. As it goes with most colleges they make promises to help with job placement, which by the way, is their way of saying that they will give you a few leads. The rest is up to you to make it happen.

A few weeks had passed since my graduation and I was filling out job application forms everywhere it seemed. My first school loan payment was quickly approaching and I had nothing to pay it with! The pressure was on and I was getting pretty discouraged. I called dad and whined a bit to him but dad was not all that helpful.

"Girl, you need to go over to the police academy and get enrolled!" he said loudly.

"What!?" I exclaimed.

Where did that comment come from? Obviously he was not in tune with his own daughter! After all I had just finished college and the idea of becoming a police woman was the furthest thing from my mind!!! His remark made me even more discouraged!

After a few days of interviews I finally landed my first job when a fashion buyer from an upscale department store was willing to take a chance on me. I was hired on the spot to work in the ladies fashion department in sales and that was my first break into the exciting world of my new career!

## NINE

# My Slow Descent

*Do you not know that your body is a temple of the Holy*
*Spirit, who is in you, whom you have received from God?*
*You are not your own; you were bought at a price. Therefore*
*honor God with your body.*
1 Corinthians 6:19-20

### I Was Off and Running!

It was just pure joy working at that department store in Wichita. I was in sales heaven in the ladies fashion department. The ladies that worked in the department were much older than I and most were from affluent backgrounds. I looked up to the others as mentors and yes, they were ladies with all the formalities of grammar, manners, and proper etiquette.

I had never seen so many beautiful clothes in my entire life! I'm surprised that I even had a paycheck left to take home! I loved getting all dressed up and accessorized. I had come from a background of not being able to afford such fashions let alone having more than a few outfits to wear.

The clientele that shopped at that department store were usually upper-class ladies. I was able to work with and admire some very outstanding women who were leaders in the community and my job was to meet their needs on the sales floor and in the fitting rooms. I would bring them clothing that I thought would fit their figures and their societal occasions. Basically I provided the best customer service that they had come to expect and were accustomed to.

Shortly after I began my new job three of my friends had secured an apartment which was less than a block away from the department store that I worked at and they wanted to know if I would be interested in moving in with them. That was an ideal situation because I wouldn't have to drive across town any longer. A perfect solution!

The apartment complex where I moved to, the condo tower next to it, and the shopping center where I worked at, were all owned by a prominent Wichita family. The widowed woman of that prominent family lived at the top of the condo towers and would occasionally shop at the store. She was such a lovely kind lady and not what you would expect from someone who was one of the wealthiest women in our community.

My grandparents had helped me move and they even loaned me a few pieces of their furniture that the apartment lacked. The apartment was on the third floor and was spacious. It had two bedrooms, two baths, a combined living room and dining room, a balcony, and a good sized kitchen. I had heard that at one time these apartments were sold as condos but just recently had been converted to apartments. Of course we had the use of the clubhouse plus a large swimming pool.

My roommates and I had fun times there and I was designated as the fix-it person when anything broke. Even though there was a handyman we could call if anything needed repair we were kind of *weirded* out by him. On one of his fix-it excursions in our apartment we found evidence that he had gone through our dresser drawers while we were all at work. I ended up fixing as much as I could just to keep him from coming into our apartment.

One time I had to fix the garbage disposal. The girls didn't know that you couldn't wash your hair over a disposal. The hair wraps around the moving parts and freezes everything up. That was a successful fix after I dug out all of the hair. There was one time when my fix wasn't so successful. One of the girls had dropped one of her contacts down the bathroom sink and I had to take the pipes apart so I could find it. Found! And before long I had put the pipes back together and voila all was fixed, right? *Wrong*! We had all left the apartment for the evening and when we returned we saw water leaking from the third floor down into the second story outdoor hanging light and then down onto the sidewalk! Above that hanging light…was our bathroom!!! Oh no! We went running up the stairs as quickly as possible and discovered that the pipes were leaking. I hadn't sealed the pipes when I had put everything back together again. Duh!!

## I Fell In Love with the Night Life

Working in retail sometimes requires crazy long hours and it was hard for me at times to do things with the friends I lived with. My trying to find time to spend with my roommates was almost impossible. My work hours were sometimes the exact opposite of their working hours.

When I came home from work one Friday evening, my roommates asked me if I would like to go out to a club with them. Even though we were all really good small town girls I think our curiosity got the best of us and the curiosity took over. My roommates had heard that a good band was playing at a local club and they wanted to go check it out. When they asked me, I was a little bit weary that it was not a good idea. As a matter of fact I was quite hesitant about that idea especially since we were not all that familiar with the area of town where the club was located. But with a little coercing I agreed to go.

My roommates were right. We ended up having a blast and I tasted beer for the first time ever…yuck! The band was great as they played all the popular music of that time and I danced my legs off.

Everyone seemed to be so friendly at the club and I became friends with some of the regulars. I found myself falling in love with the night life. I kept going back to the club by myself and meeting up with some of my newfound friends. Each time I drank beer I managed to hold my breath because the smell and taste was awful, but I wanted to be social.

My new friends also introduced me to some other popular and fun dance clubs around town and before long I was able to sneak into the twenty-one clubs. To get into these clubs, you had to be twenty one years of age but I was not yet twenty one. The friends I went into these clubs with were much older than me and for some reason I was never carded. In these twenty-one clubs I no longer had to drink that yucky beer anymore; I started drinking the hard stuff.

In the beginning of my drinking days I usually only went to the clubs on Friday or Saturday nights. But before long I started going out every Wednesday night as well, and then pretty soon every night of the week, but never on Sunday; because that was the Lord's Day, *after all*. Eventually even the Lord's Day didn't matter anymore and I was at the clubs partying on Sunday's. It was almost like I just didn't care and was living a dare.

Each step I took seemed to take me further into an abyss. It was as though I was getting away with it so what else was there to do but up the ante! With each first step further down, nothing seemed to happen. I wasn't struck with lightening and there weren't any repercussions that I could see, so what was holding me back from going deeper and deeper into the abyss?

## I Needed a Change of Venue

Even though I loved my job working in ladies fashion it just didn't pay enough. I eventually found a position working at the courthouse in the Sedgwick County Auto License Department which paid a much better salary with benefits. My roommate situation didn't work out so well so I ended up moving back to my grandparent's home and into the studio apartment that they had in their home. My brother eventually moved to Wichita to attend college and took over my grandparent's guest bedroom. Our living with our grandparents didn't last very long as we needed a bit more freedom to live the way we wanted to without questions.

My grandmother worried about us all the time and rightfully so but it proved to be a bit bothersome to us. My staying out till all hours and sometimes all night was a bit too much for her.

"What will the neighbors think?" she asked me one time.

When she asked me that question, I pretty much lost it and I told her that I didn't *care* what the neighbors thought! I had lived under that rule all of my life and *I was done with it*! My brother and I eventually found an apartment together and it happened to work out just grand for us.

## The Intimidation Ploy

After my brother and I got an apartment together I had already started working for the auto license department which proved to be very interesting. Some days working with the public was *fun* I'll sarcastically say. We had to type every form needed to make a title transaction or to renew auto tags. There were no computers back then.

Some days the lines were so long and the lines would last all day until close. It became a bit frustrating for those who were waiting in line forever, only to discover that when their time finally came to be waited on they didn't have everything that they needed to complete their transactions. There were laws and rules that people did not want to obey and that was when the fights would start!

I remember one particular day when I had had enough of one person. It was a day when the lines were long and the people had become grouchy at best and one lady really stood out that day. Everyone could tell that she was drunk and she was annoying everyone around her. I just couldn't move the line fast enough to get her out of there!

When she finally arrived at my window she hung herself over my counter and stared at me and she reeked of alcohol.

"Can't you type any faster than that?" she slur idly said.

Okay this is my story and I am sticking to it…I typed at least eighty words a minute. That's pretty fast for those of you who don't understand typing speeds. I stopped typing.

"If you think you can type any faster, than go for it!" I exclaimed to her.

"Well!" she exclaimed huffily.

She turned around and walked out of the building never getting what she came in for. As she left, everyone standing in line clapped.

Some days were slow and it allowed us to catch our breath and get some paperwork done. On one such day I remember seeing a face out of the corner of my eye that I had hoped that I would never see again. Remember earlier on when I spoke about a young man that held me at knife point? Yes, it was *him*…again!

I never looked at him directly so he wouldn't think that I had seen him. He sat down in one of the chairs and watched me for about an hour but I kept on working as if I had not noticed him at all. I was finally able to work my way over to a phone and called my dad who was at the police station in Kingman. He told me not to leave work without an escort. He called the sheriff's department which was just upstairs from the auto license department to let them know what was going on. He had asked them to please provide his daughter with an escort after work. The man eventually left and without an incident. After he was gone I began to realize that his being there must have been one of his intimidation ploys. After all, he had a history of intimidating and abusing many women but it didn't work on me. Since he didn't get any satisfaction out of his attempt to rattle me, it simply wasn't any fun for him. After he left, I never saw him again.

## Upping the Ante Persona

You might be wondering how I could possibly hold down a job and do all of the partying that I did. It was because I took my career very seriously and remained very professional at all times, except for the few occasional times when I thought it was my duty to help adjust the attitude of a few folks, like the drunken lady who came to my window. No one from work ever knew how much that I had been drinking. I was always on time for work and performed well enough to advance throughout my career. I tried to never let on that I ever suffered from a hangover. I was basically living two lives, or was it more like living *two lies*?

I remember growing up with the phrase "Sex, Drugs, and Rock 'n Roll", and it didn't take me long to be involved with all of the above. Yes, I had upped the ante and my night life was very much different than my daytime persona. My style of dressing and appearance was even different.

My night life allowed me to meet a lot of people and that included some men that I would occasionally date. Two of the men that I had met during that time contributed to two major impacts that happened in my life. I just couldn't see them coming. Or could I have? I will talk about these men much later in my story.

## My Reflexes Took Over

Let me give you an example of who I used to hang out with. There was one man in particular that I dated for a while and although he wasn't much to write home about he was a nice man, but a little bit dangerous. He was fun to hang out with and had a motorcycle that we would go riding around town on from time to time. One evening he started messing around with his gun (thinking that it was unloaded) and pointed it at my head as he was joking around. When he lowered the gun it went off putting a bullet in the floor! Yep, that was definitely a close call! He was as shocked as I was!

Several months after we had been dating he was involved in a very serious motorcycle accident. I wondered what had happened to him because I hadn't heard anything from him for a few days. I called his boss and that was when I found out what had happened. His boss told me that my boyfriend's family was trying to find me because he had asked for me when he would go in and out of consciousness. I called the hospital to speak to his mother who asked me to come to the hospital right away as they didn't think he was going to make it.

When I arrived at the hospital I saw a horrible sight! My boyfriend's head was horribly swollen and almost every bone in his body was broken. He had several major internal injuries and he was in need of brain surgery right away. Once he saw me and I spoke a few words to him it seemed like he was at peace and was ready for the surgery.

He did make it through the operation. He was in the hospital for about three months recovering from his injuries and his recovery was a slow go. He had to learn how to walk and talk all over again. With his physical therapy he had to learn other daily tasks that most of us take for granted. The doctor had told us that when people survive such experiences like that one, they sometimes come back differently. I just didn't see it coming and he *did* come back differently.

When he returned home from the hospital we tried to pick up where we had left off but he was a bit different and needed help with a few things yet. The accident also left him with a personality change. One night while we were out on date, out of nowhere and for no reason, he threw me up against a brick wall and slammed his fist into my stomach. Silly person, he should have known not to have done that! My reflexes took over and with a few quick moves I left *him* lying on the ground! While lying on the ground he kept hollering out to me about how sorry he was and for me to please come back, but I just *kept on walking*.

He called me the very next day and apologized for his actions. He told me that it would never happen again and I told him that he was right, it would never happen again because I would never see him again... EVER! I may have tolerated a lot of things from the men in my life but physical abuse was not one of them!

## I Gambled With My Life

With my trying to live two lives, or was it two lies, I was truly playing with fire as I made my slow descent into the abyss. It had all started out so innocently by my going to see a band play at a club. Who knew that I would be so captured by that one night! Who knew that the beliefs that I had held so dear while I was growing up would eventually wear down to rubble! I was constantly walking the line of danger.

I had dated men who had the potential to be dangerous. Some of them even threatened to kill me when I left them and some even stalked me for a while. I had made some decisions that could have turned out very, very badly. Most of the moral things that used to matter to me were all basically gone! The *"things"* of this world slowly took over my soul.

The *career* me was climbing the ladder of success at any and all costs and I even became ruthless in some cases. The *night-life* me...well it appeared that I was trying to be as bad or as daring as possible. I took so many gambles with my life.

Although things were getting all messed up I still maintained a bit of likeability and charisma. I was still trustworthy and I always saw the good in people and I still took up for the underdogs of this world. Basically, I still had a small amount of moral thread left in me. It was hard to see it or even find it.

## TEN

# My Mr. X

*Do not be yoked together with unbelievers. For what do righteousness and wickedness have in common? Or what fellowship can light have with darkness?*
**II Corinthians 6:14**

### Life Became A Roller Coaster Ride!

Mr. X was one of the men that I had met during that crazy time who played a major role in my life. He became my first husband. Don't worry; this is not going to be a tale of a bitter ex-wife-bashing-her-ex-husband kind of a story. A long time ago I had forgiven him for what had happened between us and I hope that he has done the same for me. I have to laugh at myself, which is easy to do now, and wonder *what on earth I was thinking.* My life with him was a roller coaster ride that just never seemed to end. It was exciting, dangerous, crazy, and insane as there was never a dull moment. I think I was star struck with him because of his fast life style and with how he spoiled me with anything that I wanted. I will reflect back and share some of the details of what I lived through with my high-roller husband Mr. X.

## Mr. X Came to My Table

My club friends were always trying to find someone to set me up with but they never could find anyone that they thought was worthy of me. Maybe it was because I was so much younger than them that they kind of looked out for me in a protective sort of way. They certainly did not like some of the men that I had picked out for myself! A man that I wanted to go steady with was one of the bouncers that worked at the club I frequented the most and my friends approved of him. He was really my first love and I fell hard for him. We simply became *just friends* because he really didn't want any more than that at that time. Many years later though, that would change and you will hear more about him in a later chapter.

*Anywho*, one of my men friends was a regular pool player with Mr. X and got to know him a bit. Eventually he thought that Mr. X and I would make a nice match so he told me all about him and asked me if it was okay to introduce us. He then brought Mr. X over to my table and the rest was history.

Mr. X was dressed in a suit and tie and I could tell that he was the flashy type. I had never met a man before that had professionally manicured fingernails which led to the obvious; his image was everything! He had short dark brown hair with brown eyes that smiled. He had a very outgoing personality and he was jovial, full of charm and charisma, and was the happy-go-lucky type. He loved having a good time and had a very positive air about him. By all outward appearances he looked like he could have a lot of money. We began to date right away.

## Hob-knobbing with Mr. X

For our first date he invited me to his apartment for dinner. He even picked me up at my apartment in his brand new car and drove me to his apartment where the aroma was wonderful! I could tell that he was a good cook and he explained to me that he had at one time attended culinary school. He also told me that he had learned some basic recipes that were full-proof. Our conversation that evening allowed us to get to know one another a little better.

He was from the Kansas City area and was four years older than me. What brought him to Wichita was that he had been a district manager for a large restaurant chain in the Kansas City area and had been transferred to Wichita. Previously he had been in the military where he had received a Jet Engine Mechanic's Degree. The story he told me was that when he was ready to be deployed to Viet Nam and was on the plane ready to go (or so he claimed), the war had ceased. He also had his private pilot's license and he liked to fly for recreational fun.

When we met he was selling insurance for a local insurance company and traveled the state of Kansas full-time. Mr. X seemed to talk about his work a lot and what he did for a living. And yes, he was able to make a lot of money.

I later found out that he had been divorced about a year or so before we had met and was told that his ex-wife had taken him for everything. His apartment was furnished beautifully with expensive furniture that matched the rest of his image. He made sure that I knew that his furniture was made of solid oak and that his sofa and chairs were made of real leather.

He was the oldest of three boys. His middle brother had married into money and lived in a mansion in Kansas City while his youngest brother, still in his teens, was living at home with his parents.

I believe that I was quite taken by Mr. X's personality and especially his business sense. He was quite the business person and was great with numbers. I found out much later after we were married that he didn't always use his smart business talents for the good, but I was at the time star-struck with him anyways.

I hadn't dated anyone before that dressed in a suit all of the time but I always loved the way men looked when they dressed up in them.

We dated for about a year and he always took me to the finest places in Wichita and even in Kansas City. He definitely spoiled me and there wasn't anything that he wouldn't do for me or give me.

It was fun hob-knobbing with the rich. It sure opened my eyes up to a whole new way of living. We hung out with folks who were on their way *up* as well as with those who had already arrived. By all appearances Mr. X was on his way up as well because it was all about the image. Too bad it took me a few years to see below the surface and figure out what was really going on!

By the way did I mention that he was great at playing pool? In fact, he never lost a game *ever*! Keep that information in the back of your mind because it will be significant later on.

## Not Everyone Liked Mr. X

The insurance company that Mr. X worked for was a great company. Every Friday evening everyone that worked for the company was required to attend the weekly sales meeting including the wives and significant others, and dressing up was one of the requirements. It was a rah-rah time to acknowledge the top sales people for all of their accomplishments for that week and also to help keep the others encouraged so that they would strive for greater achievements. The managers were great at dangling carrots in front of everyone to help spur them on.

With the dangling carrot always present, one by one the sales people would be encouraged to list out loud everything that they wanted to be able to purchase with their income such as cars, homes, boats, fur coats, diamonds, and the list went on and on, again because of the dangled carrot. It was a great strategy and it's used by many other companies even today. All I could see in that strategy was that it was one way to keep everyone in debt so that they had to work even harder to make the company more money!

My Mr. X was consistently one of their top sales representatives and his goal was to someday have his own office. That was becoming a possibility according to his higher-ups. As I look back, I really think it was just another dangling carrot.

I really enjoyed the weekly meetings. Sometimes they would do sales training and when they did, I learned a lot about sales and business dealings. To me the group seemed like one big happy family. We all became familiar with one another and I became fond of the wives and the girlfriends that came to the meetings. After the meetings we often would all go out to eat together and of course at only the best places in town. It was at one of these dinners that I saw a different side of my Mr. X for the first time.

We had been dating for quite some time when an incident occurred between us in a restaurant and I'm not sure what had really set him off. He started yelling at me right in front of everyone in the group! I was in shock and so was everyone else around us. I was so surprised that I did nothing. One of the men at the table came to my defense and called him on it.

I really did fit in with the group very well and became great friends with some of the ladies. But as time marched on I discovered that not everyone liked my Mr. X.

## Meeting the Parents

Mr. X wanted me to meet his parents who lived in Kansas City. When I met them for the first time I thought that they were great people and I especially liked his dad. His dad reminded me a little of my own dad as he was so down-to-earth. His dad owned a TV repair shop that had made him a living for many years. His father also had previously worked in a secret government program. I'm not sure what the work was about, but I think it had something to do with nuclear experiments. The details were not talked about.

His mother was a very tiny feisty woman and she was a little snippy sometimes, but friendly. She seemed a bit stand-offish in a way and it appeared to me that she just didn't trust me. His parents were a little old-fashioned but in a good way.

There was no drinking allowed in their home except at Christmas gatherings when hot toddies were made for everyone. His mother did have a twin sister that had a problem with alcohol and I had learned that her twin sister had died in a horrific auto accident that involved her drinking. Her death was a very sensitive topic.

When staying at Mr. X's parent's home in Kansas City before we were married they had me sleep in an upstairs bedroom while Mr. X slept in the basement along with his brother, who was on guard duty. It was pretty quaint I thought!

His parents were a great couple but during the time that Mr. X and I were dating, their past had caught up with them and it started causing a great deal of pain in their marriage. Mr. X's dad didn't know that his own wife had had a child before they were married. Apparently she had been raped and when the baby girl was born she was immediately taken from her. Mr. X's grandmother had taken the baby and given her away! Over thirty years later the daughter shows up and wants to meet her birth mother!

Come to find out the daughter had been given to a relative!! Yep, there was some...'splaining to do! Even though Mr. X and his brothers were excited to know that they had a sister it just wasn't a good relationship. The daughter would only show up and play the sympathy card to have access to all of their money. She was eventually asked not to come around anymore when it was discovered what she was really doing. Over the next several years Mr. X's parents would fight and sometimes it became very intense, but they stayed together.

*Now this will be very short.* When my parents met Mr. X he did not leave them with a good impression, so my parents did not care for him at all. And that was the way it was!

## Suspiciously Absent

Our first year of dating was full of fun. I really liked traveling to Kansas City with Mr. X and experiencing all the night life and eating at fine restaurants. It was so enjoyable for me to be around the positive goal oriented people that we usually hung out with. I also liked hanging out with a few of the wealthy folks we knew because they were so interesting; some were even heirs to some very well-known fortunes. I liked being around the money or so I thought!

Mr. X traveled quite a bit in his business and sometimes the sales team would travel to a certain area in the state together. There were times when he would be gone for about a week but he would always keep in touch with me. There were no cell phones at that time so I would usually receive a call in the evenings when he made it back to his hotel room.

On one of these trips Mr. X disappeared! I hadn't heard from him at all for a week! I even called his office to see if they had heard from him and they hadn't heard from him either. They thought that maybe he was working out in an area in western Kansas somewhere. More days went by and his office was calling me wanting to know if *I* had heard from him. It was all highly suspicious especially since he had not contacted anyone.

Mr. X finally showed up for work and offered everyone a very vague explanation as to his whereabouts. From the office he called me to give me an explanation which I simply did not buy and I told him I didn't want to see him again. I also told him that it was rude to not have any contact with anyone, especially me, the person who he had talked to daily shortly after we had started dating.

## Dating a Psycho

Mr. X and I broke up and I did just fine without him. I started losing weight just because I wanted to. I realized that all of those visits to the fine restaurants had put a few extra pounds on me. I hung out with my friends at the clubs more and I went back to drinking majorly. During that time I had also changed jobs and started to make some new friends from work. I felt I was doing great. Yep, I was just doing just *peachy*!

For a while I had hooked up with a man who turned out to be somewhat of a psycho! After dating for a while it sure seemed like he was the possessive type and early on he told me of *his* plans for me when we got married. *What? Married?* We had only known each other for a few weeks and he was talking about marriage already? I certainly did not like the plans he was making for me; living in the secluded mountains somewhere, barefoot and pregnant! But wait a minute! I didn't *even* want kids? That guy was *nuts!* I broke up with him. Or at least I tried to. He didn't listen very well.

After I had tried to breakup with him he threatened to kill me and went on and on with the threats. He said he would even kill anyone who tried to date me. *Oh, whatever*! I just thought to myself, good riddance! He did stalk me for a while and even tried to cause some major problems especially when he found out that Mr. X was trying to get back into the picture.

Several months had passed and I was still trying to get Mr. Psycho to understand that we were not a couple and to leave me alone! Then, as if I needed any more weirdness from guys, I was out partying one evening with friends at a new club when Mr. X showed up. *Now what? Great! Just Great!* He walked directly to me and asked me to dance and after dancing we spent most of the evening and even into the wee hours of the morning talking. We discussed what had happened between us as we explored the idea of seeing if the relationship could be fixed.

### Me, Sign a Pre-nuptial?

Mr. X and I became engaged a few days later and we decided to get married over the Thanksgiving weekend. That was just a little over a month away! I should have run, but I didn't. Hindsight is 20/20, right? I found myself with some major planning to do and not much time to do it in!

First of all, I realized that I was engaged to two men at the same time, Mr. X and Mr. Psycho. Well, let me put it this way, Mr. Psycho was engaged to me but I wasn't engaged to him. I somehow had to get Mr. Psycho to understand that he was out of my life! Yep, things got pretty creepy as he threatened to find and kill me and Mr. X, but Mr. Psycho eventually gave up and moved on! Thank goodness!

When we broke the news to our parents his parents were thrilled but mine were not so thrilled at all. I would never receive my parent's blessings, ever. My dad even wrote me a multiple page letter explaining his opinion. Mom basically stated at first that she wouldn't support me in any way towards my wedding. Even my aunt invited me to her house for lunch and tried to talk me out of it. The family thing just wasn't working out very well.

When we broke the news to our friends some were surprised while other seemed to be thrilled. Some, well, you could tell that they had an opinion but weren't going to say anything. Basically, it was a mixed bag of feelings coming from all directions.

Next, Mr. X and I went shopping for our rings. We visited several local jewelers and happened to find some rings that were perfect, very nice, lots of diamonds, but not overstated. He then asked his best friend from Kansas City to be his best man and I chose my best girlfriend to be my maid of honor. When we asked Mr. X's boss and his wife to be attendants they accepted and stood up with us as well.

Since we only had a month to plan the wedding I spent most of that month working on my dress. I was a seamstress so I quickly got to designing. Our wedding colors were cream and light blue. Then there was the cake to pick out, and invitations, and so much more! We didn't have to plan a honeymoon because Mr. X had won a sales contest for a trip to Acapulco which we took several months after we were married.

During our short engagement period we had several heated discussions in which he wanted me to sign a pre-nuptial agreement. Mr. X wanted me to sign one to protect his interests. I was pretty ticked off at him for even asking and refused to sign. I told him if he didn't trust me then we shouldn't get married. He eventually caved as I promised him that I would not take him for everything or even anything if things didn't work out.

### Mr. X Lied to the Pastor

Mr. X wanted at least a verbal agreement with me that in five years we would re-evaluate where we were at in our marriage and discuss at that time if we would want to continue on. *Fine*, I agreed to it. I was so glad that I had agreed to that one because it proved to be very beneficial for me later down the road.

I had started attending what used to be my home church mainly because I wanted to get up enough nerve to approach the pastor to ask him if he would marry us. The pastor agreed but only if we would come and take sessions in his marriage counseling. Of course the pastor had to call my parents to see what was *really* going on, but after private conversations with them they agreed that the pastor could perform the wedding.

*"After all, they will just go find someone else if you don't,"* my parents responded.

The church had just finished building a new sanctuary and we were going to be the first wedding in the new facility. Several years later it made me sad to think that the first wedding in their new facility was ours, a wedding that was not based upon anything godly at all.

Our counseling sessions went well I suppose; we suffered through them. I about died though when the pastor brought out some sex books and recommended several other good titles that we should go and purchase. I wasn't expecting that and I'm sure my face showed it. I was quite embarrassed.

Mr. X even had to brag to the pastor about an uncle of his whom at that time was a very well-known televangelist. The trouble was, the closest Mr. X ever came to religion was bragging about his uncle, as if knowing his uncle had him covered for *fire insurance*!

After our sessions, the pastor asked us to attend his church but Mr. X lied to him and told him that we would be moving away shortly after our wedding. Mr. X told the pastor a story that held only an ounce of truth because he did have his eye on opening an office in Salina, *some day.* By the way, it never came to pass.

We had everything planned and in place a week before the actual wedding day and we had everything paid for. I wanted to place an announcement in the local newspaper but Mr. X didn't want me to. I thought that it was a little bit odd that he didn't want an announcement made. He simply said that he didn't want to make it easier for people to find him. What? I didn't quite understand his remark! At least not until much later when I started putting two and two together.

My attendants had their dresses made and the fittings went well and the men had gotten their tux fittings done. I was putting the finishing touches on my dress even up until the last minute. I met with the church wedding planner several times and everything was all set at the church as well. The wedding planner was a bit rigid when it came to the rules but I really appreciated her help.

## I Was Mortified!

My friends put together a wonderful bridal shower for me and a lot of friends and family were invited. The shower was a huge success. It was held in my apartment complex's club house and my friends had decorated it so lovely. There was a great turnout and we played fun games and had the traditional cake and punch. I had so many gifts to open as everyone was so generous.

My shower attendees consisted of my close friends, church friends, family members, and all of the wives from Mr. X's office. My mother came to the shower under protest, I'm sure. My grandmother was in attendance and was instrumental in trying to smooth things over with my mom.

What happened at my shower, however, I did not see coming and I was mortified. As I was opening my presents the room was all a buzz with all kinds of conversations going on. Everyone was laughing and having a great time when out of nowhere one of Mr. X's co-worker's wives asked me if Mr. X had made it to the early morning meeting that had been held that morning. I told her that I didn't know.

"You should have kicked his "BLEEP" out of bed, and made sure that he got there!" she loudly stated.

The room went silent! Everyone in the room had heard her. I was stunned and my jaw dropped. Everyone began to stare. There you have it, the whole truth laid out there for all to hear.

When some of my friends saw how embarrassed I was, they quickly started talking to get the room buzzing again with conversations. That co-worker's wife still hadn't caught on; except that she must have said *something* wrong. I recognized my mom's stare as *the look of death*, and I just knew that she was going to go explosive on me when we got alone together. And, she did!!

## My High Rolling Mr. X

Mr. X and I decided to pick up the tuxes the day before the wedding. I was driving and I decided to stay in the car while he went in to retrieve the tuxes. It was very quiet in the car and a thought slammed into my brain. *This is not going to work out well.* I just brushed the thought off as I didn't know what to do with it; after all, it was the day before our wedding!

Our wedding day came and I was surrounded by friends helping me to get ready. My dress was not a traditional wedding dress. It was a long dress but with very simple lines. It was made out of taffeta with a short train in the back. It had long lace sleeves with a scoop neckline. The coverlet that covered the shoulders was made out of lace and scooped up to create a tall neckline. The coverlet flowed all the way to the floor in the back to make a very long lacy train. I wore a halo of white flowers in my hair and carried a beautiful flower bouquet made out of daisies and roses.

Daisies had been a significant flower to me when I was growing up. When I was in grade school I had a favorite daisy perfume and lotion that I really liked. One of my prom dresses that mom and I had made had white flocked daisies in an allover pattern. I constantly drew the daisy flower in my sketches and as young girls we would play a game with the daisy flower. Each time we would pull a petal from the flower we would say "He loves me" and with the next petal "He loves me not." With the last pull of the last petal you would know if your beau loved you or not! Just a silly girl's game. *I should have pulled a few petals that wedding day; it could have saved me several wasted years!*

The day of our wedding was a horrible day when it came to the weather. It rained and stormed the whole entire day but the wedding itself went off without a hitch. We had a traditional reception at the church that followed the wedding with wedding cake and punch. Although we were not allowed to throw rice as we left the church, our car was filled with it! What a mess! My new husband's boss held the *real* party at his house after the reception with the traditional booze and plenty of food. Of course we stayed at the most expensive hotel in town for our wedding night with champagne and all the trimmings.

It didn't take me long after our marriage for me to discover some very interesting things about my new husband Mr. X. He was truly a high roller and unbeknownst to me and for the next several years, he would use me in his schemes and just about took me all the way down with him.

## ELEVEN
# The Root of All Evil?

*For the love of money is a root of all kinds of evil. Some people, eager for money, have wandered from the faith and pierced themselves with many griefs.*
**I Timothy 6:10**

### My First Home with Mr. X

I took a week off from work after our wedding to help get us settled into our new home. Since the two of us already had established separate apartments before our marriage we were trying to merge two households into one and that proved to be quite a challenge. We had to figure out what was staying and what had to be sold or given away. There for a while we were wall to wall with stuff!

Because of the stress of getting through the wedding, the move, and getting our house all set up, I ended up in the emergency room at the hospital one evening. My heart had started running away with itself and I began hyperventilating! The hospital determined that I had a heart murmur and recommended that I not get all stressed out and that I should slow down a bit. That was easy for them to say!

Mr. X and I moved into a very plush town home on the east side of Wichita. The two story town home featured a very large kitchen with a Jenn-Air stove and grill. Our dining room featured wall sconce chandeliers with a skylight that allowed light to flood into the room from above the second floor. The living room was rather large with a wonderful fireplace and we had a half bath on the main floor. A private patio could be entered on to from the kitchen or the living room and the green foliage that surrounded the patio added an extra ambiance to the exquisite abode.

We had a guest bedroom upstairs and a master bedroom. Our bedroom had indoor shuttered windows that opened up to allow us to look straight down into the dining room located on the first floor. We had a large closet that had mirrored doors and there was a full bath. The upstairs hallway was lined with a railing on one side that resembled a French terrace which also provided an overlook to the dining room below.

When I married Mr. X I was twenty-one years old, and I just have to say for the record I didn't ask how much it cost for us to live in that townhouse. I never knew. And for my age and background I had never known such luxury; it was a bit overwhelming.

## My Flash Temper Flared!

We had a rocky start to our marriage. I happened to awaken early one Saturday morning to cook breakfast for my Mr. X. I had already organized our place and was ready to have a wonderful breakfast time with my new husband. The table was formally set with most of the food already cooked as I finished up with the eggs. The aroma of breakfast being cooked awoke my husband and he came downstairs to see what was going on.

He proceeded to sit down and developed a big grin on his face which quickly turned into anger as I brought him his eggs.

"What is *this*, I can't eat *these* eggs!" he yelled. "This is not how my mother fixed them so you better take a few lessons from her!" he ranted on.

I let him rant for a while. I had a flash temper problem myself back in those days, but Mr. X had not seen it yet, until then! I proceeded to walk over to the table where I immediately picked up all of the food and threw it into the trash!

"What are you *doing*?" he asked. "The rest of the food is still good!"

I answered him by telling him that if the eggs weren't good enough eat then the rest of the food wasn't good enough to eat either. I told him he could fix his own breakfast from then on!

## They Read Him His Rights

We had been married for only about two weeks when we had a rather disturbing incident happen late one evening. We had been relaxing and watching television when all of a sudden we started hearing the sounds of a helicopter hovering over our townhouse complete with spotlights shining down upon us. In a few moments we heard banging on our front door and I could tell that the noise was created by a police rod hitting the door.

When I opened the door I realized that our place was surrounded by officers. Three of those officers forced their way into our living room and asked me to sit down. They asked my husband if he was indeed Mr. X and as he responded, they handcuffed him and read him his rights. The next thing I knew they were out the door!

I caught up with one of those officers and asked him where they were going to take my husband and he explained to me that I would need to call a bails bondsman. They still gave no other explanation as to the reasons why my Mr. X was arrested. I decided to drive to the county jail by myself worried the whole time as I wondered what I had gotten myself in to.

When I arrived at the county jail the stench of that place brought back many memories of my younger years when my family lived at the jailhouse in Kingman. I was not allowed to see or visit my husband and

I still was not being told what he was arrested for. I asked the clerk for some names of bail bondsmen. I was somewhat familiar with a few of them from my working days at the courthouse. I looked through some of the names and found a familiar name and gave him a call.

That bail bondsman had a reputation, you might say, for hitting the sauce, so of course I was able to reach him across the street at a local nightclub. When he showed up he *was* a bit tipsy but still had enough wits about him to be able to handle the transaction needed to get my husband out of jail.

He was released and we drove home. He tried to explain to me that the reason for his arrest was because of some fraudulent checks that he supposedly had written somewhere out in the middle of nowhere Kansas. He further explained to me that he had a habit of leaving his checkbook in his car. When we got home he went to his car to see if his checkbook was still there and he found several checks missing. These missing checks were not all in a row, but every so often throughout the stack one would be missing! He then put two and two together and realized that a man that he had been training and traveling with must have taken some of the checks!

My husband had to appear in court the very next day with his lawyer and stand before the judge to plead his case. Unfortunately my Mr. X was arrested again, on the spot, for unpaid parking tickets and was escorted from the courtroom. You see, my husband was a very arrogant man and he would park wherever he wanted to and he didn't care if there was a time limit or if it was a no parking zone, and he even often parked in handicap spaces. He simply would wad up the ticket left on his car and throw it down on the curb! Well his arrogance had finally caught up with him! I received a phone call from my husband telling me that he was sitting in jail, again.

Later that same week, one of the investigators took my Mr. X to nowhere Kansas and visited the same retailers that those checks had been written to. The investigator did not tell the retailers that the person standing in front of them was the person who supposedly had written the fraudulent checks, they just acted as if Mr. X was one of the investigators. The investigator asked for the description of the person who had written the checks and the description matched the person that my husband had been training!

I don't remember how the case turned out except for the fact that my Mr. X was exonerated from those crimes. I do not know if the real culprit was ever apprehended, and yes, my Mr. X paid for all of those unpaid parking tickets!

### If You Ever Want Out, I Can Help You

I had only been married to Mr. X for a short time when one of the wives that I had met through Mr. X's office told me of a job opening that she thought would be perfect for me. She was working for the national headquarters in the research and development department of a well-known pizza chain. I decided to go for an interview and when I did, I got the job. The position paid much more than my previous job and it had better benefits. My desk sat on the same floor as the co-founder's office! Wow! I couldn't believe it!

I received a phone call a few weeks after I had started my new job from the best-man who had been in our wedding. My husband was on the road that week and wasn't at home. I just thought that his call was a friendly check-up-on-us kind of a call since he had been the best man at our wedding. I was telling him about my new job and a few other things that were going on in our lives. I thought that our visit was about over when out of nowhere the tone of the conversation changed.

"You know, if you ever want *out*, I will help you," he quietly said.

I was floored by his remark and responded by asking him why he would think that I would want out. Mr. X and I had just gotten married after all! He made the statement again with a heavier emphasis on the word *out*. I went silent and there was a long pause. He finally spoke again.

"You really *don't know*, do you?" he inquired.

"*Know* what?" I questioned back.

There was another long pause.

"Uh...he's connected to the Kansas City mob," he stated.

I was angered by his remark as I tried to assure him that my Mr. X was not connected at all to the mob.

"Ask him, and he will tell you," he somberly said.

At that point I didn't know what to do. His statements floored me but I decided to sit on that information for a while at least until the time was right. For several weeks after that phone call conversation I would catch myself staring at my husband trying to see if I could get my thoughts wrapped around the whole idea of him being tied in with the mob. *Could that be why he disappears sometimes* as I wondered to myself? Could that be why we spent so much time in the Kansas City area? Was that why he didn't want our wedding announcement in the newspapers? I decided to wait a few more weeks before I asked my Mr. X about his possible involvement.

Eventually I was finally ready to confront him and he was a bit upset with my questions. He was also upset that his friend had spilled the beans, but he finally came clean and began to tell me the whole sordid story.

### Bubba Came To the Rescue

The game of pool was my Mr. X's specialty. He had started playing the game as a teenager and because of his math skills and his ability to fully grasp the game, he never lost! A talent scout for the mob discovered him playing in a pool hall one day and liked what he saw. He approached Mr. X and asked him if he would like to make some money and since Mr. X was all about the money it was a perfect fit. He started out that new lifestyle during his last few years of high school. Every rendezvous was a complete secret and his parents were none the wiser.

Mr. X would receive phone calls telling him where to park his car and usually he would park it in a large parking lot. A limousine would then pick him up and take him to wherever the game was being played or drive him to a private jet so he could be taken somewhere in the United States to play. He was provided with women that hung off both of his arms and he was provided with a body guard they called Bubba. He never knew how much money was on the game so that it would not affect his ability to keep winning. He just knew that there was a lot of money at stake and that he would be making a lot of money himself, and in cash!

Mr. X was living the high life when things went wrong one evening. If you have any knowledge about gambling you know that you have to let the other players win every once in a while so that they have a chance to win back some of their money. However, Mr. X was ruthless and wouldn't let anyone win, *ever*!

On one particular evening one of his contenders had had enough of losing and grabbed a knife. He was about ready to cut off Mr. X's hand when Bubba stepped in just in time. The knife ended up missing Mr. X's hand but sliced all the way down his leg and laid it wide open. Bubba then picked up the man welding the knife and threw him down a flight of stairs killing him instantly. Bubba was arrested and eventually went to prison for murder. Mr. X was rushed out of the building before the police arrived and was taken to a mansion somewhere in Kansas City where he was sewn up by a doctor who was owned by the mob. It was rather hard for him to hide that kind of an injury from his mother but he came up with some crazy story that his mother believed.

Mr. X continued working with the mob not letting that one event stop him. He was able to hide all his cash except for one evening when he carelessly left a wad of money in his bedroom and his mother found it while cleaning his room. She was furious with him but he never told her the real story of where it came from.

To fan the fire even more, as a teenager he had gone down to a local car lot and bought himself a brand new sports car right off of the showroom floor. His parents were furious, but once again, they still were not told the real story.

I listened intently as he explained to me his story and even the part where he said he had played the game with the legendary Fats Domino, and beat him as well. Fats Domino was a pianist, singer, and songwriter who was born in 1928, the Big Easy era, and sold more than sixty-five million records. It was Billy Diamond who gave him the nickname of "Fats" because at that time he weighed two-hundred and twenty pounds while standing only five-feet, five inches tall!

By the time my Mr. X had finished telling me his story he assured me that he was no longer involved with the mob. I was left silently wondering if anyone really *ever* gets away from the mob.

## The Air Was Thick and Balmy

We were so excited when my husband won a trip through his company to Acapulco. We decided to use the trip as our honeymoon get-a-way. His company had booked us at the best hotel and in the presidential suite! We could hardly wait for the trip, but the day before we were to leave my boss called me into her office to tell me that she could not let me go. I was floored! I reminded her that when she had hired me she had already approved the trip in advance! I also reminded her that she had told me that she had lived in Acapulco for several years and had mentioned to me several places to visit while we were there. Still she was not buying anything that I told her! In fact, she informed me that if I took off from my job I may not have that job when I returned.

I could not believe what I was hearing and didn't know what to do. My Mr. X and I had been waiting for that trip for so long. I was in a dilemma and decided to call my husband. When I told him what was going on he offered to come and speak to my boss.

When he showed up at closing time, so that the other employees would not be able to overhear our conversation, he told my boss that I was in fact going! He was quite the persuader but nothing he said worked either! She simply told the two of us that she would deal with the situation when we returned from our trip.

Our trip to Acapulco was a very long flight and it was my first time to fly. We made a safe but rough landing in Mexico City and because of the rough landing my stomach became quite ill and I wasn't the only one. At the airport I quickly found a restroom but since the airport was under construction there was only a communal restroom in place. I was in shock! Yes, men and women had to use one restroom with no doors on the stalls! *Great*! I had to have my husband stand in front of the stall for me so I could take care of business; some of the native people were not as modest as me!

We were able to catch the next flight out of Mexico City to Acapulco only to have another rough landing once again. These pilots had to be very skilled to be able to fly into that airport. The plane had to maneuver over the top of the mountains and bam, there was the landing strip! The airplane had to come to a complete stop pretty fast on the runway so that we wouldn't head off into the ocean. Again, my stomach took another beating. There were a lot of barf bags used that day!

It was winter back home but not there! Breathing the air there took a bit of getting used to because it was so thick and balmy. It also seemed like the sun was so much hotter than back home and it was very easy to get sunburned. We even saw a few people who had not heeded the warnings given to them concerning the sun and they were severely burned and had to be hospitalized.

## The European Folks Shocked Me!

From the airport we caught a bus to downtown Acapulco and on the way passed the hotel that Howard Hughes had built and lived in.

Howard Hughes was an American businessman, a movie producer, and an aviator; however, he was perhaps best remembered for spending his later years as an eccentric reclusive billionaire. His hotel sat just a few miles outside of town and we decided later on to go visit his hotel to see what it looked like. It was gorgeous of course!

However, the hotel we stayed in was also just as beautiful. Upon our arrival we were greeted with a huge basket of fruit and a bottle of champagne. Our room was very high up and faced the ocean. Two of the walls met in a corner with double sliding glass doors that opened out onto a terrace. We could open those doors and catch the ocean breeze while the long white curtains flowed with the current of the wind. The floor was made of slab marble as were some of the walls. It was simply beautiful!

One day while swimming in the hotel pool, I noticed some Europeans. I had always heard how differently the Europeans looked at things than we Americans do but never in my wildest dreams did I think I would experience it first-hand. And boy, are they different! I tried not to look shocked but I'm not sure I was able to conceal it. When these Europeans had finished swimming they changed out of their swimsuits and into their street clothes right there and in front of everybody. Yikes, I thought to myself as I wanted to poke my eyes out!

## We Experienced Acapulco

One morning I thought I would get up early and get to the beach to beat the crowds. I was running as fast as I could to make a big splash landing in the ocean when I realized that about ten Mexican men were running after me and yelling something. I knew that they probably did not want to go swimming with me so I stopped and turned around and looked at them wondering why it appeared to me that they were about ready to tackle me! Finally I began to realize what they were trying to say to me.

"Sharks, sharks!" they were screaming.

When the red flags on the beach were up, no one was supposed to go into the water! *Apparently* there were rules for the beaches. Silly me!

Mr. X and I went on several tours of the area. We rode in a glass-bottom boat, went deep sea fishing, where my husband caught a fourteen-foot swordfish; that was sure interesting. We decided to donate the meat to an orphanage. We sailed on private yachts to see some of the splendors of the area from the ocean view, watched the cliff divers dive off of the cliffs, watched native dancers perform, shopped at the markets, learned how to barter, and took a midnight run on a yacht that dropped us off on an island to experience a beach party. Afterwards we waded in the ocean…in our evening clothes! Okay I was young and it was fun to ruin our clothes! We also took tours to see some of the Hollywood stars' homes that were in the area.

We also attended a bullfight. Okay, so it made me ill! To me it was nothing more than pure torture for the poor animal and I would never go again, but there was one redeeming factor; the meat was donated to an orphanage.

I went parasailing and loved it! I wore a parachute that was attached to a boat by a long rope. The boat would take off as I ran on the beach and the next thing I knew I was high up in the air flying over the ocean. It was only about a ten minute sail but I started getting a little nervous as I looked around and realized how high up I was! I could also see clearly down into the ocean below where I saw a few sharks swimming around!

Coming down from so high up took a bit of skill. I had to pull on one of the ropes to gradually let the air out of the parachute so I could land safely without crashing or breaking a leg in the process. It was fun and I did it! It has only been recently that I have read reports of how some people have died in parasailing accidents. Glad I was naïve!

## The Culture Was a Real Eye-opener

In and around Acapulco the native people are basically very poor. Many lived on dirt floors with just a cooking pot on the ground. Some of the homes were only thatch type roofs held up by four poles and that was basically all it consisted of. I watched a few mothers teach their small children how to beg in the market square and watched as they were sent out to beg. If their children came back without money, they were often beaten and sent back out again.

We vacationed two more times in Acapulco but the last time we visited Acapulco the government had seized the banks and the Americans were not looked upon as kings and queens any longer. There was a strange feeling that I felt the whole time that we were there. I remember going shopping by myself one day and I was stopped by one of the natives who told me to go back to the hotel because a white girl had no business walking on the streets alone. I didn't let that deter me and went on shopping, although I did look over my shoulders a few times.

We were all encouraged to lock up our valuables in the hotel safety boxes. One couple we knew of had their safety box key held for ransom at a local restaurant. The couple had eaten at the restaurant and the man had accidentally left his key lying on the table and when he went back to retrieve it, the waiter dangled the key in front of him and asked him for a large sum of money to get it back. What does someone do in a case like that? You pay the ransom!

## It Was Scary Going through Customs

I basically fell in love with Acapulco from our first trip that we took there. It was such a beautiful place to visit. During our last vacation there Mr. X had placed us in some danger. I don't know who he was making the purchases for but he was asked to bring back four switch-blade knives that he knew were illegal to bring back into the states. My husband disappeared one day in Acapulco and lurked around the underbelly of the town and when he returned, he had the knives. Apparently, as he had tried to explain to me, he had to meet a person in some back alley and ended up in a room full of arsenals. At that point I didn't want to know anything more.

My Mr. X was able to sneak those knives into the states without incident. I was scared the whole time that we were going through customs.

Oh, and by the way, the boss who would not give me permission to go on my honeymoon after she had originally approved it, yep, I was fired.

### "Way to Go Debra, You Showed Him!"

My Mr. X's boss had just built a brand new house and held a Super Bowl party that same year, and of course the whole office was invited to attend. It was just another one of those bonding times to help keep everyone close together so they could help encourage each other in the business. At the party most of the guys were on the lower level with all of the food and watched the game on TV. The ladies just sort of hung out together on the main level talking about life in general.

During half-time everyone had decided that they wanted tacos, so I and some of the ladies drove over to a local fast food taco shop to order some up. I knew that my Mr. X had a dangerous allergy to cheese so when I ordered his food I would always make sure that the cooks were careful to never let any cheese be a part of his order. We ladies purchased the food and quickly re-joined the party and then *it* happened! When Mr. X opened his tacos to eat them there were a couple pieces of cheese that had gotten tangled up in the shredded lettuce. Not much cheese was in it at all, mind you, and it could have been picked out. Mr. X gave it to me full blast! He went explosive in front of everyone, and it wasn't very pretty.

"You march yourself right back to that taco shop and you get it right this time!" he screamed at me. His tantrum startled everyone in the room.

Okay. I calmly told myself that I would take that opportunity to adjust his attitude. That would certainly be the last time that he would treat me that way in front of everyone. I quietly excused myself from the room and drove back to the taco shop. I explained to the taco shop server about the problem with the cheese and they apologized. They fixed the whole problem by giving me a new order for my Mr. X and I returned to the house. I found several children playing hoops outside in the driveway and asked one of them to please take the food to Mr. X. I quickly drove off and left him there to deal with his own embarrassment in front of all of his co-workers! After leaving, I caught up with one of my girlfriends and we hung out together for the rest of the day and evening.

It wasn't until about ten p.m. that I decided to call and see if my Mr. X had cooled his jets yet and to see if he was in need of a ride home. His boss answered the phone.

"Hey, it's Debra!" he shouted to everyone in the background.

Then I heard everyone chanting, "Way to go Debra, you showed him, good job!"

I was chuckling as I asked if my husband was still there and found out that he wasn't. Apparently he had hitched a ride home with someone from the party, but I not only had his car keys, I had his house keys too! I wondered how my husband was able to get into our house. When I called home my Mr. X answered the phone.

"How did you get in?" I asked.

"I climbed over the privacy fence!" he snarled.

By that time I was laughing so hard inside just to picture my Mr. X in his altogether climbing the privacy fence, and in our neighborhood! I informed him that I would be home shortly and he hung up.

Yep, it was pretty cold around our house for a while! He even threatened to divorce me because of that episode. But guess what, *he didn't*! His ego was bruised as he realized that his co-workers would always come to my aid. He also learned to never yell at me again in front of other people.

## Avon Calling!

After I lost my last job because of our honeymoon trip to Acapulco, my Mr. X informed me that I didn't need to work unless I just wanted to. So for the next six months I didn't, but I was bored out of my ever living mind! How many times could a person go shopping? My second home was at the mall! All my friends worked, my husband traveled a bit, and I was getting fidgety! I decided to look into selling Avon products. My mother had sold the products for a while when I was a teenager and I could still remember how much fun it was for her. I called a local representative and met with the area manager to sign up.

At first I was given one territory to work. Back in those days the Avon ladies walked their territories knocking on doors and leaving brochures hoping that they would get an invite in to show their samples. Every once in a while a few strange people would greet me at their doors. An example was a man who basically came to the door with no clothes on! There were also a few other creepy invitations that I decided to decline as well for obvious reasons.

It wasn't long after I started working with Avon that I asked to add on another territory. I had gotten the first territory established and the second, so I asked for more. Altogether I had three territories and loved it! I achieved the President's Club right away and won a diamond locket. My territories were adjacent to each other on the east side of Wichita and mostly in what was considered the wealthier neighborhoods. I felt pretty safe walking the streets and peddling my wares.

## The Victim Was The Stalker!

One day I was working in one of my new Avon territories and found myself in a house having a very friendly conversation with an elderly woman. She was having fun looking through my Avon brochures and making purchases. I asked her if she knew of someone else on her block that might be interested in visiting with me as well. She informed me that most everyone wasn't at home that day or was working except for the one lady across the street and down a ways.

She then asked me if I was familiar with the latest news headlines about a woman who was being stalked and who had been stabbed in the back by the stalker at the mall a few nights before. I informed her that I had been following the news on the case. That was the same woman who lived right across the street! I said to my customer that maybe I should try and call on her neighbor at another time especially with what she was going through. My customer assured me that her neighbor would love the company, so against my better judgment I headed across the street to meet with her.

As I approached the house I noticed a dark car parked in front of the house on the street with a plain clothed detective sitting inside. I assumed it was for her protection. I didn't know if that detective would even allow me to go to the front door but he did. He probably had been watching me walk up and down the street and figured that I was just an Avon lady calling.

I had read where that woman had been stalked for weeks. She would find letters on her front porch or on her back porch from the stalker. Other strange incidences were happening as well, but the ultimate attack had happened a few evenings earlier when the stalker hid in the back seat of her car while she was shopping at the mall, stabbing her in the back when she returned. It was an unbelievable story as the stalker had escalated his anger with each incident.

When I reached the front door I rang the doorbell and her husband came to the door. He allowed me to come in while he proceeded to grab a dining room chair and sat it in the middle of the living room. He asked me to have a seat on the sofa. He then went to another room and got his wife and slowly walked with her to the chair that he had placed for her in the middle of the room. I thought that the whole scene seemed weird.

When she was seated she sat on the chair with a very queen like posture and was rather demure. She was very well put together and was dressed in a simple blouse and skirt. I could see some of her bandages from the recent stabbing protruding out from the neck of her blouse. She was very kind and carried the conversation quite well. I never physically approached her without asking because I just had a feeling inside that something was not right about her. I never asked her what had happened to her as I figured that it was none of my business. If she wanted to talk about it that would have to be her call. She did offer a few details on her own.

I knew that her husband and another detective were somewhere in the house for protection and when I walked away from that house I was thinking how strange that encounter was. I knew that something was not right at that house and it wasn't the whole stalking thing, it was something else, *but what?*

I think the police department came up with some startling conclusions about the case themselves. For months I knew that the police department was publicly on the hot seat for not being able to find the stalker. How was it that the stalker could leave items at the house and not be seen! And the letters that were actually mailed to her had no fingerprints on them.

Soon after her attack one of the detectives followed the woman and he watched her mail herself a letter! Yes, she was her own stalker and she had stabbed herself in the back! It's hard to know what mental state a person has to be in to be able to bring all that attention upon oneself and to do such harm as well. It saddened me to know that such a beautiful person who offered nothing but kindness to me had such troubles going on inside of her.

I eventually gave up my job with Avon. Mr. X kept taking my money and it was making it harder for me to pay for my samples and products. I decided to quit so I wouldn't have to leave on a bad note.

I was starting to see more of the real Mr. X.

## A Shell of a Car Became a Jewel

I knew that my Mr. X belonged to a car club and I had seen many pictures of his collectibles. He particularly liked to collect the rare Shelby vehicles that were manufactured by Carroll Shelby, not the Shelby manufactured by Ford. Mr. X was without a collectible car when we were first married but within the first year of our marriage he purchased one.

He had found a rare find sitting on some farm land in another state and struck a deal with the farmer to purchase it. Mr. X briefly described the car to me and explained that it was a fixer-upper and that he was spending five thousand dollars to purchase it. He was so excited about the find and I was excited for him!

When my husband arrived home with the car he burst through the front door to exclaim to me that he was home and rushed me outdoors to see the car. I was greatly disappointed. It was basically a shell of a vehicle! Chickens had been roosting in it, the rag top was shredded, the passenger seat was missing, the leather interior was ruined, one of the quarter panels was missing, and I could see through the floorboard to the pavement below.

"*Oh my goodness*, you spent *how* much money for this rusted piece of junk!?" I exclaimed.

It took the better part of a year to restore that vehicle. The GT 500 engine was in perfect condition and no repairs were needed for it except for a tune up. Because the car was so rare my husband had to search for parts all over the United States. We even drove to another state just to borrow one quarter panel from another vehicle so that a mold could be made to reproduce the fiberglass panel that we needed. The interior and convertible top was completely replicated by a local company in Wichita that specialized in car interiors. All in all, the vehicle turned out to be quite a jewel! It was totally restored to its original beauty. I had to admit that I loved that car.

It did take me a while to learn how to drive it because it was so powerful. I often left skid marks when taking off from a stoplight at least until I learned to let the car drive itself away from the stops. The car always did well at the car shows and won a few trophies.

Mr. X went on to collect a few more show cars while we were married. We did hang onto that first car though for several years and finally sold it for a mighty handsome profit.

## The Mexico City Cathedral

My first year of marriage to Mr. X was definitely eventful leaving me wondering what was going to happen next. That was the way it was until our marriage ended. Over the next several years I was able to get back on track with my career while riding the roller coaster with my husband.

We liked to travel and had visited the Indy 500 several times. We attended the World's Fair and traveled with his business for special events and traveled to the home office in Des Moines when required. We also spent a lot of time in Kansas City enjoying the shopping and the night life there. Of course we so enjoyed our several trips to Acapulco as they were the highlight of our traveling.

I remember one time during the Easter holiday that we flew to Mexico City for a visit. The city was all a buzz. I wanted to go and visit the modern cathedral and was totally amazed as I watched person after person walking on their bare knees to the cathedral, sometimes for miles doing penance. In most cases though, it was the father of the family that walked on his bloody knees as his family walked beside him. The cathedral itself was very busy with people as they walked in and out, and all the while mass was going on.

We found ourselves venturing into the town square where we visited the famous Metropolitan Cathedral; it is the largest and oldest cathedral in the Americas and the seat of the Roman Catholic Archdiocese in Mexico. I was totally amazed at all of the gold that was in the cathedral. The walls were lined with it! A lot of the inside was barred off, probably to deter looters. I thought that if they were to melt down one of those walls of gold they could feed the poor of that country for quite some time!

On the outside of the cathedral a rare find had just happened. They had just discovered that there was a pyramid buried under the cathedral! The excavation was privately fenced with no way to look inside to see what was actually going on. It was also heavily guarded with the militia. Of course Mr. X could not resist knowing what was being hidden from public view. While I was across the square looking at another building I noticed out of the corner of my eye a military truck being let out of that fenced-in area. Mr. X stood next to the gate and he jumped up and started taking pictures, one right after another. I was horrified as he was basically held at bay by the military while his film was destroyed! Lucky for him, he wasn't killed instantly!

### The Mayan Pyramids

We next traveled outside of Mexico City to see the Mayan Sun and the Moon pyramids. The Sun pyramid was the taller of the two so I set out to climb it and it took a long time to reach the top. It was a bit steep and in some places it was almost like climbing a rung ladder but I made it all of the way. A few of the people that had attempted the climb that day didn't fare as well and some even had to stop to throw up! The air was a bit thin being that high up, but I could see for miles in all directions.

Yes, my Mr. X and I did have a lot of grand times jet-setting around in our first few years of marriage. I learned a lot from him about business and about positive thinking. I think we owned *everything* Zig Ziglar! He encouraged me in my career but there was still a dark side to him and the ulterior motives that drove him that sooner or later I would have to deal with.

## Addicted to Greed and Drink

Mr. X really did have a bit of a dark side which only grew more apparent as he became immerged in the addiction to money and drinking. He could no longer social drink without going too far. I still partied when I could, but my career didn't allow too much time for that. I would hang out at a club on occasion and party it up.

It became very evident that I was estranged from my family. We weren't exactly on the guest list for special family gatherings because they didn't want Mr. X around. It was more of an invite because they had to. They didn't want anything to do with my husband or want him around at all. I couldn't blame them. There became a time when I didn't want him around either and would sometimes hope that he would just simply die.

Mr. X and I eventually moved further east in Wichita to another townhouse. We made the move a little over a year after we had gotten married. I didn't like it as much as the last townhouse, but it was still a very nice home.

One day my husband's boss called Mr. X and me into his office. Apparently Mr. X had discovered a loop hole in writing insurance policies that allowed him to take home more commissions that the other salesmen. His boss warned him, in front of me, to stop doing it or he would be terminated. Like I said, my Mr. X was a smart man when it came to numbers and he always found a way to finagle the system. After our meeting with his boss I asked him what he was going to do and he stated to me that he would continue with operating in the same manner until they fixed the loop holes. Needless to say, he was terminated several months later.

With him being without work and the kind of life style we were living we eventually ran out of money within a few months. I was still working but my pay only took care of the food and gas for the cars. We were going without heat, electricity, no phone service, and all of that took place in the middle of winter! I used baking soda for toothpaste and took freezing showers. I grew up being poor and I was a very resourceful person so I knew I could survive if I had to. Mr. X didn't fare as well, you know, with a bruised ego and all.

We used our fireplace for a source of heat and managed to keep warm day by day at least until our property manager found out how we were living and we were asked to leave. I think the embarrassment of that incident was what drove Mr. X to even higher levels of greed which amongst obvious other things eventually ended our marriage.

We then moved to a very small apartment all the way to the west side of Wichita. It was quite interesting trying to fit all of our stuff into a small apartment. Luckily, we weren't there for very long! Mr. X and I found new jobs and for all appearances he was back on top of the world again.

## He Started Chanting My Name

During my life with Mr. X he introduced me to all kinds of things that take place in the darkness of this world, dark things that most people would never have any opportunity to even know about. I won't even go into detail to describe those things in this book so you won't have the visuals that I have had to live with. All I can say is that we people live in a very depraved world.

His lifestyle led him to become a frequent flyer of the gentlemen's clubs, which aren't so gentlemanly as far as I was concerned. His thirst for gambling on the pool table increased even more. His love of money increased at any and all costs.

Through his acquaintances, Mr. X introduced me to some swingers. That was a big NO for me! I did however watch young naïve couples experiment with that lifestyle only to find their lives and marriages grossly shattered. Mr. X also introduced me to strippers, pornography, and many backroom operations for gambling. I was surprised to learn of the many businesses that were only fronts for gambling and other illegal operations! All of which I wanted nothing to do with. He even suggested that I become a dancer.

"*Really*?" I sarcastically asked him. "Oh *berrrother*!" I said as I rolled my eyes.

On one of our many day trips to the Kansas City area Mr. X wanted us to stop at a club that he had heard good things about, which I found out was only a ploy to get me there. Lo and behold, that club was having a wet t-shirt contest, a rather ridiculous fad of that time and one that I felt was very demeaning to women. All the girls were lining up on the stage wearing their white t-shirts that had been provided for them getting ready to be sprayed down with water. The announcer was making a last call for any girls who hadn't made it up onto the stage to please come on up. The next thing I knew, Mr. X had started chanting my name and had the whole club chanting my name as well! I was mad and disgusted just to put it mildly, and I excused myself and went outside to sit on the curb. If it wasn't for the fact that I didn't know where we were at, I would have driven off and left him there!

## I Became His Arm Candy

If that wasn't bad enough, Mr. X introduced me to my first biker bar. For some odd reason he just had to visit that one bar. I was a bit hesitant, especially with us being all dressed up in our eveningwear fineries. Not a smart move I must say! You are just asking for a fight. When we walked in the door we immediately got the glance overs by everyone. Mr. X left me sitting at the bar while he visited with some people towards the back of the club. I never put it all together as to what was actually going on but I did figure out that I was being used as a shield.

In fact it turned out that I was being used for all kinds of schemes. *I just didn't know it.* It just took me a while to figure out his game. After a couple of years I started to see a pattern and put it all together. I had noticed that we didn't keep couple friends for very long. Mr. X would always bring me along for the first few meetings when he was getting to know his prey. He became a member of the Downtown Optimist Club which was where he met most of those folks. I can't tell you how many known community leaders were at our dinner tables. He would become friends with well-known or wealthy people, then after meeting with them a few times, he would try to get them to invest in oil wells or other business opportunities. Most of the time he was trying to entice them to become a business partner with him in *some* investment deal.

But once people figured him out or had him investigated and determined that he was a risk, well we will just say that he was not liked very well. I was kept in the dark and never knew about all the schemes he was dreaming up until I was able to put two and two together. In the meantime, he knew that people trusted me and liked me so he used my character to try to build a relationship with others. In other words, I became his arm candy to open doors that he wouldn't have been able to do on his own when he needed to impress his prey. Once I figured it all out he abruptly discovered that I was no longer available to be used in such a manner.

### "I Don't Do Menial Labor!"

We finally bought a house, or should I say Mr. X finally bought me a house. A friend of my husbands offered to sell us his home. We had visited there a few times in the past and I had fallen in love with it. The home was built in 1910 and it had some very special architectural surprises inside that supplied a lot of charm. There were a few things that needed to be updated or fixed up but for the most part it was ready to go.

It didn't take me long to figure out that I would be the one doing all of the work around the house including all of the yard work. Mr. X told me he bought me the house only because I wanted it. He never wanted a house because of the upkeep. He didn't have time for it which was why he had always lived in condos or townhouses where the properties were taken care of.

I remember one day when a huge amount of snow had fallen during the night. I had asked him to help me clear the driveway so we could get our cars out.

"I don't do menial labor!" he firmly stated. "That's why I make lots of money, so I can hire people to do that kind of stuff," he snarled.

All righty then I thought to myself, and shoveled the driveway by myself so that I could get to work on time!

I really enjoyed decorating the house and made some interior and exterior changes. I fixed up the yard and planted a large rose garden in the back yard. It was fun making improvements to the property but it also caused our house to become a target.

### I Surprised the Burglars

One day I had taken my grandmother shopping. The store I worked at hosted senior days where the elderly could shop early before the store officially opened for business and they would receive a special senior discount. That particular day, I will never forget for as long as I live, because not only did my grandmother bless me with a brand new set of dishes for my upcoming holiday party, I also had a surprise waiting for me at home.

After our shopping excursion I took my grandmother home and I made a quick stop at my house to drop off my packages. Because I was in such a hurry to drop something off at my husband's office, I entered only into our living room and left all of my packages lying on the floor. Nothing seemed out of the ordinary as I hustled off to Mr. X's office which was only two minutes away. I had made it back home in less than ten minutes. As I entered the front door I could see that the back door leading out from the kitchen was wide open. It was then that I realized that my house had been broken in to. There was shattered glass everywhere and some of my crystal pieces had been broken as someone tried to make a quick get-a-way. I immediately called the police.

According to the police, when I had dropped off my packages I had surprised the burglars who were probably hiding in my house! Evidence showed that someone had been in one of the closets because a space had been cleared for someone to hide in. I must have scared them with my quick entrance and exit. The police had noticed too that the thieves had run past a diamond ring, an expensive camera, and many other valuables that they hadn't taken with them. The warning that came next was scary.

"Now that the burglars know what is in here, they may come back," stated one of the officers.

*Wondermous* I told myself, just *wondermous!*

Yep, we became a target. I had put a load of nice white rocks in the gardens in our front yard and when I came home one day after work the neighbor from across the street came over to let me know that he had witnessed some people loading up the white rocks from our yard into a truck and taking off.

"*Really*?" I exclaimed with amazement.

We also had hamburgers taken off of our grill one evening while they were being cooked! And then there was the time that our lawnmower, the lawn chairs, and I could name a few more things had disappeared. Apparently we *were* the supply house for many!

## It Was the "Where Else" That I Wondered About

Mr. X had a really odd way of looking at money. I was never allowed to save any as his thoughts on the subject were that everyone works hard all their lives to save up for their retirement years but most never get to live to use it. He was going to live it up and use it up as he earned it, and he did!

After we were married for some time I realized that Mr. X wasn't paying any bills. After I received a few phone calls from utility companies and I started to realize that he didn't forget to pay them he just didn't pay them. If he created a bill he never would pay it. It wasn't as if he didn't have the money to pay the bills he was just going to enjoy the money he had made and spend it on what he wanted to!

As it ended up, I paid all the household bills and any other debt that he racked up. The only thing good about the setup was that for the most part we bought everything we wanted with cash. We did not have credit cards and we didn't need credit cards. His income came from many different sources such as his job, his gambling, flipping cars, his money schemes, and who knows from where else. It was the "where else" that I always wondered about.

## I Was None the Wiser

I remember one time when Mr. X decided to sell one of his show cars. It was one that I had driven on a daily basis. The trouble was, I loved that car. It was a red convertible with white leather interior and top. I had no idea that he had it up for sale. On Valentine's Day Mr. X sent a boat load of roses to me at work. When I got off work and was driving home in rush hour traffic mind you, I ran out of gas on a bridge! *Great*! Luckily someone stopped and helped me push my car off the busy bridge and I was only a half a block away from a gas station. I knew that I had gas in my car when I started out that morning so what happened to it?

I walked to that gas station and I called my husband at home and told him my dilemma. He told me he was too busy watching his TV show and I would just have to wait until his show was over before he would come and rescue me. By then I was really steamed up, roses or no roses! I walked back to my car with a gas can in hand, put gas in my car, and then I opened up the hood and put a little gas on the carburetor and started the car up and went home. Mr. X was still watching his TV show when I got there! By the way, I still refuse to watch any re-runs of that TV show to this day!

The next day when I returned home from work there were people standing in my driveway with Mr. X waiting for me. My husband had sold my car out from under me and with no warning whatsoever! By the way, I figured out where my gas had disappeared to.

The day before, while I was at work, my husband had handed that couple his keys to my car and had them take my car out for a spin. They took it from the parking lot where I worked and they took it for a long drive. When they returned the car they parked it back exactly where I had parked it and I was none the wiser, well, until I ran out of gas.

Great, I was without a car and on foot. Every morning Mr. X had to drive me into work and he was supposed to pick me up when I got off work. That didn't always work out well. One night it was snowing and it had started to come down pretty heavy when I got off work. I waited and waited in the dark empty shopping mall parking lot and in the snow for my Mr. X and he never showed up. Luckily one of my co-workers had stayed with me and she offered to take me home. The next time it happened I had to call a taxi. Where was he? He had a couple of falling-down-drunk episodes and had forgotten that he needed to pick me up.

Mr. X eventually bought me another car and to make up for all of my inconveniences he bought me a brand-new sports car right off of the showroom floor.

He was good about that, buying me expensive gifts when he knew he had messed up. I guess he thought that those gifts would always fix everything.

### I Threw Him for a Loop

Mr. X did another one of his disappearing acts one weekend. I never heard from him at all for three days. Apparently he had taken one of his friends with him because early that Saturday morning the wife of that friend called me. She was in panic mode. She was speaking very fast and asked me if I had seen her husband or if I knew where he was. She kept going on non-stop and continued on with her thoughts and ramblings; maybe these two men were together or what if something bad happened? She finally stopped long enough for me to speak to her. I told her that I had not seen her husband, nor mine.

"*Well, aren't you worried*?" she asked.

I told her nope, I wasn't worried at all. I also told her that my husband disappeared all of the time. She was flabbergasted by that remark!

At the end of the weekend my Mr. X finally showed up and was throwing money all over the house. Good heavens, it almost looked like he had robbed a bank or something. He hadn't. He had found a bunch of fools to gamble with and he played with them all weekend.

It also had become apparent that I was just another resource for his money. One time he had inherited about a thousand dollars from one of his relatives. He asked me what *we* should buy with it and I told him that the money was his and that he could do with it whatever he wanted to. That sure threw him for a loop.

"No, it's *our* money," he insisted.

"Nope," I said, "it was from your relative, so it is *your* money."

"So," he said, "is that how it's gonna' work with *your* inheritance?"

I asked him what inheritance and laughed.

"You really don't know how much money you are inheriting from your grandmother, *do you?*" he asked.

"What are you *talking* about?" I asked him.

Can you believe it? He actually had gone to my grandmother and asked her how much she was worth and asked her how much she was leaving to me! I was furious, and by the way, he bought a thousand dollar watch with *his* inheritance.

On two different occasions Mr. X had not paid his taxes. On two different occasions my paycheck was being threatened with garnishments to pay those taxes. That was why he was always self-employed, because his income couldn't be garnished if something went wrong. His initial reaction to my possible garnishment did not settle well with me.

"Oh well, let them garnish your checks," he said nonchalantly.

By that time I had enough on my own husband to put him away, so not one of my paychecks was ever garnished! He paid his *own* taxes!

### Okiedokilie!

I had a couple of detectives show up at my work one time and they started asking me all kinds of questions about Mr. X. I was very cooperative even though they didn't tell me what the questioning was all about. They wanted to know where they could find him and I told them where his office was. They warned me not to call him and give him the heads-up that they were coming. I never did find out what that was really all about. It surely had something to do with...you guessed it, money!

Weird things were going on in our banking accounts. One day they were filled to the brim and the next day they would be empty then voila, there it was again and plentiful the following day. I'm not sure what was going on but I had my suspicions.

Mr. X was spending more and more time away from home. His business luncheons where he made all of those deals always involved alcohol. Those business meetings would evolve into a game somewhere, and then that would lead him to the gentlemen's clubs. The next thing I knew I had strippers calling me at home looking for Mr. X.

"He promised me five hundred dollars," they would say.

He always felt sorry for the dancers because they just didn't have the same opportunities that I had had, to get an education and all. *Okiedokilie!* I thought to myself as I rolled my eyes. By that point I wasn't surprised by anything that he said.

### I Gave Him The Stink Eye!

Mr. X was deteriorating more and more each day. His drinking was on a daily basis and to the point that it was obvious to me that he had become an alcoholic. I confronted him about it and of course like most alcoholics, he denied that he had a problem. It was becoming worrisome for me cleaning up after his drunken nights. It was getting old driving around town trying to help him find his car because he couldn't remember where he had left it.  It was usually found at the strangest places and I would often ask myself what on earth was he doing in *that* neighborhood?

His demeanor started changing and he told me one day that I just wasn't as fun as I used to be. *Gee, I wonder why?* Then he told me he was going to sell another one of my cars. For fear of being left on foot again I hid the title. I almost took a hit from him in the face one day when we had a fight about it. In our years of marriage we had never fought like that. The fight had gotten very heated up and he flipped me around to face him as he reared back his fist. I looked at him with my stink eye and *double dogged dared him* to hit me! I knew that if he had hit me I was going to be knocked out cold! And there I was double dog daring him? Well, I also knew that my dad had threatened him on our wedding day. If he ever hurt me, he would have to deal with my dad and my brother. I could see the wheels turning in his head as he held that threatening pose. He then let me go and dropped his fist.

I never did let him have the title to the car so he just applied for another one and sold the car anyway.

## It Was Our Five Year Marriage Evaluation

A few months before our fifth year anniversary I reminded my Mr. X of our verbal agreement that we had made before we were married. I knew that it was time to evaluate our marriage and see if we should continue on. He was stunned at my decision to end our marriage. He laughed at me and told me that I would never leave him. He told me that I liked my lifestyle too much to leave and he dismissed me and my thoughts. I, however, started right away saving up money on the sneak without him noticing. I had saved well over a thousand dollars and was hiding it in the house where I thought it would be safe.

In the meantime, my dad had resigned from his police duties and had moved to Wichita. He had been trying different jobs to see what he might like to do in his retirement years. Mr. X had changed jobs as well and had been working in the home improvement industry in sales. Somehow, and I am still not sure how it happened, Mr. X had talked my dad into working with him selling home improvement products. My plans to leave Mr. X had to be put on hold. I didn't want to risk my dad's position especially if it was something that he was good at and wanted to continue doing.

I kept on saving money while I was waiting it out with Mr. X. Apparently he had caught on that not all of my money was going into the bank so he tore through the house to try and find my stash.

When I got home from work one day he cornered me and wanted to know why I was saving money. I lied to him and told him that it was for a new dining room set. He proceeded to take my stash and went out and bought a new dining set without me! Great! What was I going to do?

Dad finally decided that he didn't like the sales position with Mr. X's company all that much and moved on to something else. Many years later when I told my dad what my initial plans were when he started working with Mr. X he felt terrible. He couldn't believe that he had spoiled my plans to leave Mr. X, someone that I should have left a lot sooner that I did.

Basically I was pretty much living my own life separate from Mr. X. He wasn't home much and my career had taken off so I wasn't around much myself. I had my own friends that I started hanging around with. When I partied, I partied! That was the time when drinking and smoking those *special* cigarettes seemed to take me away for a while. And yes…I inhaled!

## I Unleashed My Fury upon Mr. X

Remember the bouncer I spoke about earlier? Well he was a fireman by trade and when I married Mr. X, the fireman had voiced his opinion about the marriage as well. He kept in contact with me by showing up where I worked, just to make sure that I was okay. He wasn't being bothersome at all, just concerned.

As my marriage was totally deteriorating and completely falling apart I began spending time with the fireman on the side. We were very discrete as it could have cost him his job. Mr. X was never around and when he was he was usually drunk, so he was never the wiser. Yes I was a married woman seeing another man! Where else on this earth could that lifestyle have led me?

Mr. X and I made one last trip to Acapulco. It was a very miserable trip being there with someone that I didn't love anymore. I tried to make the best of it because I so adored being in Acapulco, it was always so magical.

When we returned from our trip Mr. X decided to start his own home improvement company. He set out to getting everything put together with the banks and landed property to operate out of. He came to me and wanted me to sign with the banks but I refused. I found out during our divorce that he had forged my signature on all of those documents that he needed to get his company started with.

While my Mr. X was gathering all of his start-up capital he showed up at my work one day. He walked directly up to me and in front of all of my co-workers he caused a very volatile moment.

"I need you to go to your grandmother and ask her for your inheritance," he stated.

Okay, I told myself, that was *it*! My flash temper went into a rage and I marched him into the back room and closed the door where I proceeded to unleash all of my fury. When I was through I opened the door and all of my co-workers were standing at the very front of the store as far away from the back as possible. They were mortified at Mr. X's request and even more horrified to see my temper totally unleashed!

Mr. X somehow got his operation up and going without my help and by all appearances it was a success. I was still trying to figure out how I was going to get away from him and when to make my big move. Mr. X had a trip to China planned for us and I didn't want to go with him. I had a feeling that going out of the country with him could have been dangerous for me; I needed to make my get-away before that trip. Then another incident happened that helped me to make my decision even faster.

### The Convict Came To My Door!

One afternoon there was a knock at my front door. When I opened the door, standing in front of me was someone that I had known from working at the courthouse several years earlier. I was stunned to see him standing there, and he, just as stunned to see me. I knew he had been sent to prison several years earlier and I asked him what he was doing at my house. He told me he was there to see Mr. X but Mr. X was not at home, so he told me he would come back later.

Let me give you a little bit of background about that person. He was one of the security guards at the courthouse. He had a very young son who needed to have cancer treatments that the guard could not afford so he embezzled a lot of money over a period of time and was caught. He was sent to prison for a while. *Why did he want to speak to my husband? I wondered. And how do they know each other?*

When Mr. X arrived home I told him about the visitor and I wanted to know how they knew each other. Mr. X told me that he had hired the man to work for him. He just didn't tell me the whole story and for *what* he was hired to do.

When the visitor returned I was asked to leave the room. I decided to hide in an adjacent room where I could eavesdrop. Oh my, did I get an ear full! The visitor was actually working at a competitor's office and was hired by Mr. X to steal their sales leads and other important business information. That meeting was to pass off what had been stolen; I watched the hand off through a small open sliver in the door. I thought to myself, o*h my, we are into corporate theft?*

I knew right there and then that I had to make my move very quickly whether I was ready or not. The next morning I remember standing in the middle of my house looking around at all of my pretty stuff and decided that no amount of money or things that I owned was worth the risk any longer.

# TWELVE

# Mr. X's Shenanigans

*The acts of the flesh are obvious: sexual immorality,
impurity and debauchery; idolatry and witchcraft; hatred,
discord, jealousy, fits of rage, selfish ambition, dissensions,
factions and envy; drunkenness, orgies, and the like. I warn
you, as I did before, that those who live like this will not
inherit the kingdom of God.*
Galatians 5:19-21

### The Two Week Notice

Galatians 5:19-21 pretty much sums up what my life had become. Things in my life had deteriorated quite a bit and not just with my marriage but with my person as well. It may sound kind of funny, but I gave my Mr. X a two week notice! I informed him that I would be out of our house by the end of two weeks. It was pretty much a formal yet business kind of an escape I suppose and I went out to find a studio apartment to move to and started making arrangements for moving day.

I carried on during those two weeks as I would normally. I cleaned the house, I did Mr. X's laundry, I did the yard work all the while I was wondering why I was behaving like that. Maybe I was just filling my time up until I could move out?

I told Mr. X that we needed some space and that I was moving out for a while. After all I wanted to make sure that I could have a safe get-away. If I had told him that I was leaving so I could divorce him I don't think he would have let me go without an incident. He was not a happy camper to say the least. He was especially taken back at the thought that I would even consider leaving him before we took our trip to China!

During the time of my two weeks' notice Mr. X went into overdrive trying to keep me from leaving. He had made arrangements for us to look into the possibility of adopting a child. *What?* Where did that come from? Maybe he thought that I was leaving because we didn't have children? I didn't know about his plans until one day when we were both at home and the phone rang. It was someone from an adoption agency. I had the look of shock written all over my face as he discussed the issue on the phone. He eventually told the person on the phone that he needed to see what his wife felt about the idea before he went any further.

At the end of the two weeks I packed up only my personal belongings and left. However I had left my piano behind with the understanding that I would be able to come back for it as soon as I could make some arrangements to have it moved. I asked Mr. X if I could use one of the cars at least until I could find another car to purchase and he allowed me to take the Lincoln.

When I left, I left behind all of the furniture and mostly everything else that had been given to me over the years that were from friends and relatives. I didn't take my oil paintings, wedding or vacation pictures, or the checkbook. I just wanted out! I didn't want to give any ounce of leeway for him to state that I had taken something from him. I took absolutely nothing from him, *period*!

Because I was estranged from my family they knew nothing about my moving out and living on my own for several months. Eventually they did find out. Because of the size of my apartment, it became apparent that I would need to store a few boxes at my parent's home and they agreed that it would be okay. Dad met me in the driveway when I arrived with my boxes. While we were unloading the boxes, my grandmother joined us and proceeded to sternly tell me that I needed to *remember my raisin'*! I thought my dad was going to lose it!

"She *has* remembered her *raising*," he growled, "that's why she stayed with him for so long in the first place." He continued on, "She is doing the right thing, *now leave her alone!*"

I think I had my dad's blessing.

## Mr. X Tried Harassing Me

I found a very small furnished apartment that was complete with a kitchen and a living room that doubled as a bedroom. It was cute and small but it was my new home. It sure didn't take me long to get settled in! I had already worked out a budget that I knew would cover all of my expenses and I was ready to go it alone once again.

When Mr. X asked me where I was moving to I declined to tell him but it didn't take him long to find me. Once he knew where I lived he was constantly calling to harass me and trying to find ways of forcing me to come back. Our conversations always ended up with me in tears. He would follow me around town and leave notes on the car not only to let me know that he had been watching me but also to let me know that he knew where I was hanging out and with whom. He wanted me to know that he would always be able to find me.

I also started hearing about the lies that he had told my family and friends about me. I could not believe some of the stories that he told; crazy, ridiculous stories. And most of these were stories had been told to folks all throughout our marriage! I could not believe the betrayals and on so many levels, mostly done in order for him to look better in other people's eyes. I was so glad that folks finally felt that they could ask me about the stories so that I could clear things up.

He claimed that he really didn't know why I had left! I did tell him that one day I would tell him the reasons why I left but I never did. I felt he wasn't ready to hear the truth then nor would he ever be ready to hear what I had to say.

## Where Was the Key?

Several weeks after my leaving I had made arrangements with Mr. X to retrieve my piano while he was in China and he told me that he would leave a key at the neighbor's house. I contacted my friend, the fireman, to meet me with his truck so we could move the piano to my dad's house. My studio apartment just wasn't large enough to handle a piano. When we arrived at Mr. X's house and asked the neighbor for the key, Mr. X had not left a key! Mr. X had not even mentioned anything to the neighbor about leaving a key!  It was obvious that Mr. X was trying to keep me from getting my piano.

My fireman friend and his fireman buddy just chuckled and stated to me that they were experts at breaking into homes. When I told them that I really didn't want them to use an ax, they both laughed!

I watched as the firemen gently took a window apart and proceeded to crawl into Mr. X's house. It was genius I thought to myself and I won't tell a soul how they did it.

They were able to load up the piano and put the window back together. Then we left to take my piano to my dad's house. Don't forget this part of the story about the piano because I didn't know, nor could I have known that this moving-of-the-piano story would be very significant in my life many years later.

## The Unexpected Discovery

I had only kept my house key for about a week after I had moved out just in case I would have to return to retrieve something that I really needed. On one of my trips back to Mr. X's house I found myself looking through some paperwork in a metal lockbox that Mr. X kept at the bottom of one of the closets. I thought that it only contained his pilot flight logs. When I opened the box and starting looking through it I found a letter. It was from his ex-wife.

As I read the letter it was apparent that she had written it sometime during their divorce many years earlier. The letter sounded almost as though I had written it. Her parents had come from out of state to rescue the poor girl. They laid in wait for Mr. X to leave for work and after he left they quickly entered the premises and loaded up their daughter and everything that she owned and escaped. It was then that I realized for the first time how fortunate I was to get away on my own and how thankful that I didn't end up being committed to a mental health facility like she had to be. Maybe because of my strong personality and feistiness I was able to get out in pretty good shape! Mr. X had worn me down though. It took someone close to me to help me to understand and realize that I had been in a verbally abusive relationship with him. I hadn't seen it that way because mainly I had never viewed myself as a victim.

I decided to close the letter and place it back in the envelope. When I looked a little further into the box I found some life insurance papers. I wondered what I was staring at. But since I didn't have much time to investigate further I took those papers with me so I could examine them later.

It appeared to me that Mr. X had taken out a life insurance policy on me! I couldn't tell for sure if what I had in my hands was for real but if so, would he have followed through with something like that, take out life insurance on me? Did I somehow ruin some kind of a scheme that he had conjured up? I decided not to investigate any further on that one because I just simply didn't want to know.

### Credit Report Showed That I Didn't Exist!

I went car shopping because I needed to give back the one that Mr. X said I could borrow. Soon I found a car that would work fine for me and it was within my budget, but something unusual happened. I knew that I had established excellent credit before Mr. X and I were married but when the dealership tried to pull up my credit record I didn't exist, *anywhere*! How could it be that I just did not exist anywhere! Certain suspicions started to rise up in me. *What did Mr. X do?* The dealership decided to take a risk on me anyway and I was eventually able to work out a loan for the car.

A few months later, one of my friends came to me to inform me that Mr. X was selling my long mink coat. I started to laugh and told her that I didn't own a long mink coat. Well apparently I did because my friend was the same size as me and she had actually tried it on. My Mr. X thought that maybe my friend would want to buy it. He told her that I had special ordered the coat from a furrier and had stuck him with the bill! I began to realize that he probably had purchased the coat to give to me as a gift to try and lure me back. Yes he did try luring me back.

Mr. X started sending roses to me at work and even to my hangouts. I remember I had to drop something off to him at his house one time and he met me in the driveway. I stayed in the car and handed the item to him, and as I started to pull away he handed me a set of car keys.

"I purchased that convertible you had been looking at before you moved out," he said. "All you have to do is go to the dealership and pick it up, it is there waiting for you."

I just glared into his eyes while I dropped the keys at his feet and drove off.

### She Was Bright and Spunky

Shortly after I had moved out I started searching for a lawyer. The only problem was, Mr. X knew a lot of the local lawyers so I had to find one that had no connections to him at all. One of my friends suggested someone and I decided to set up an appointment with her. At my initial meeting with the lawyer my first question to her was if she knew Mr. X or anything about him. She said she didn't know him at all. She seemed to be quite honest, bright and spunky, so I went forward with the divorce using her counsel.

She was just what I needed to go to war with Mr. X and go to war we did. Of course Mr. X retained one of the best known lawyers in our community who later became a judge. I didn't want a war I just simply wanted out. I was willing to leave the marriage with absolutely nothing just to make it easier and faster to end it. Mr. X did not want the divorce at all and did everything in his power to throw a wrench in the works to hold up the process. The battle lasted for two years!

Mr. X first tried holding up the proceedings until the following year so he wouldn't mess up his taxes. I wasn't really interested in helping him with his taxes so the proceedings went forward as planned.

My lawyer informed me that she could not draw up divorce papers if I was not willing to take anything from the marriage. She knew the judge and she knew that he would not grant the divorce under such circumstances. She was able to come up with some items that I should have, knowing all the while that I didn't want them. She listed my collector's plates, alimony, and for Mr. X to take on my car payments. We even listed the house so if he did put it up for sale I would receive half of the proceeds. The main point being was that I was not forcing him from his house. If and only if it was sold would there be a division of the monies.

We were separated for six months before I was able to appear in court to get the divorce. The judge just about did not allow it, however. Once he saw the list of all of the assets that I brought to the marriage and the combined income we brought to the marriage he just about didn't grant my wishes.

He tacked on a little more to the alimony and granted my request for a divorce, but it was still not over! There were a lot of other details that had to be worked out concerning other property and his business. It was during the investigations that I found out that he had forged my signature on his business loans and some other paperwork that I had nothing to do with.

It took two years before the dust settled and we were completely divorced. Of course I only saw a few months of alimony and a few months of car payments just as I would have expected from him. I didn't pursue the matter, I just dropped it. I wasn't after the money, especially his.

## Who Were My True Friends?

After the money dries up you find out who your real friends are. It was kind of funny to see how that worked out. Money was not a problem when I hosted fun parties for my friends, and yes, we would often get into all kinds of trouble at those parties! If my friends wanted a party all they had to do was ask. Like I said you find out who your real friends are when you are no longer the party house! Only a few friends stuck it out with me while I was going through my divorce.

I began to figure out whom my *not-real* friends were when I found out that some of them were holding a bet. One of them called me one day to see how my divorce was going. They all knew it was a messy one and that it was taking a while; they also knew that it was taking a toll on me. She finally came clean and told me that there was a bet going on amongst them. They didn't think that I would really go through with the divorce and even if I did, I would eventually go back to him.

"*Why would you think that*?" I inquired.

She answered, "Because we don't think you can live without the money!"

Apparently they didn't know me very well. But then again, they were the *not-real* friends.

## Mr. X's House Burned Down

About a year after I had moved out of the house that Mr. X and I had lived in I received a phone call one morning from his little brother. He told me that Mr. X's house had burned down the night before! I just couldn't believe it so I drove over to his house and entered where the front door used to be. It was obvious that the fire had started in the kitchen area because it was totally gone, floor and all. The rest of the house had major smoke and water damage and was a total loss. My suspicion radar went up!

It just so happened that I had found out through the grapevine that Mr. X had gone to a loan shark to borrow quite a substantial amount of money and I knew that the loan was due the month that the house burned down. The fire was ruled as an accident but I knew better. I tried to get the case re-opened but the fire department was going to stick with their initial ruling.

Over the next several months Mr. X called me from time to time to get prices on items that were in his house in order to settle with the insurance company. Since I basically had purchased all of the items for that house I had a good memory of what I had spent on everything.

Then one day Mr. X called me and needed pricing for some draperies. I asked him when the insurance company was going to pay and how they were going to pay. I asked him if there would be two checks because of the property division and asked just how all of it was going to work?

"The divorce decree states, 'when the house *sells*', now the house didn't *sell*, did it?" he snidely remarked. And with that he hung up on me.

I immediately called my lawyer to tell her what he had said and she went silent for the longest time but then she quietly told me that Mr. X was right. She felt awful for me mainly because she knew what kind of a person he was and secondly she knew that he had found a way to get away with it. She immediately went to work and put a lean on the property that the house sat on so that it could not be sold without the monies being split between us. Mr. X and I showed up to sign those papers as well. It didn't matter though because he found a way around all the legalities, sold the property, and took off with the money. Yes he made out quite well on the deal!

## Did She Do Me a Favor?

After about two years of being in and out of court, the barrage of legalities, and dealing with Mr. X and all of his shenanigans, my lawyer's bill was quite substantial to say the least. When it was all finally over my lawyer called me to tell me that she would cut my bill in half if I would pay her in cash within the next couple of weeks. I thought that sounded like a pretty good deal. She told me that she didn't like handling divorce cases because they are messy and complicated. During my divorce she had gotten to see firsthand who I had been married to because she, herself, had to deal with him for two years.

"Debra, in your case," she said, "I did you a GREAT BIG favor!"

## It Was Finally Over!

Mr. X eventually left town and quickly, so it seems. I assumed that he went back to the Kansas City area. I found out later that he had sent his teenage brother into harm's way to pay off that loan shark to whom he owed a lot of money. I was called by investigators several years later who wanted to know if I knew the whereabouts of Mr. X because he had left town with many homes unfinished through his home improvement company and the monies to complete the homes were missing as well.

He did show up back in town many years later and on one of my birthdays. At that time I owned a business and he had found out about it and called me to wish me a happy birthday. Fortunately I was out of the office at the time, but I was stunned when my secretary asked me who he was as she gave me the phone message. I knew that it was just another one of his ways to let me know that he could always find me, *as if I was even trying to hide from him!*

He showed up in town one other time at my brother's house for who knows what reason. My brother was not very happy at all to see him standing in his yard. Mr. X was lucky he didn't have to leave in an ambulance!

My lawyer eventually put some kind of an order in place to have him arrested if he came back into the state of Kansas. She even called me ten years after our divorce to see if I wanted to renew the decree she had set in motion but I told her to drop it. It really didn't matter to me anymore because it was finally over. As I have recalled this closed chapter in my life, all I can say is, it is what it is!

## A Note of Care – Especially for Ladies

Today as I mentor young ladies about relationships I make sure that they understand that there is a difference in *needing* a man in their lives and *wanting* a man in their lives.

As little girls growing up we are groomed, dream, plan and prepare for our wedding days. Girls in, some cases, become all consumed about what their prince charming will be like. Tall, dark, handsome, loving, and caring are just a few characteristics that little girls are looking for. They want to be told that they are pretty and that they are loved. They want to feel like a princess, feel safe, and they want to be taken care of. And they want a lot of babies.

Ladies, please, please make a plan on how to take care of *you*. I have seen so many women never make plans for their own futures leaving themselves without a means of support. They forgo an education and other opportunities all in hopes that some man will take care of them. They *need* a man in their lives to survive, or so they think.

Soon they find themselves with several children and the man who was going to take care of them for the rest of their lives totally bailed.

Women who think that they need a man can oftentimes find themselves trapped in abusive controlling relationships with nowhere to go and with no means to support themselves.

When you are needy you make mistakes; regardless for the reason of your neediness. You can scheme and plot to get your man and all the while you overlook traits, characteristics, and *"things"* that should send up all kinds of red flags and warning signs about the man.

Even if your world is perfect and you have found your prince charming *life* can still happen. You may find yourself widowed or caring for your husband because he has become an invalid. He may lose his career and his identity along with it. You may *have* to become the bread winner for the family.

Just know that if you have found yourself in any of these situations there is hope and there is help.

Ladies if you are just starting to look for prince charming, regardless of your age, please consider praying to God to provide for you an upright godly man; one that will be His gift to you. Ask for wisdom and guidance as you date and look for suitors. Be patient and wait on God.

In some cases it is better for us to remain single. Again wait for God's answer and will for your life. Your ministry may be best carried out by remaining single. I like to empower women by validating and encouraging those who have chosen to do so.

Their choice is not to be questioned or demeaned in any way. They are not any less of a woman for their choice. Some of the most powerful and influential women that have made a difference in this world remained single, totally dedicating themselves to a cause near and dear to their hearts.

Ladies, first and foremost, you need to know that you are loved by God your heavenly father. You are beautiful in His eyes and you are His princess. He is your provider and protector. Once you have truly gotten this, and only then, will you be strong enough to rely upon his help, his wisdom, his timing and guidance, and his will for your life.

### THIRTEEN

# The Fireman Was a Gentleman

*Let him kiss me with the kisses of his mouth – for your love
is more delightful than wine.*
Song of Solomon 1:2

## It Started With a Phone Call

I was only nineteen years of age and was actually underage to be hanging out at some of the local clubs, but somehow these establishments always allowed me to come in without question.

To be quite honest I wasn't paying too much attention to the bouncers, but I found out that one of them was a fireman one evening. He approached me while I was sitting alone at one of the tables. My girlfriends had gotten up to dance so he took the opportunity to come calling.

"I really like tall girls," he said as he leaned over me.

He then handed me a piece of paper with his phone number on it.

"If you would like to go out sometime, give me a call," he quietly stated.

I just stared at him as he turned around and left. I was taken back a bit but I could tell by his request that he was sincere. That was how it all began.

When my friends returned to our table I told them what had just happened.

"You should give him a call!" they excitedly exclaimed.

All of us found ourselves staring at him trying not to look too obvious. He sure seemed very nice. And that he was!

The bouncer and fireman was a tall very muscular man with blonde hair and blue eyes. He was the quiet type but he could bring to order any situation very quickly if he needed to. Nothing about him seemed to scream *run the other way*! It took me a couple of weeks before I finally got up the nerve to give him a call.

After our phone conversation we decided to go on our first date to a local restaurant that he had frequented often. He arrived in his corvette on time and was very well mannered. At the restaurant we shared some really good food and some awkward conversation, at least until we got to know each other a little better. It was at that time that I discovered that he was seven years older than me and that he had joined the fire department after returning home from two Viet Nam tours. He not only worked part time as a bouncer but in construction as well to earn extra income.

## He Was Referred to as Hulk Hogan

My fireman friend not only drove a corvette, he also owned a Harley. He shared a house with a few other firemen as well as with other friends, most of whom were also bouncers at the same club. He was a body builder and I found out that some people referred to him as Hulk Hogan.

After our dinner he drove me home but we were both rather quiet, which created a kind of awkwardness for us once again. I didn't know if he would really ask me for another date or if it was the end of the road for any future dates. At the age of nineteen I had no way of knowing how that relationship was going to impact the rest of my life. It wasn't the end of the road!

Our friendship grew and I was falling head over heels in love with the man. You might say that he was my first love. There were times when

I found myself daydreaming and writing my last name as his, but deep down inside, I knew that the relationship would not be anything more than just a few fun times together. Even though I went on to date other men and even got married, there was always that *something* between us.

Many times while frequenting the clubs with other dates I would catch him staring at me and we would often run into each other at different places as well. The apartment that I was living in before I got married was only about forty feet from the fire station where he worked so he would often come over to my balcony to talk with me in the evenings. He was pretty up-to-date as to what was going on in my life. It just seemed like our lives had always been intertwined somehow.

I mentioned earlier in a previous chapter that he was not happy at all when I got married. Not that he wanted to marry me at that time, but because he could tell what I was getting myself into. He did not have any respect for my husband at all.

## I Read Between the Lines

In the summer of 1980 I helped open a major discount store when it came to the Wichita area. That summer held the record for being one of the hottest summers ever. A lot of work had to be done to get that mammoth store open and ready for business and we worked without any air-conditioning, so it was quite a sweat factory. There were many inspections and sign-offs to be carried out to meet specific building codes including the fire department inspections before the store could open.

The store was located in the same fire district that my fireman friend worked in, and lo and behold, he came out for a tour during the inspections. It had been a while since I had seen him and I was a sweaty mess! He then knew where I was working.

Several times he would be on duty when we had to call 911 for people who had gotten hurt at the store or for other medical emergencies. Many times he would make occasional shopping trips to the store and we would get caught up with each other. My marriage had been disintegrating but I never told him anything about it, I didn't have to because he had pretty much figured out what was really going on.

One time, while he was visiting with me at the store, he made mention as to where he was hanging out at. He didn't invite me to come to that club or initiate anything, I just read between the lines. It was many months later but I finally showed up at his hangout.

## While Mr. X Was On a Mystery Trip

When I showed up at the club that my fireman friend had told me about, I was scared to death. I was as nervous as a cat on a hot tin roof. Would he even be there? Not knowing what to do or even if he would know what to do if I showed up, I was secretly hoping that we could begin to have a relationship again. Oh yeah, there was just one little problem, *I was married!*

The club was crowded and the band that was playing was great! It took a while but our eyes finally met from across the room. He seemed surprised to see that I was there. We danced the night away and talked for many hours. He left it up to me to decide if we should start seeing each other again. There was no pressure or strings attached. I went home afterwards to an empty house because Mr. X was out of town on one of his mystery trips once again.

I had told Mr. X many months earlier that I wanted a divorce long before the affair stuff started. Mr. X had dismissed any and all divorce ideations as he laughed at me.

It took me a while, but I finally made the decision to start seeing my fireman again. We met up with each other secretly for several months before I finally left my husband. No one ever knew because we told no one!

## He Gave Me a Key to His Home

My fireman friend was quite the gentleman as he always treated me very nice. He was kind and would offer me great council at times; he was a wise man in many ways. He was very strong and I felt safe and protected when I was around him. He was the quiet silent type, a gentle giant, but when he spoke it was worth listening to. He really liked women and respected them. He made every woman that he met feel special, but unfortunately, his kindness sometimes led to a few fatal attractions.

After my divorce from Mr. X we started to become an item and it took me a while to run off all of the other women! Sometimes I would watch the women as they would fall all over him at the clubs. One woman in particular would fall at his feet the moment he entered the club and she would beg him to see her again. It was very embarrassing for me to see that woman beg as I watched her sad display. He was embarrassed as well as he would try to get her to stop making a spectacle of herself.

One of the reasons that I think our relationship worked was because I was not like the other women. I didn't need to throw myself at him because we had a genuine relationship. I treated him with respect for who he really was and without going all *gaga* over him. He could have had a great big huge ego that played right into all of that attention, but he didn't. As a matter of fact, he was a bit disgusted by the way some of the women acted around him.

One of the very first gifts that my fireman gave me after my divorce was a key to his house. By that time he had purchased his own home. He presented it to me in a felt ring box and told me that I was welcome to use his home anytime I needed to. Wow! That was a very significant gesture I thought.

There was one woman in particular, I found out about, who was a little bit harder for me to get rid of. He was seeing her on the side, and that didn't sit too well with me. When I was at his house I would do some snooping through his mail. I found several letters from her because she wrote him quite often. I discovered that she was going to be in town for a visit and wanted to see him. I saw a date, time, and a place where she was hoping to meet him. Ornery as I was, I decided to show up too! What an interesting night that was! I knew who the woman was and what she looked like, but she had no clue about me.

I arrived a bit early at the club and watched when she arrived. She sat down at a table all by herself so I approached her and asked if I could join her because I was all by myself too. I led the conversation asking her what she did for a living and where she was from. Of course I already knew all of the answers. She talked about how she was in town to meet up with her boyfriend so I asked her all about him. Yes, I had quite a bit of fun with it. *Are you smiling yet?*

A short time later, I noticed that my fireman's best friend had been observing what was going on and I could tell that he was having a total coronary! When I got up to visit with some friends he followed me.

"What are you doing?" he quietly asked me.

"Just having a friendly conversation is all," I replied back with a wink.

"Do you know about her?" he asked me.

"Yep," I replied.

"Does she know about you?" he asked me as his face drained.

"Nope," I said as I grinned from ear to ear. "I am getting a lot of interesting information for sure though!" I exclaimed.

"Oh, my!" he said as he sternly continued on, "You are playing with fire girl and you know that he is not going to show up if he sees your car outside!"

"Yep," I said very confidently, "I know that."

I eventually had all the fun that I could muster up and I left. My fireman never showed up but he called me the next morning, as he sometimes did to check in on me. I told him how I had met one of his *friends* the night before at the club and how she was *so* disappointed that he had not shown up. There was a bit of silence on the other end of the line. He was not amused by my silly game. After a few more times of me pulling some secret interceptions and actually catching them together, she was no longer a problem!

## He Became My Best Friend

My fireman and I were falling in love. It wasn't a surprise at all that it would eventually happen. Even some of my friends who had known the both of us for years stated that it was about time! He was the type that usually kept his feelings at arms-length so I think that was why he had such a hard time realizing his feelings at first and to realize that what he felt was real. It took me some time to get him to understand *what* he was feeling and for him to just let go and let it happen. We dated for a few years and as with any relationship, we had our ups and downs while we worked out the kinks.

We were out on a date one evening when out of nowhere he told me that he couldn't provide for me the way that Mr. X had done. I think he must have thought that I would leave him because of the crazy lifestyle I had grown accustomed to. I was a bit shocked by his remark but told him not to worry about such trivial matters. I told him that the lifestyle that I had with Mr. X was not worth it. I also told him that all he had to do was to simply love me and that was all that I needed.

In reality, he was a much better provider than Mr. X. He was very responsible with money as he invested it and saved it. After he had purchased his house he added on a very nice garage with a workshop improving his property. He didn't have any debt and he didn't flash money around or try to impress anyone with it.

After a couple of years of dating and while we were at a restaurant he asked me a serious question.

"Did you leave your husband for me?" he quietly asked.

As he asked me the question, he looked right into my eyes. I honestly told him no, he was not the reason why I had left my husband. I also explained to him that the marriage had totally fallen apart and that my health and well-being was why I had to leave him. My leaving my husband was going to happen, regardless. I assured him that it was very nice to have had him there to help me pick up the pieces.

Everything else just started falling into place as my fireman and I rediscovered each other. We began to have so many fun times together. When he was working at the fire station he would call me every night around ten o'clock and we would talk forever. We would laugh and make plans, and I would always hate it when we had to hang up. He was really my best friend. We enjoyed going out to eat together, going to the movies, dancing, and working on our tans at the lake. One time we even took a trip to New Orleans.

I had never been to New Orleans so I didn't know what to expect. It was quite an eye-opener for me and I remember a comment that I had made to him about one woman who was performing on stage. I thought that she was just absolutely beautiful. He quietly informed me that it was not a woman, but a man! Oh my! Yes, I got quite an education while in New Orleans.

### He Was Very Protective of Me

Because we both stood over six feet tall and were pretty fit, we often got stares whenever we were out in public together. We exercised and ate properly and were into health and vitamins big time, so we looked very healthy. When one of us discovered some new health item we would share it with the other and give it a try.

He didn't like going shopping with me mainly because I knew everybody, as he would say, and I would have to visit with everyone I came into contact with making the shopping extravaganza drag on even longer.

He became very protective of me and a bit jealous as well. He didn't like it when I talked with other men, regardless of how innocent it was. It was best that we didn't party at the same club on the same night as it usually wouldn't end well when his jealousy would show up.

He didn't like one of my girlfriends that I hung around with, and he had every right to not like her. Maybe it was because she was pretty rough around the edges. I had met her through her parents who Mr. X had known. She came from a very prominent family and was a likeable gal. She was a single mom with one child and she had made some pretty poor decisions concerning the men in her life. Maybe it was because she liked the biker bars and the biker type of guys. One night she talked me into going with her to one of those biker bars, again. We weren't there for very long when a fight broke out. It just seemed like there always had to be a fight when I went out with her.

Before I realized it, the fight ended up in the parking lot with my friend right in the middle of it! She loved action! Bullets were flying and a driver of a truck was getting his head bashed by someone who was hanging off of his truck while he was trying to make a get-away. I was standing in the parking lot while bullets buzzed my head and I almost got run over by the truck! I was very ticked off at her after that night and that was pretty much the last time that I saw her.

I did run into her many, many years later and enjoyed hearing how her life had changed, and all for the better. To this day, she will leave you with a blessing! She was someone from my past who eventually found the Lord.

## I Needed Some Rest

My fireman also did not like my career much either as I had a very demanding job. He became frustrated with trying to share his time with me and my work. My work also took me away from him for nearly a year. I ended up being transferred to another state but I had given him ample time to ask me not to go; he never did. I could tell he didn't want me to go but he was smart enough to let me leave and not interfere with my career. It was sad when we had to part ways, but he would still continue to call me on occasion to see how I was holding up and I would see him when I would come back to Wichita for visits.

I soon discovered, after doing some investigating on my own, that the company I was working for was about to go under. It was then that I decided to make a get-away before I got stuck in another state without a job. For nine months I had been working ninety hours a week and that job had taken everything out of me!

When I returned to Wichita I was exhausted. My brother and his family welcomed me into their home until I could recuperate and get my footing. My health had declined and I was at my lowest weight ever looking quite waif. My mental state was not good as well; I just needed a rest.

My fireman knew that I was back in town and he started calling me on the phone. At first I refused to take his calls. I just didn't want to start up a relationship again until I felt I was mentally able to handle it. I wanted to make sure that our relationship was really what I wanted to pursue. I didn't want to jump right back in until I had some time to myself to think.

Several weeks went by before I knew that I was ready to talk with him and I surprised him by showing up at a business that he worked at on his days off from the fire department. The meeting was sort of awkward, especially when he wanted to know why I hadn't taken his calls. As he looked me over and saw my condition I think he understood why.

### They Gave Him a Razzing!

We resumed our relationship and our love for one another grew so much so that we could look at each other and know exactly what the other one was thinking. We could even look into each other's eyes and carry on a conversation and not say a word. There were times when we could finish each other's sentences and other times, and without saying a word to each other, we could feel each other's joy, pain, and even sorrow.

By all rhyme and reason we were soul mates, and it was obvious that we were headed towards marriage.

My fireman had been a bachelor for all of his adult life and marriage was a tad bit scary for him. He pretty much dragged his feet the whole time we were dating. I wasn't in too much of a hurry myself and was patient.

He loved to buy me cards and gifts. I remember the first gift he bought me for one of my birthdays. It was a carved stone elephant. I opened the gift and thanked him. He stated that it was for my elephant collection and I watched as his eyes quickly darted around my apartment looking for the collection. I busted out laughing!

"What elephant collection?" I said, as I roared with laughter.

He had mistaken some of my figurines as elephants! We had a great laugh on that one!

He liked buying me very beautiful gold jewelry pieces for different occasions and he enjoyed teasing me with hints on what he had bought. He did things like that to help build up the suspense so I would keep guessing. For one of my birthdays he bought me a beautiful necklace with a diamond and ruby pendant, my birth stone. He teased me about having the most expensive birth stone, *ever*!

Whenever my fireman would shop for household items he would buy two so that I would have one also. He bought me a VCR and a microwave oven amongst other things. The men at the fire station could see where all of it was headed too and they started giving him a hard time about it; they gave him such a razzing! They did, however, voice one sincere concern about us getting married.

"She doesn't know how to *cook*, does she?" they snickered.

I admit that my cooking had made for a bit of fun to toss around at the station!

One time I had made the guys at the station some cinnamon rolls from scratch. Making cinnamon rolls is not as easy as it sounds, and that's my story. I did follow the recipe to the tee and they sure did smell good and look good, so I delivered them to the fire station for the men to enjoy for their breakfast the next morning.

When I talked to my firemen the next morning and asked him about the cinnamon rolls, he started laughing.

"Well, the guys are out in the parking lot right now using them as hockey pucks!" he exclaimed.

We both started laughing so hard and to the point of tears. Yep, those little critters were as hard as hockey pucks!

On another occasion I brought a blueberry cobbler into the station and it was quite obvious that I also had trouble with that recipe. Actually the cobbler had bubbled out all over the place and it made such a mess, but at least it was edible!

Yes, the men had a right to be concerned about my ability to cook because heavens forbid, their co-worker might have starved to death! But, because of him and his co-workers' willingness to be my guinea pigs, I eventually learned to become a pretty good cook.

### Viet Nam Left its Mark

Sometimes I pride myself in being able to identify people by their personality types using my many years of experience of working with the public, but my fireman was often a mystery to me. He kept a lot of himself locked away, especially the pain that he had experienced in his life. I knew better than to pry so I learned to be very patient with him. Although over the many years that we were together he did start opening up to me revealing to me some of his past experiences, and that helped me to understand him better.

I always wondered why it was so hard for him to freely love and to show sincere love, but then I discovered that he had been deeply hurt in the past. I also wondered why he would never set foot inside of a church, regardless of whether the occasion was for weddings or funerals and even if they were for immediate family; he wouldn't go inside of a church.

When I would attend church he would always ask me to pray for him, but I never would get a real explanation from him as to his reasons for not going. It was not until after he explained to me about the time that he spent in Viet Nam did I place the pieces of the puzzle together. It took many years before he finally opened up to me about 'Nam. It was there in that horrible place that he would eventually discover that he wanted to be a fireman when he returned home.

He started out in air traffic control during his first tour in Viet Nam. That wasn't exciting enough for him, so he asked to be put on the front lines where he became a gunner. He then flew in helicopters where he hung off the sides with a machine gun and gunned down the enemy ground forces. I could only imagine the toll that the war had taken on him with all of the men that he had to have killed.

There were times when he opened up and told me many stories about what happened while he was there. He brought out pictures for me to look at that showed him with his buddies in their tent cities. He also showed me his medals and honors and asked me to use my skills to arrange them in a display case for him. All of it had been tucked away safely, either in his mind or in the closet where he kept all of his mementos.

One of the mementos that he brought back was a skull. Not just any skull, but the skull of a Vietnamese man with a bullet hole through the forehead. By the way, it was totally illegal to have! He had told me the story of how he was able to smuggle it back into the states. If his mother only knew what she had in her possession when his boxes arrived home!

For years he used it as an incense holder when he was living with a bunch of roommates. In his new home he had it wrapped up and in a box in the closet. That skull brought a whole new meaning to having a *skeleton in the closet*! He told me that if anything should happened to him that I was to make sure that it was properly disposed of. How could

I dispose of it? Throw it in the river or a trash can? Anything I would do to dispose of it could cause quite a stir if it was found!

As he told his story he talked about one of his missions that he was on where some troops had been shot down. Their helicopter hit the ground and burst into flames. There is one rule that all servicemen hold dear and that is that no one is to be left behind during a war. My fireman arrived at the scene and went into that helicopter with fire all around him and brought every one of those men out, even though none of them had survived the crash. It was then and there that he knew that he wanted to be a fireman when he returned home.

## Being a Fireman Takes a Toll

Being a fireman takes a physical toll on the body. But that isn't the only toll that it takes. Like my dad with all of his years in law enforcement, it takes its toll on you mentally as well. I know only too well what policemen and firemen have to experience during their careers because I kind of grew up in it. One of the things that bothered my fireman the most was the little children who sometimes perished or who were horribly burned.

He worked many accidents and crime scenes that were horrors as well, sometimes only to find out that they were someone that he had known. There were times when the only way to recognize a victim was through reading their identifications.

He told me so many different stories and some of the stories were about those who annoyed him. There was one story in particular about a woman who liked calling in her suicide attempts in the middle of the night. And as he put it, it got old really fast.

It was obviously a sad attempt on her part to get attention from the men in uniform. Finally one last time, they went to her house in the middle of the night to assist her. My fireman, totally annoyed at that point, was in conversation with the woman in her kitchen when he decided to pick up a kitchen knife. He stabbed the kitchen counter with it and the knife stood straight up.

"The next time you do it, do it right!" he firmly stated to her.

...She never called them again.

## Bullets Buzzed By My Ears!

He had a very interesting group of friends, most of whom he protected me from. Some were firemen that he had met on the job while others were folks he had met through his contacts in the motorcycle world. But there was a tight group of close friends with whom he hung out with. They were pretty much rough and tumble, raw, macho, motorcycle types. He was a bit different than they were really, and was not like them at all. I never thought that he really fit in with them but they were still his buds.

He never took me on a motorcycle ride. He was very protective of me and stated that he would probably never be able to forgive himself if something should happen to me. He usually did not take me around his friends that much either and I figured that they would probably just give him a hard time about me anyways.

He did take me to one of his yearly get-togethers that his friends held. One of the men owned a nice spread with a lake. These friends would have a barbeque, do some fishing, and drink *a lot*. All of the wives and significant others were invited as well. I watched and learned firsthand that you stayed right next to your man.

*Another thing I learned quickly was to not let drunks have guns!*

All of the fishermen had put their lines in the water and secured their poles in the sand. That's pretty typical in the realm of fishing. The bobbers were floating with not much action taking place. I walked to the beach just in time to watch a turtle swim by. The next thing I knew there were bullets buzzing right past my ears! Those silly fools were shooting at their own bobbers! What does one do when you are standing between the guns and the bobbers? *You stand perfectly still!* I knew that at least some of those men were great marksmen, as most had served in 'Nam, but I didn't know how good of a shot they would be if they were all tanked up! Luckily for me, they were all great shots!

## I Wasn't "Mrs. C" Yet

My fireman and I had known each other for about thirteen years and we had become a serious item for at least seven of those years. I was starting to become a little antsy over when we would tie the knot! Even some of his friends had given up and just started calling me "Mrs. C". I ended up telling him that I was going to give him until the end of the year, and he wanted to know what that meant. Simply put, I was going to move on if something definite was not in the works. Would I *really*? After all, we were so addicted to each other and I don't know if I would have *ever* followed through with my threat when the time came.

We started making plans together in the direction of marriage. His house needed some major upgrading and we knew that I wasn't going to move in until everything had been fixed up. He asked me to draw up some plans to help modify his house so I drew up some sketches. We worked together on the plans and decided that we would start the project the following January, a few months away, so that the house would be ready for me to move into after our May nuptials.

We made all kinds of plans and had many dreams for our future together. We even joked about how we would be as we grew older together. He had lost some of his hearing in Viet Nam, and I was as blind as a bat! We made up all kinds of funny stories about our deficiencies and what we would be like in our old age. We might even have rockers on the front porch!

We discussed what his dream home would be like and maybe someday he would be able to build that home out in the country. He had some very good ideas for his new abode and how to make it economically efficient. His plans also included the fact that he didn't want me to work.

My fireman wanted me to stay home and take care of our place after we married. He was very old fashioned that way. I had been working hard to regain my identity, career, independence, and my credit history and I didn't want to leave myself unprotected again. I was not going to give any of that up, even to marry. Also I had already started building my first company and told him that I would probably always work. It took him a while to get his head wrapped around that idea, but he did finally agree.

He didn't want a big fuss with a wedding and I had already been married once and didn't want a fuss either, so we pretty much decided that we would just go to Las Vegas to get married. Of course he had a small battle on his hands with my mother! She wanted to be at our wedding, even if it *was* held in Las Vegas!

He had met my family and had even spent a few holidays with all of us, but his taking me to meet his family that lived in Wichita was well, you might say, a *very* big step for him.

After all the years that we were together it finally looked like we were moving in the same direction, so I sat down and started designing my wedding dress!

# FOURTEEN

# A Life Given, Not Taken

*Greater love has no one than this, that he lay down his life for his friends.*
John 15:13

### We Had a Plan

I remember hearing a saying once that said that if you want to hear God laugh, tell him *your* plans. And that was what I had been doing for most of my life, telling God my plans.

I was developing and building a growing business and had assumed that I was also going to build a life with a man with whom I had loved for many years. We were going to spend the rest of our lives together. In all of my arrogance I thought that my life was perfect and that I had the world by the tail.

It was November and it seemed like everything was moving forward. We pretty much had the plans for the house figured out and we both liked how it was going to look. The remodeling would begin in January, just a few weeks away.

My fireman had me help him write checks for all of his bills so that I would become familiar with all of the household expenses. He even shared with me what his investments were and other financial information as well. Because of his career we had made a verbal agreement that if he died before we were married, I would get nothing. He was very specific in how he wanted his mother to be taken care of and also what items his two brothers were to receive. He even showed me where he kept his full-dress fireman's uniform just in case it was ever needed.

There had been a situation that lurked in the background for many years and we knew that possibly someday we would have to deal with it. When we had reunited after my divorce from Mr. X, my fireman had shown me a picture of a small young boy.

"Do you think he looks like me?" he inquired.

I told him that indeed it did look like it could be possible. He then explained to me that the young child and his mother had appeared at the fire station several years earlier and as it was told to me, the introduction went something like this.

"Son, this is your dad, dad, this is your son," the mother had stated.

The statement was a jaw-dropper for my fireman! He never had a long term relationship with the woman and he had never been told, until then, about the boy!

Many years after that shocking introduction, the State of Kansas started going after dead beat dads and wanted proof as to who the real father of the boy was so that they could collect monies due to them. The mother had married a man shortly after she had found out that she was pregnant and let her husband think that the young boy was his own son, so he had been raising him and supporting him only having been recently told that he was not the boy's birth father. It was a tangled web.

I told my fireman that regardless of how it all turned out we would get through it. We had already agreed that we would not have children together and that was our plan. I did however state to him that if it was required for us to take the boy in, it would be alright if that was what it came down to. He on the other hand wanted nothing to do with the whole situation and I understood very clearly as to why much later on.

We weren't really sure where this was headed with the State being involved or what the outcome might be, but maybe a paternity test would reveal the truth. One had been scheduled for January 2$^{nd}$, just a few weeks away. We figured that it was only a bump in our plans because we just knew we could wade right through it.

It is imperative that firemen know that their co-workers have their backs; they have to trust them with their lives. That is just a reality! A co-worker had just been transferred to my fireman's station, one that I had heard him complain about in the past. After my fireman told me about the difficulties that others had had with that person, I told him that the co-worker was going to end up getting someone killed. There recently had been several firefighters killed in the line of duty that November in a single fire incident in the Kansas City area. The headlines brought to the forefront the reality of the dangers of being a fireman.

### He Was Not Himself

When December finally came and Christmas was fast approaching, my fireman was simply not himself. We had a wonderful Christmas together but his anxiety about the scheduled paternity test was starting to wear on him. I thought that was all that he was worrying about, but I was wrong.

About a week before Christmas he had let himself into my apartment one evening, totally unannounced, and just stared at me. That was one of those times that we held a conversation without speaking. All I could do was hold him as I watched my big man start to crumble from the stress.

He had nothing to worry about from me. I had known about the young lad for years and knew that he was just part of the package when I married my fireman. I didn't want to add to his stress by having him think that I might bail. I wasn't going anywhere.

I soon found out that there was more on his mind that was adding to the stress.

The week of Christmas he wanted me to make a promise to him, but I needed to know what the request was before I could make any promises.

*"If I burn in a fire, I need for you to make sure that I do not live,"* he firmly stated.

With his request I must have looked stunned and told him that I couldn't make that promise. I just could not honor his request.

*"You must,"* he insisted, "I will not have a cheese scraper used on me."

After being with my fireman for so many years I had learned a lot about the brotherhood and fires. I learned what happens inside of burning structures and more importantly, what happens to the human body in a fire, as well as what happens to the surviving burn victims. It just isn't pretty!

I think that he had had a premonition that his life would be ending soon.

Even with such a request and the gloom that was hanging over our heads with the paternity test, the week after Christmas leading up to New Year's was an exciting time for us. We were making plans to spend our first New Year's Eve together! That may seem pretty strange, but in past years I would have to work or he would have to work and sometimes even a blizzard would keep us apart. There was always something that came up so that we couldn't be together, but that year would be different. We were planning a simple evening together, one in which we could watch movies, eat snacks together, and bring in the New Year.

## An Eerie Smell

The day before New Year's Eve had started out as a normal day. I had worked all day and was standing at my patio door enjoying a cup of tea while I stared out at the scenery. All of a sudden I thought I *smelled* my fireman in my apartment. Let me explain what I mean by that statement.

My fireman had a second job building special motorcycle frames for racing, and he was very talented at it. I had watched him one day as he performed his meticulous art of welding. He had me put on protective gear so I could watch him safely. I was amazed at how detailed he was. Every time he came home from that job he had a very distinctive smell, almost like the smell of smoky metal. Before I turned around I had assumed that he had shown up to surprise me and I fully expected to see him standing there. But when I turned around, there was no one in the room. My entire living room was filled with the smell and everywhere I walked I smelled his presence! Then it occurred to me that he could be in trouble. *Was it a warning?* He must have gotten hurt at his second job! But the more I thought about it, it eventually dawned on me that he was at the fire station that day so he must have been alright or someone would have called.

That same evening at ten p.m. on the dot, he called me like he always did and I was relieved to hear his voice. I asked him if he was alright but he sounded grumpy. During our phone conversation we synched up our plans for the following evening and we figured out what I needed to go shopping for at the store. When I suggested pizza he came unglued and almost bit my head off.

"You know I can't eat anything like that when I have a fever blister," he stated.

In all the years that I had known him, I had never seen him with a fever blister nor had he ever raised his voice at me! He told me that he only developed fever blisters when he was stressed out. Our conversation came to an end and we both said "I love you" and that was the last conversation that I ever had with him.

### Their Faces Spoke Volumes

I was awakened the next morning by a knock at my door. It was so early and I thought that maybe my fireman had come straight from work to see me which was not at all what we had talked about the night before. I made my way to the front door and looked through my peep hole and saw my mother and my fireman's best friend standing there.

*What?* These two don't even know each other, I thought to myself. I was puzzled. Later I remembered that he had helped my fireman deliver my piano to my parent's house many years earlier. That was how he knew how to get a hold of my parents.

When I opened the door I just knew it was about my fireman. The look on their faces spoke volumes; those faces simply said it all. I invited them in and as we stood around the dining room table they delivered the news to me. My fireman had died in a house fire a few hours earlier trying to save someone's life. The lady he was trying to save had also perished. I went numb.

With that news I had to sit down so we made our way into the living room. I asked them what had happened but the investigation was still too early and there were only speculations as to what had really taken place. I couldn't even cry. I just sat there. I simply could not get my mind wrapped around what I had just been told. The fireman indicated to me that the fire department needed to notify the next of kin and needed their phone numbers as soon as possible. I told him that I would take care of it.

After they both left I felt that I needed to go lie down for a while before making a few phone calls to some close friends, but when I got to the hallway my knees collapsed under me and I fell to the floor in a heap. It was then that I was finally broken. My ego, my arrogance, my life was all stripped away. I wept uncontrollably. I cried out to God because it felt like my heart had been ripped right out of my chest and I had never felt such pain like that before.

I really didn't think I was going to be able to make it through that one.

### God Has another Plan for You

Little did I know how much strength I was going to need to get through the next couple of weeks, months, and years; and it was only the beginning of a nightmare! I could not have made it through without the strength that I gathered from God and the wonderful caring support of my family and friends.

I knew that I needed to go over to my fireman's house to get the phone numbers that the fire department had requested. They had already called me once to see if I had found them yet. I was dragging my feet because I was dreading going over to his house to retrieve the phone numbers. One of my best friends and my mother decided to go with me.

When we arrived at his house his vehicle was parked in his driveway just like he would have parked it himself. When we entered his house his gear was in one of the living room chairs, including his helmet that had his name stenciled across the front. The fire department had cleaned out his locker and had brought all of his belongings to the house. It was eerie for me to see his helmet sitting in the chair as if that was all that was left of him. I found the phone numbers and then returned back to my apartment.

When the fire department called again, I at least had the phone numbers that they had requested. They were not able to get a hold of my fireman's brother who lived in town, so I told them I would break the news to his mother and find out where his brother was. *I would have to say that it was one of the hardest things that I have ever had to do in my life.*

My fireman's mother lived in New York at that time so I had to call her and tell her about her oldest son over the phone. I asked her if her husband was with her and she told me that he wasn't. Then I asked her to please sit down while I proceeded to give her the news about her son as gently as I could. I couldn't stop crying as I told her the information that I had. His mother couldn't stop crying either. It was awful.

His mother booked a flight to Wichita and arrived the next day. His mother, immediate family members, and myself all came together to console one another. The second hardest thing that I had to do was to break the news to the family about the young boy who could possibly be my fireman's son. I had to break the news that day to them because that bit of information was starting to go public the day of his death and I wanted them to hear it from me first. It was just another grief added on to the already difficult grief that they were all dealing with.

The next week was a whirlwind blur because so much was happening, and in the midst of all the craziness a really good acquaintance of mine had made a profound statement that was, at that time, very hard for me to hear

"Debra, God has another plan for you; a good and perfect plan," she stated with care and wisdom.

I needed those words and I would repeat them over and over again in my mind. Those words kept me from going off of the deep end on several occasions, especially when I had suicide ideations.

## My Instincts Were Correct

When the family and I gathered for the first time and after I had delivered all of the shocking news to them, I also told them that we needed to go to my fireman's house so that we could gather up all of his valuables and vehicles and store them in a safe place. I just knew that his house was going to be broken into, and exactly by whom.

When all of us were at my fireman's house to pick up all of his valuables for safe keeping, the phone rang. I didn't answer the phone and I was so glad that I didn't. It was a lady from his past who was trying to convince my fireman's brother to have a necklace buried with him that he had given to her for Christmas. The brother explained to the lady that nothing was going to be buried with him. He then looked over at me when he hung up. I asked him who it was and he told me her name. I knew who she was and I just grinned and shook my head.

"We need to make sure that his casket is sealed," I stated. "That will not be the only person calling with such a request, and by the way, he was with me at Christmas." I continued, "He did not give her a necklace."

Little did I know, but his casket had to be sealed any way. His family just didn't want me to know that just yet.

I am so glad that I went with my instincts to have the valuables removed for safe keeping. The house was broken into by the person who I had suspected would do the dead.

### He Loved Me, Not Her!

The fire chaplain and the fire department representatives met with us at his brother's house to determine our wishes for the funeral. Because my fireman died on duty all of the funeral expenses were covered. We were given a choice. We could plan a simple service or have a full-blown ceremony with honors. My fireman's family was so gracious to me and allowed me to help with the decisions that had to be made.

"You know, he would not have wanted a bunch of hoopla…that just isn't his style," I said. "But, I feel that he deserves to be honored."

And, so it was! The Fire Department took it from there and made all the necessary arrangements for the funeral.

Then I was asked by the mortuary to bring his full-dress uniform with me to the meeting at the mortuary.

I drove over to his house all by myself. When I entered inside I felt really uncomfortable. It was almost spooky. I was genuinely creeped out, like he was watching over me and I could feel his presence everywhere! I immediately knew where his full-dress uniform was, but *how did I know that*? Then I remembered back to when we had conversations more than a week earlier about where to find it. Then I started wondering, w*ere all of the preparations and conversations about marriage really about preparations for his death and burial*? I shook off the feelings and quickly headed for the front door, uniform in hand.

Before I could reach the front door, there was a knock. It was so quiet in the house that the knock scared the *bejeebies* out of me! When I opened the door I saw a small-framed young lady standing in front of me. I decided not to open the door very far because I didn't recognize her at all. She told me she just wanted to come by to offer her condolences. Then she had a puzzled look on her face.

"Who *are* you?" she inquired.

I told her that I was his fiancé. The look that developed on her face well, I just cannot describe it. It was a mixture of shock and devastation, all in one expression. I still didn't quite understand her visit as she turned and left immediately. How strange. I waited for her to drive down the street before I opened the door and headed for my car.

My fireman's family, fire department officials, and I met at the mortuary to finish up with the details for the funeral. I soon found out that if you were a fiancé you don't have any rights. You cannot even be listed as one of the survivors for the newspaper obituary. But again, the family was so gracious to me and allowed me to help with all of the arrangements.

When all of the arrangements had been made, I pulled his brothers aside and told them what had just happened back at the house with a young lady. Apparently I had just missed the brothers as they had arrived at my fireman's house shortly after I had left. The same lady had approached them as well. In fact, they had just arrived and were getting out of their vehicle when she came running up to them. She had asked them all kinds of questions about me. Apparently she became hysterical.

"He loved *me*, not her!" she exclaimed.

*The circus was just beginning.*

### People were Honoring Him

His funeral was held January 4th and it was a warm day; no one even needed to wear coats. It was sunny with hardly a breeze. The funeral was held at the fire chaplain's church. The church was barely large enough to handle the crowd that came that day. People had to stand in the corridors and the news media was located all around. A sea of uniformed firemen from all over the country also attended the fallen hero's service. It's a brotherhood, you know.

My nerves were shot by the time the service began. I just couldn't stop shaking inside and I allowed a few tears to fall. Here I was walking down the isle of that church arm-in-arm with his mother between me and one of her other sons; I just about lost it when I looked up at the flag draped coffin ahead of us.

During the mortuary viewing I did not get to see my fireman because it had been a closed casket for obvious reasons. That just made it harder and more complicated for me because I felt like I couldn't say a proper goodbye. All I could do was touch the flag on his coffin with kissed fingers.

His service was lovely but I don't think we were prepared for the overwhelming response he received nor were we prepared for all of the news media that was in attendance. As we exited the church the flag draped coffin was lifted up onto the back of a fire truck. The procession took us past Station No.1 where the longest procession I had ever seen began. We then drove to the highway so that we could head to the cemetery for a mock internment to finish the full honors ceremony.

While the procession was on the highway people had pulled over, had exited their cars, and were saluting the hero as we drove by. Citizens who never even knew him were honoring him. The over-passes had saluting firemen on them as we drove under each bridge. The entire route was full of people saluting as we drove by. *It was so touching and unbelievable.*

At the cemetery there had been a tent set up for the family to sit under. The reason for the mock internment was because my fireman was to be buried in another state in a family plot. There were people everywhere when our limo pulled up. One boy in particular seemed to stand out as he had such a likeness to my fireman. I wondered if he indeed was my fireman's son, but only time would tell. We were seated and the service began.

## Together Forever

During his service there was a fly-over, a full gun salute, and the dispatcher made the *last call* for my fireman that was heard over the fire truck radio and at every fire station. The American flag was then neatly folded and handed to his mother. She was so grieved that she buried her face in it and cried.

We were then greeted with the procession of people to meet his family and to give them their condolences. I knew that it could turn into a three-ring circus so several days beforehand I had asked my fireman's best friend to help weed out any potential trouble makers, i.e. fatal-attraction women, or women with children. He did just that because he ended up stopping a few, however one did make it into the line. She probably didn't think that I knew who she was, but I did. She did behave herself and did not cause a scene.

When we left the cemetery we headed back to Station No. 1 where a wonderful meal had been prepared for us. The fire chief sat right across the table from us. In visiting with those around me and listening to their comments I had mentioned that my fireman and I had had a strange discussion just two weeks earlier, the one about making sure that if he was ever burned in a fire that he wanted me to make sure that he died. The silence was deafening and unreal. The fire chief stopped eating and just stared straight ahead. *Was he thinking what I was starting to think? What exactly did he know?*

The next day we traveled out of state to lay my fireman to rest. The small country cemetery was located near his family's farm where his grandmother resided. It was a very quiet sunny day in the country and it rendered a very peaceful feeling as we all repeated the twenty-third Psalms in unison.

I only went back one time to visit his grave and that was five months later during the Memorial Day Weekend. I wanted to lay a wreath by the black granite tombstone that had his name and the family name chiseled on it. The ribbon on the wreath that I left behind read "Together Forever." It was a phrase that we had repeated to each other on many occasions.

Yes, it was a life given and not taken. He was a fighter and a hero from the very beginning of his life, only weighing in at one pound when he was born. His life had meaning and purpose as he dedicated himself to serving his country and his community.

# FIFTEEN

# Was I Being Tested?

*And God is faithful; he will not
let you be tempted beyond what you can bear. But when you
are tempted, he will also provide a way out so that you can
stand up under it.*
1 Corinthians 10:13

### Another Profound Statement Was Made

The following two years after the death of my fireman, and the whole event surrounding his funeral, had definitely been a life-changing experience for me. My story continues with danger, bewilderment, intrigue, and of course I was left with a lot of questions. A profound statement that was made during the planning of my fireman's funeral helped to set me on the right course for the rest of my life.

When the fire chaplain had first met with all of us before the planning of the funeral, he had offered his condolences and mentioned that he also wanted to help with the planning of the services. Before he left us that day, he asked a question.

"I know that you are not particularly a religious family, but I wonder if it would be alright if I pray for you before I leave?" he inquired.

My insides were screaming! What did he mean by that statement? *I'm a Christian!* Who are you referring to? I'm not sure about the other people in this room, but I *certainly* am! It was as though a knife had been inserted into my chest and twisted. Of course, he prayed with us.

At that point in time, my life did not resemble any likeness to a Christian life. It was simply not visible. The statement that he made that day helped me to see that no one had a clue that I was a Christian! As the years passed on I wanted to thank that chaplain for his statement. I never remembered his name or what he looked like and I certainly did not remember what he said at the funeral, but his remark became a wake-up call for me.

Many years later the chaplain and I ended up working together and for nearly a year we had no idea who each other was! We always had morning devotions at work and one morning, after I had finished leading devotions, my co-worker spoke up.

"*I know who you are!*" he exclaimed.

To my amazement, it was him, the chaplain! Now isn't God good? I was able to thank him for how he had been instrumental in changing my life and the lives of others as well that day. Many lives were changed by that man, and for me it was from one simple statement that he had made. He didn't even know what an impact he had made until I was able to tell him face to face. I am forever grateful for this angel here on earth!

### Was it More Than I Could Bear?

The Bible clearly states that God will not let us be tempted with more than we can bear. That is only part of the verse and it is somewhat loosely translated so you'll have to read the full version of the scripture that is referenced at the beginning of this chapter. I just wish He hadn't placed so much trust in me! He and I had plenty of conversations during that trying time in my life and I was working with him on a mountain of issues, and even though he was forgiving me in every way, I still was dealing with some very bizarre consequences that surrounded my fiancés death that put my newly rediscovered faith to the test.

The days and weeks that followed his death were very hard for me. It seemed like every local TV news channel kept playing the events surrounding his death over and over. I wished that they would have stopped playing the tape of the paramedics working on him while his lifeless arm fell off of the gurney. They kept showing his photo on TV over and over again while they were discussing his death.

Someone had told me that the first official written report presented to the fire department had to be torn up and rewritten. That bit of information led me to wonder who they were protecting. Were they protecting my fireman and his reputation, or were they protecting the city trying to deter a law suit? Yes, *I knew things;* I just didn't let anyone know what I knew.

Lawyers were crawling out of the woodwork wanting to know if we were going to sue. When I was asked about it, I had only one answer.

"He went in and he didn't come out," I stated. "Nothing will bring him back, so the answer is no."

I also knew what was going on in the background at the coroner's office but I never really wanted to see or hear about the report. Unfortunately, a newspaper reporter confronted me several months later and tried to exaggerate the causes of my fireman's death as he told me what was in the report.

I never wanted to visit the scene of the fire and even to this day, I have never gone there. Two people lost their lives that day. A lovely lady who was a mother and a wife also perished in that fire. What I did find out was that the fire originated with a brittle Christmas tree when hot sparked cinders from the fireplace caught it on fire, and because of that bit of news, I would never have a live Christmas tree in my home ever again.

## Crazy Events Became a Circus

Strange things started happening only one week after his funeral. First, I received a wedding planner date book in the mail that was sent to me anonymously. My first thought was, who could be so cruel?

Then I received a phone call from the fire department telling me that there were several women wanting to get a hold of me. One of those women wanted to send me pictures of her with my fireman. It was then that the fire department official told me that they would do all that they could to protect me and under no circumstances would they give out my personal information. He also told me that there was so much money paid out on a firemen's death that women would come crawling out of the woodworks with all kinds of claims. He also told me not to pay too much attention to all of it.

My fireman's family was also becoming quite concerned for me with the circus of women trying to make their presence known to all of us. They were wondering how I was holding up under the strain of the claims that these women were coming out with.

You know, at that point, it really didn't matter. I wasn't concerned about any of it, even if the claims being thrown around had even an ounce of truth to them. What were these women trying to gain or accomplish? Did they need to be validated because they knew him? Did they think that it was important for me to find out about them? I knew how popular he was with the women; none of it was a surprise to me!

He had trusted me with all kinds of personal information about his life and had trusted me with all of his financial information. My job at that time was to get his family and myself through all of the grief and through all of the entanglements of settling an estate. I had to pass on any information to the family that could be important to them in the future. My focus was elsewhere, not on all of the women.

One day while I was walking past my car I noticed that items were missing off of it and I wondered who would take things off of my car, and for what reason?

Yet another day, while I was doing my laundry, another interesting experience happened. I had to walk several feet across the courtyard to go to the Laundromat where I lived in order to do the laundry; I felt as though someone was watching me but I dismissed the idea. After I had placed my clothing in one of the dryers I left, only to come back and find that all of my clothes had been taken out of the dryer and thrown all over the place. When other things began happening, it finally became apparent to me that I was being watched and sometimes followed. What were the reasons, I wondered.

My parents were becoming quite concerned for my safety and insisted that I move to another apartment complex. I definitely am not a scaredy-cat and no one was going to have such control over my life by trying to threaten me, but I really did want to move because I needed a change of scenery.

It didn't take long at all for *"things"* to start happening again after I had moved, and even though I knew in the back of my mind at that point as to *who* was behind the attempts to intimidate me, I still didn't know the *why*.

## The Paternity Test Results

The paternity test was still going to happen even though my fireman died two days before the scheduled tests were to take place. The coroner had to grow brain cells in order for the paternity to be proven; it took several months before the test could be accomplished. We were all anxious to have the truth revealed.

Why the mother of the child got it in her mind that I was a threat to her and her child's future, I don't know. Maybe she thought that I would be inheriting my fireman's money. Nothing could have been further from the truth. All she had to do was asked and it would have saved her a bunch of scheming, time, and trouble! She went so far as to find out everything that she could about me, and used some very bizarre ways to do it. Strange things continued to happen.

One day I was at a client's house making an inspection visit. As I was leaving I noticed a small child out of the corner of my eye as I started to back out of the driveway. The child started to cross the sidewalk behind me so I quickly tried to stop, but I had no brakes! Thank goodness I missed the child. *No brakes? Great!*

As luck would have it, my mechanic brother's house was not far away so I drove very slowly to his house using my hand brake all the way. He discovered that my brake lines had been cut in three different places.

When the paternity test results came in, yes, my fireman was the father of the young boy. The results became a sad day for me because I knew that my fiancé died before knowing whether or not he was the father of the child. The boy didn't even get a chance to know his birth father. The results also changed the dynamics of the inheritance because soon after the results came in, several representatives from the city paid a visit to my office to have a meeting with me.

These representatives wanted to know if they could somehow consider me as my fireman's common-law wife. They knew that if they could prove common-law then I would be able to split the inheritance with my fireman's son and I could then in turn give my portion over to his mother as my fiancé had requested. I knew that proving common-law was not an option and unfortunately my fireman's requests had all been verbal agreements with me. He didn't have a written Will, but fortunately he had listed his mother as a beneficiary on most items. The bulk of the estate had no directives for a beneficiary along with other monies that were to be paid out that came from state and federal funds.

The court system took over once the paternity test was in. I never wanted to attend any of the court proceedings and legally and at that point, it was none of my business, but I was kept abreast of the hearings by his family. It turned out to be such a soap opera but I feel that it is not my place to speak any more about it so I will not reveal the details. Even months after the courtroom drama had started, I was still being stalked, but in a much weirder way.

## A Parade of Episodes

After I would run a help wanted ad for my business I would notice that several women coming to my office to apply for work came from the area of town in which my fireman's son and his mother lived. In some cases, these women lived on the exact same street. Yes, I did a little bit of my own investigating and knew quite a bit about his son's mother as well. I had become quite suspicious of everyone at that point and I just couldn't believe all the trouble that she was going through to try to plant a spy within my company!

Finally I had had enough of the charade and the parade of women coming into my office under the guise of seeking employment and unfortunately one poor soul caught my wrath one day.

During an interview, I sat listening to that perspective employee while she answered my questions. My gut feeling began to tell me that she was one of the gang, a spy. So I confronted her and asked her how long she had known the person that had sent her in to see me. The look on her face was priceless and she started shaking! She was busted! Yep, I gave her a little message to take back to her friend.

After that episode I thought things were starting to calm down and then another weird situation occurred, but I didn't realize it at first as being connected to the drama.

I found a note one morning on my car when I was leaving work. The note read as follows: "If you would like to go out sometime, give me a call."

There was no name only a phone number. Needless to say, I was not interested in dating anyone at that time. I hadn't had much time to grieve over my loss when all of the weird stuff had started happening. I found myself always having to look over my shoulder most of the time. But I was really curious as to who might have left that note on my car.

Luckily, I was very resourceful person and I had friends in high places. By the time that I had applied that single phone number to my investigative skills I knew all about that man and learned that he lived in my apartment complex.

One day while I was walking over to the apartment complex's Laundromat to do my laundry, the same man who had left the note on my car was out in the yard playing with his dog. At first I just walked passed him to see if he would say something to me, but he didn't. So I turned around and walked back to him and confronted him.

"So, do you make it a habit of leaving your phone number on girl's cars?" I asked sarcastically.

He stopped in mid-motion as he looked at me. He was speechless!

"Uh, how did you know that it was me?" he nervously asked.

I continued to inform him of his own name, his address, and where he worked. I told him how much money he earned a year and some other private information about himself as I went on giving him the rundown about his life. By that time he started to get very nervous.

"Are you a cop?" he inquired.

"Nope, just a very resourceful person who you don't want to mess with," I firmly stated.

That neighbor of mine was a much older man and almost the same age as my father. He seemed very old fashioned and had great manners. He did apologize for leaving a note in that way, and asked if we could start over. He then introduced himself in a proper manner and we became acquaintances. Again, I was highly suspicious of anyone new coming into my life, so I stayed on guard.

He often took walks with his dog and when he passed my apartment he would yell up to my balcony with a hello. Eventually I would go for walks with him, but I would never tell him much about myself. I even evaded some of his questions on purpose. One time he asked me if I had ever been married before and I told him yes, and that was all I offered. I purposely left out the story about my fireman. He eventually asked me to go country dancing with him. On many occasions we went out to eat together. None of it was dating; we had an understanding between us and we were just friends. Besides, I was way too young for him and he wasn't interested in me in that way either.

I had known him for many months and it was during one of our evenings at a restaurant that I began to develop an awful gut feeling about him. It was an instinct that roared up inside of me and all of a sudden I just knew that he was a spy. He was just about to take a bite of food when I couldn't contain my suspicions any longer.

"How long have you known *her*?" I blurted out.

He immediately dropped his fork in his plate and was left speechless. The look on his face was priceless. Once again, my instincts were right. It took him a while to gather his thoughts.

"How did you *know*?" he quietly asked.

I told him that he had better come clean and that he had better do it right then and there. I also told him that his big mistake was that he never once asked me about my fireman, even after seeing his portrait hanging on my living room wall. The only way anyone wouldn't have known who he was, was if they had lived under a rock! Everyone recognized that picture from the news coverage.

He then confessed and told me the whole sordid truth of how he had known her through a friend and that she had paid him to befriend me. I found the whole plan revolting and couldn't believe that when I had moved to that apartment complex, I had landed in the vipers den!

He said that it didn't take him long at all to figure out that I was not the horrible person that I had been made out to be and that he realized quite quickly how obsessed the other woman was with me. He told me that I was the kindest person that he had ever met and felt absolutely terrible thinking that I was the one with evil intentions.

He did end up apologizing to me for meeting me under false pretenses and he even met with my father to apologize to him for his involvement in the whole scheme. He really did turn out to be a decent kind man who himself was being used; operating under the lies and false stories that he had been told thinking that he was helping a distraught woman and her son whose lives were being destroyed by me.

It took about two years for everything to get sorted out in the courts and for the estate to be settled. Finally all of the attacks on me were over with as well leaving me with another unbelievable chapter in my life that is what it is.

Unfortunately, because there was not a written Will, I could not oversee how the monies were dispersed according to my fireman's wishes. All possessions and property were ordered to be sold by the courts and if any one of the family members wanted anything, they would have to purchase it at auction. My fireman's son inherited the bulk of the large estate since he was the only legal heir and it was ordered to be governed by a local bank so that the monies were guaranteed to only be used for his care. Many years later I was thrilled to learn that the boy became a college graduate and that the money was used mostly for the betterment of his life.

I certainly do not intend to oversimplify the story of the estate settlement. It took a long time, it seemed, for the courts decisions to come through. There was a lot to sort out. In the meantime, the whole harrowing ordeal took its toll on the family, both financially and mentally.

## Honors Were Given

The news media had been very good to us as they respected our privacy and our requests that our faces not be shown during the funeral services. They also provided us with a montage of film footage from the funeral coverage that they had gathered and created a very nice video for us to have as a gift.

The year following his death contained a couple of events that honored him for his years of service. In April, only a few months after his death, he was honored by the Veterans of Foreign Wars, the Disabled American Vets, the American Legion Ladies Auxiliary, and the American Veterans. His brother received a plaque and a medal in his brother's honor. A Children's Miracle Network Miracle Fund was set up in his honor, and the monies received helped supply one of the local hospitals with an infant warmer for their burn unit.

My fireman's mother also received a letter from President Regan, who was the president at that time.

On July 4th of that year, he was honored as one of the "Home Town Heroes" at Cessna Stadium. A few days before the award was to be given though, I had received a phone call from a newspaper reporter. The conversation was friendly at first, but then it started turning, we will just say, ugly.

The reporter started asking me questions about my fireman's health. And then the *big* question was asked that the reporter really wanted to have the answer to; if my fireman knew that he had a heart condition and hadn't told anyone about it in order to save his job. I became enraged! He even asked me if I had read the autopsy report, in which I told him, that as a matter of fact I hadn't. I continued on to let that reporter know that I really did not want to know what was in the report. He dismissed my request and proceeded on to quickly blast out all of the information that was in the report including the fact that his death was caused from a blocked artery that resulted in a heart attack.

## I Was Horrified by the News

What the reporter was telling me made me horrified and mad! He continued on with the report that my fireman was found in a bathtub with his mask off and that his tank was out of air, all with a window being located only a few inches above him. I did not want to know any of that because it only caused me to have more questions. The conversation continued on.

"Why didn't he go out through the window?" he asked me.

I was quite annoyed at that point and coarsely told him that he obviously knew nothing about house fires or he wouldn't have asked me such a stupid question. To try and clear up a thing or two I then continued *my* conversation with *him*. I knew that my fireman would have never, *ever*, put his fellow co-workers in harm's way. If he thought for one second that he had a heart condition, he would have never risked going into those fires. I made it quite clear to him that my fireman was the picture of health, a body builder, and that he had passed all of the yearly doctor examinations required by the city to be on the fire department.

I was horrified to hear how and where my fireman had died. Why was his tank empty? He was responsible for filling it himself. Removing his mask was sure death, he knew that. How could a twenty year vet of the department make these mistakes? Was he so distraught over the weeks leading up to his death that he made some unforgivable mistakes? What really happened that day? I hated that the reporter had called me and opened up that can of worms.

The news reporter published his story the day before the Cessna Stadium event was to happen. The story brought into question about how many firemen possibly could know that they might have a health condition but forgo telling anyone so that they wouldn't lose their jobs. I was quite annoyed.

I was a bit worried about how the story could impact the crowd attending the ceremony at the stadium but the worry was for nothing. As we stood up on stage to accept the honors the crowd gave an overwhelming and enthusiastic response as they stood and clapped and cheered.

Now that I had heard another part of the story of how my fireman was found I wondered if he did in fact kill himself. Was he under such stress that he wanted to die? Did the fireman that was transferred to the station, the one that started working there in November, contribute to the breakdown in communications during the fire causing bad judgment on the part of my fireman?

I knew a lot about what had transpired secretly behind the scenes, but I also knew my man and what he stood for. These were just some of the questions and thoughts that darted through my mind and all at once it seemed. These were questions that I will never have answers for, or even need or want the answers to. It really doesn't matter in the whole scheme of things. He went in, and he didn't come out. He was a hero. That was the real story and nothing else mattered to me.

## The Interview

I only granted one official interview for one of the local newspapers. I trusted the owner and writer of the newspaper because she had written a feature story on me a few years earlier and I trusted her to do the story justice and to write the story well. I gave her, and only her, the exclusive rights to the story. She later told me that the article created the largest selling circulation that she had ever had.

Below are some excerpts from the story that was written by Marlene Smith-Graham of the Westside Story in the March 1989 edition.

### "He Put His Life on the Line—and Lost"

"Throughout the day on New Year's Eve, on radio, television, and in the newspaper, many Wichitans heard the tragic news of a firefighter who had died in the line of duty —in a futile attempt to rescue the mother of two trapped inside a home on North Meridian."

"While the news tugged at the heart of many, it ripped through the heart of westsider Debra Todd. The firefighter was her fiancée. He was a man she had waited fourteen years to marry; a man who died just months before they were to be wed and just two years short of retirement. He is a man who will always be dear to her heart."

"Debra doesn't have many pictures of C.C. — he didn't' like to have pictures taken she says —but she does have a scrapbook of articles about the firefighter gathered from those terribly difficult days following the incident. She's proud to show them off...

"*Firefighter dies in burning house; Fireman lived as he died, a hero; Peers to honor fireman at funeral; Family, colleagues pay respects to firefighter; A life given, not taken.*"

"Deb is the first to admit that she doesn't think the tragedy has hit her fully. She even says one evening when the phone rang at 10:00 p.m., about the time C.C. would normally call her, she smiled and jumped up, just for a split second, forgetting that he was gone. That he wouldn't be on the other end of the line."

"...Deb says she knew C.C. was in a very dangerous job, but somehow she just couldn't see anything happening to him. He was so strong, so sure of himself. And, too, Deb who grew up as the daughter of a policeman knew it was futile and unproductive to worry. Perhaps it was her knowledge of his job and the way that she handled it, which made their relationship hold firm through adversity."

"...About the televised reports and pictures taken, she has mixed feelings on the coverage of something so personal: "If you see it on TV and it's not someone related to you, it's kind of interesting to see what process they go through to try and save someone; but if it's someone you know and you're watching them suffer and die, it's really…it's hard, it really is."

"But Deb is doing her best not to remember C.C. that way. She wants to remember him as the really easy-gong and quiet guy he was. She says in their relationship they seldom fought, and when they did it was more of a mental test of wills."

"…She also wants to remember him for his quick wit. She says he was funny at the least expected times."

"He'd be real sophisticated," she says. "Not the dress up type, but when you were in public, you had to conduct yourself in a good manner. That was important to him. But then suddenly he'd do something really stupid and just crack you up, totally out of character."

"She recalls once when they had gone out to Red Lobster."

"We were having a nice dinner…and you know he was real particular about how I looked in public, about how he looked in public; I mean we looked sharp together. We had to, after all we were two giants walking through; everybody turns their heads to look." She laughs, then continues the story: "Well we were having this dinner, and he ordered dessert. Here I am stuffed to the gills, I couldn't eat anything else, and he's saying 'take a bit, come on take a bite.' I wouldn't do it, so he starts talking real loud "Open up, here comes the airplane' and he just starts acting like an airplane trying to make me take a bite: I was just dying. Everyone was looking at us. It was so embarrassing. For him that was so out of character; but he could surprise you."

"...He was a very meticulous person, almost a perfectionist," says Deb, "and his welding was very well known around the nation. He built motorcycle frames. Sometimes we talked about him maybe opening up his own welding shop when he retired from the fire department."

"That would have been in two years. Had he lived, those two years would have completed twenty years of fighting fires."

"During a recent series of television re-ports called "In the Line of Fire' reporters talked about C.C. and the spirit that would possess a man or woman to risk his or her life in such a job. A firefighter interviewed related the fact that many of the people who work the job do so because they love it. They love be-ing on the edge, taking chances, being scared. Deb says C.C. was like that in many ways."

"He was a real go-getter", she says. "Not even just in the fire department, but also in his personal life."

"She tells about the time his neighbors' van got loose. C.C. was aware that the owners were in the habit of loading their kids into the van while it warmed up. On one snowy, icy day, the truck somehow slipped off 'park' and took off on its own."

"C.C. heard a noise and saw the van going around in circles out of the driveway and into the street," Deb recalls. "He thought the kids were in it, and here it was hitting houses, trees, knocking stuff over. So he ran out and tried to stop it. Well, heck, it knocked him all over the street, he had broken ribs, he banged himself up and bruised himself up, before he realized the kids weren't in it. He was like that. He would just get on things, go, and wouldn't worry about himself."

"…The memories go on. And Deb knows she, too, has to go on. She knows, emotionally, it will be tough to let go of the man who has meant so much to her, but at least she will always have near her, dear to her heart, special remembrances of a very special person."

"He was my knight in shining armor. I didn't have to worry about anything when he was around. It is going to be hard to let go, to not have him with me, to get over the anger and the grief. I know there's a process I'm going to have to go through; and I am working at it. I try not to dwell on what happened; I try to think that everything happens for a reason. But still…you can't help but feel a little cheated. It's like I told my mom…now my fairy tale will never come true."

## Mr. Skull

Now that I have you all depressed, I would like to take this time to lighten it up a bit. Remember the *skull* that was in my fireman's closet? Oh, lucky me! Mr. Skull and I had quite a relationship for a while...sense my sarcasm??

I was able to carry out at least one request for my fireman! Why on earth did he leave me here to take care of *that* crazy mess?? Well I took that skull and put it in the trunk of my car and left it there for a while... yep, pretty stupid! My fireman had it all wrapped up and in a box, a box the exact same size as a skull. You couldn't miss it.

And you guessed it, I was pulled over by the police while speeding down the road ten miles over the speed limit on a city street; I should have been busted. I normally would never have done it, but I pulled the bereavement card. The police officer, while looking at my Driver's License, recognized me from the funeral and let me go with a warning.

Since I had escaped what could have been a very awkward moment, I then took Mr. Skull and put him in my closet! I had no clue how I was going to get rid of him!!! I always had a few skeletons in my closet, but I had one for *real* that time!

Mr. Skull was in my closet and for quite some time as a matter of fact. I finally got tired of looking at the bizarre box and decided that I needed to figure out what to do with him.

My secretary's husband was a doctor so I inquired of him one day to get his thoughts on donating Mr. Skull to one of the medical research facilities. It was a go! So I handed off Mr. Skull to the doctor to be placed in a facility, the name of which I will not divulge, to be loved on by someone else! Good rid din's I thought, as I brushed off my hands and waved good-bye to Mr. Skull!

SIXTEEN

# Redirecting My Life

*There is a time for everything, and a season for every activity under heaven; a time to be born and a time to die, a time to plant and a time to uproot, a time to kill and a time to heal, a time to tear down and a time to build, a time to weep and a time to laugh, a time to mourn and a time to dance....*
Ecclesiastes 3:1-4

## We Were Married in Our Hearts!

After my fireman's death I tried moving on without him, but it wasn't easy. I thought that we were going to be spending the rest of our lives together regardless of what difficulties might lay ahead. Some of my friends didn't know how to respond to my loss while others quietly tried to help me pick up the shattered pieces of my heart. There were those who thought that they were helping me but sometimes their responses came out rather strangely. I knew that they meant well, so luckily I was not the kind of person who got their feelings hurt easily. I tried to over-look most of the comments but one person in particular just had to *go there* with a very insensitive comment.

"What's all this carrying on about anyway?" they stated. "You weren't *even* married...after all!"

The comment floored me! Didn't they understand my loss and my grief? We were married in our hearts! We had known each other for thirteen years and we didn't need a piece of paper to prove that our love was *real*!

For all of the fiancés out there who have lost a mate before their wedding day, I understand what you are going through. You have no legal rights and you will not be listed in the obituary as a survivor. People will sometimes dismiss your relationship with the deceased simply because you were not married. Some will not acknowledge that you and your feelings need to be validated. You need to mourn and you will need time to adjust to a future without your intended loved one. Simply put, it is not easy trying to move on with your life. You will have some bad days and you will have some good days. You will feel cheated. Don't let others make you feel like your grief should end quickly.

My grief was overwhelming as I carried on with my day to day operations like normal. I was still running my business and functioning at a level that looked like *normal* all the while I was dealing with some physical side effects from the grief. I was dealing with a lot of unnecessary drama during that time, as you have read, that contributed a lot to my stress levels.

The first week after his death it had become very difficult for me to eat. My throat would simply close up and not let the food go down. That would continue to happen later on from time to time. I was on the road quite a bit with my business and it was during those times that I had the worst side effects from the grief.

I would come upon bridges and be tempted to drive off of them. How easy it would be to do and I would even turn the wheel a bit, but those words that my friend stated to me would quickly run through my head and stop me. I have to see what God has planned for me. I can't give up.

Other times while driving I would go into a trance. That was the scariest side effect of all. I would wake up and not know where I was at.

I also dealt with many other emotional side effects and went through every phase of dealing with grief.

Sometimes you will have dreams about your loved one that died, but this is very normal. They may sometimes feel so real as if the person is right there with you. During your dream you may feel like you can reach out and touch them and when you awaken, you can become all consumed by the dream. These kinds of dreams can last for years but don't be alarmed, it's normal. As you remember the anniversary dates of those special times that you shared together such as holidays, birthdays, and special days that meant so much to the two of you, they will be the hardest. When your loved one has passed away on a holiday, you will have an instant reminder year after year.

Everything that you will encounter such as your feelings, your experiences, physical, spiritual, and mental challenges, while you are working your way through the crisis of your grief is absolutely normal. Just know that there is plenty of help out there if you need it. There are books, grief counselors, pastors and clergy that have been trained for such care giving.

A few months after my fireman's passing I received a call from a lady who told me that my puppy had been born. She wanted to know when I would be able to come by and see it. I had forgotten all about the arrangement but then realized that my fiancé told me that he wanted to buy me a puppy from a litter that I had chosen. I sadly told her that I could not take the puppy, not because I couldn't afford to purchase it, but because the puppy would be a constant reminder of the pain that I was suffering.

At the beginning of this chapter is a bible verse that gives us a reminder that there is a time for everything. I highly recommend that everyone read chapter three of Ecclesiastes because I know you will enjoy it and find comfort in it as well.

I finally had come to a point after the tragedy that I knew that I had to move on. There was no need to continue living in all the pain wondering or trying to imagine what our lives could have been like had we married. Regardless of what had happened I would always have the memories of the love and the life that we *did* have together.

## It Was Time to Clean House!

At the time of my fiancé's death I owned a home and office cleaning business. I am not sure how it all happened outside of hard work but my cleaning business started to boom. I had moved my business from my apartment to a business office and eventually I had twenty five employees while working with several contractors in the area as well. I had realized that cleaning up Wichita, Kansas, was not the only thing that needed cleaning. I needed to start cleaning up my own act as well. It was time for me to *clean house*! I commissioned my Heavenly Father and started working on my wounded soul. It's sad that it took a tragedy to finally set me straight.

The first thing I did was make a mental list of the things that I knew needed to be changed, such as my most obvious outward issues. My thoughts went back to a day when I was younger and had received so many compliments about how sweet and thoughtful I was. I really wanted that Debra back!

Some fiction writers love to have fun writing stories about time travel and time machines where a person can travel back and forth in time. The characters in the story are able to change the outcome of their lives by going back in time, but in reality this is not possible. It's not even an option. We do not get to have a redo as we can only live life once.

What we *can* do is redirect our lives and write a different ending. You *can* live a life that is not self-consumed and destructive. You *can* have a life that contributes to society in good ways while setting good examples for others to live by. I have always said that if there was ever anything going on in my life that I didn't like, I could change it. And that was exactly what I set out to do.

The first outward issue that I wanted to change in my life was my potty mouth. It just seemed like every time that I dropped something on the floor a bad word came out of my mouth, at work when something good happened I would spout out a bad word, every time…well, you get my drift. Yes I could sling out the words with the best of them and I wanted that to stop.

I'm sure that my vocabulary of bad words wasn't all that impressive to others; not showing much signs of human intelligence at all. So I asked the Lord to please help me to break that bad habit. I asked Him to seal my lips when a bad word or an evil thought would come to mind. Believe it or not, He did just that. His awesome power made me chuckle one day.

I was driving down the road when a car pulled out in front of me and that ugly thought with a word attached to it came to mind, but it simply did not come out. My mouth simply did not open almost as if it were sealed shut. Awesome, I thought. Thank you, Jesus!

At first the list of items that I wanted to work on was a short list until I started realizing that there were other things in my life that needed to change as well. I asked God to please reveal them to me as we went along. One thing about God is that he is patient and he doesn't hit you upside the head to remind you of all of your sins at once. Did I change overnight? No.

My change took years as I still made mistakes along the way. It took a while for me to become the person that God intended for me to be. By the way, I am still a work in progress!

Many years later a lady came to visit me at the store that I owned. She was in tears and had just watched the movie "Left Behind" and sadly told me that she didn't want to be left behind and didn't know what to do. She wanted to know how she could get to heaven. We had a good talk that day.

She revealed to me that she didn't think that God would be able to forgive her of her sins as she started sharing the laundry list of them, one by one. I looked at her with a smile.

"Hon, I want you to know that God *will* forgive you," I stated. "After all, I am a walking miracle myself and if God can clean me up, he can clean you up too!"

Then I continued on giving her my laundry list of items that I had overcome from my past life. Some items were very similar to hers with some of mine being much worse. She kept staring at me with such bewilderment written all over her face.

"*You did all of those things?*" she asked as her jaw dropped.

"Yes, *indeedie*," I said with raised eyebrows.

She left my store a much happier person that day. I discovered later that she and her husband had been baptized together a few weeks after our conversation.

## I Don't Dwell on Regrets

Over the years I had allowed myself to plunge into an abyss that most people don't often get a chance to come out of, and trust me my life had been a mess. Maybe you've been able to identify with some of my story, or maybe you haven't.

My laundry list of obsessions had included drinking, greed, drugs, pornography, sex, a flash temper, obscene thoughts, a potty mouth, and so much more. Did I fall from grace all at once? No. As I allowed myself to be led into that kind of lifestyle it was as though I was testing God. If I got away with one thing and nothing happened, I would up the ante.

What was I expecting, *a lightning bolt to strike me down*? God gives us free will and we can make our own choices. God wouldn't be a God that anyone would want to serve if we were *made* to worship him, *made* to do what he wanted, *made* to live the lives that he wants us to. That's kind of a dictatorship, isn't it?

The God I serve is a loving and powerful God. I was so grateful that he was there, just waiting for me with open arms for my return. He didn't judge me; he saved the day for me! I am truly grateful for his love, grace, mercy, and power and for all of the work that we did on cleaning up my life.

Maybe you cannot relate to my story at all. But you do know about the things in your life that you hide; the things that you worry that someday someone might find out about. You might harbor some hatred towards someone or you may struggle with forgiveness, overeating, under eating, and many other *"things"* that can keep you from living a full life. You see you don't have to be a bad girl to have struggles, fears, weaknesses, and major issues. We are all human and live on this side of heaven. The ills of this world are not prejudiced. It doesn't matter what social status, religion, race or creed you are, any and all peoples can stumble and fall.

And for the record, in the telling of my stories I want to make this perfectly clear; I am not endorsing anything immoral that I took part in from my past. If you do see yourself in any or all of the situations that I found myself in, I want you to understand that there is a way out and there is help. God will help you and place people in your life to counsel you, pray for you, and support you. All you have to do is ask. You must humble yourself before God, you must get past your pride, your greed, your lusts, and your ego and let God take the lead. It's hard to give up control especially when you are a control freak like I am, but once you do, it is very freeing!

I have chosen not to live a life of regret because my Heavenly Father forgave me for my past life. He gave me a hope and a future. I would only be showing Him a great disrespect if I were to continually beat myself up over my past. Instead, I have chosen to use my story and my past for the good; to help others who are struggling with issues in their lives and to help them see that they have within themselves the power to change and to move past their situations. It may take some work, but please know that there is a hope and a future that anyone can have.

You may be dealing with something that happened completely out of your control like a sudden death of a loved one or you may be dealing with consequences from your choices. Regardless of the storm that you are going through you *can* come out on the other side of it and continue on with your life. Your life may look or feel a little bit different after the storm, but you adjust, and you *can* go on!

*Trust in him at all times, O people;*
*pour out your hearts to him,*
*for God is our refuge.*
*Psalm 62:8*

# SEVENTEEN

# Bringin' Home The Bacon

*Whatever you do, work at it with all your heart, as working for the Lord, not for men, since you know that you will receive an inheritance from the Lord as a reward. It is the Lord Christ you are serving.*
Colossians 3:23-24

## My Career

During my career I have held many different positions, and in almost every case I found myself working with the public in some manner. This chapter contains some stories that relate more to my spirituality and faith. I will share many more of my very interesting career stories with you in the bonus section at the back of this book.

Even with all of the silliness that went on in my life when I was younger, the crazy lifestyle that I led never seemed to affect my career; my career never suffered any consequences from it at all. It was as though I was living two lives. I had my career life and then there was my party life. I was always religiously serious about my work and always remained professional. I worked very hard and in most cases was promoted very quickly. I also learned how to promote myself.

## The Gift of Discernment

I remember through my growing up years, and even into adulthood, that there were times when I knew that something was going to happen before it happened. That gift was given to the females in our family. Some called it E.S.P. while others called it women's intuition. I somehow could never reconcile this gift with the Bible so I never told many people about my experiences. I didn't want them to think that I was one of those *wierdees*!

One time I decided to share one of these episodes with a dear friend and she was so kind to help me see what the *intuition* experience that I had was really all about, and that it was something that I need to never be ashamed of.

"You have a wonderful gift from God," she said, "and it's called discernment."

I realized for the first time what it was so then I understood it. This wonderful gift of discernment had come in handy plenty of times during my life and career. It helped me sense danger as well as to sense when things were *off*.

"Girl, you have to go with your gut feelings!" my dad the cop would say.

Most of my early career was in retail management and I always found myself looking for those who were up to no good, especially the thieving people. That included not only customers but co-workers as well.

At one time I worked for a large department store in soft lines and they had a loss prevention team. That team would sometimes pretend to be shopping while they were watching people who they thought were acting suspicious. They would also watch the video surveillance for suspects as well. Many times they would drag shoplifters back into the building only to engage in a big scuffle knocking over merchandise and fixtures, at least until the police could arrive to help.

After the loss prevention team had worked with me for a while, they learned to act upon my gut feelings as well because many of those feelings turned out to be right.

## A Small Black Cloud Follows Me?

My cleaning business was just the beginning of a seventeen year self-employment reign! I eventually had my own gift shop, but it still wasn't that dress shop like I had wanted so many years earlier, but I did carry some clothing, does that count? I also used that shop as a ministry and I did have several encounters with people who were searching for the Lord. I sometimes found it amazing how some people just knew that they could talk with me about religious things. I also had some crazy, scary encounters with some of those who were up to no good. However, I found that I was continuously protected from harm.

It wasn't until I stepped out of the self-employment arena and back into working for others, that I gained a reputation for having a small black cloud that followed me around!

For years I would often outlive the businesses that I went to work for. One such business had been around for over sixty-five years! Oftentimes I would have a job for about a year or two, and then I would have to move on because they had to close. It seemed kind of funny after a while.

I remember during one of my interviews that I was asked why I was changing jobs so frequently. All I could do was smile and ask them to re-read my list of employers, because most of them didn't even exist anymore!

I seemed to never worry with all of the turmoil of losing jobs. I knew that the Lord would provide in his timing. It's so hard to wait upon God sometimes, but I have learned over the years that it is well worth the wait. Each position I took helped to prepare me for the next position.

I remember every day to give thanks to God for all my successes, my jobs, and my income. I regret grumbling about the days when it was so hard and difficult to do my work as my grumbling would make it appear that I was not appreciative of His provisions. So I realized that I needed to take deep breaths and offer up thanks, even during the hard days.

### Was it for Naught?

There was a time on two different occasions where discernment played a huge part as I waited and listened to the Lord concerning my career moves.

Right after 9/11 things changed in our city as it probably did in most towns across the nation. It was a sad day for all of us as we watched everything as it unfolded that awful horrific day. Lives were changed forever and life as we once knew it would never be the same. It also affected the job market as businesses were closing, jobs were lost, and people were finding themselves homeless.

I was in the middle of getting ready to expand my little shop when that tragic day happened. When my sales showed a major slump, I decided that I could "*do this*" another day. I went about praying to the Lord to see what he wanted me to do. It wasn't until a few months later that I was invited by one of my television ad representatives to visit with her at the station. She wanted to see if she could help me by going over my marketing plan to see if I was hitting the mark that I was aiming for. Even though I knew that I would probably be closing my shop soon, I went ahead and kept that appointment.

The morning of the appointment I was at a Bible study and had scheduled my meeting with her shortly after my class was over. But on my way to the meeting something told me to stop by my office and run off a copy of my resume. I didn't know why, I just thought that maybe the station was going to offer me a position or something. After running off a copy I tucked the resume in my purse and headed to the meeting.

After my meeting with her I found myself standing in the parking lot wondering why I had to run off a copy of my resume. I got back in my car and headed for home, but then I remembered that there was a cleaning business not far from where I was at that I had heard about, and they were needing some help with their business so I thought I would stop by and see if there was anything that I could help them with. Maybe that was why I had my resume with me.

As I approached the cleaning business, that same feeling came over me again, but that time I was told to keep driving. *What*? After passing the building I found myself heading in the opposite direction of home. Then I was being told to drive to a place of business, that was a ministry, and I was told to speak to the owner. I was getting scared.

"What, Lord?" I queried. "I am not going to bust in on that man's day unless you make all of this perfectly clear to me!"

Yes, I argued with God for a bit, until I finally gave in. I was nervous because I had never met the owner before. But I continued on as directed.

After entering into the building I hesitantly asked to speak to the owner and was told that he was busy, but they would check and see if he had the time to see me.

Believe it or not, he took the time to come meet with me! I knew that he was terribly busy so I was humbled that he would even take the time. During the long walk back to his office I wondered what I was going to even discuss with him.

"All right, here I am…what am I to say?" I asked the Lord.

In his office I started up a conversation about business, a subject that I was familiar with. We then discussed what was happening in our town and how the sales had been affected. Several minutes went by when all of a sudden my hand reached down into my purse and out came my resume. I watched that whole scene as it appeared to be unfolding in slow motion. The air glided my resume right across his polished, slick desk.

"So, do you think you can use me in your business?" I asked.

*What just happened here*? I was really scared. What just came of my mouth? Then the look on his face…I just knew that he was going to throw me out of his second story window for sure, but I misread his look.

"Wow!" he exclaimed, "This has been happening to me all day!"

I, of course, had no idea what he was talking about.

"My buyer just came in and told me that she was not coming back to work after she has her baby and I had no idea what I was going to do for a buyer," he said. "And here you are, you've been running your own store and you even know the vendors and representatives already."

I was amazed at his response and would be quite honored to get a chance to work for that person, but we both decided that we needed to think it over for a couple of days before making any decisions. After all, I had my own shop to close down and according to when he needed me and I didn't have much time to do so.

Several days later we agreed that I would come to work for him so I set about shutting down my store. I was not sure how I would accomplish that task in such a short time, but everything fell into place.

It was such an honor for me to work for that business. I loved my new job and I felt that I could have stayed with that company for the rest of my life, but it was not to be. Was it for naught? No. I learned so much while working there and I grew spiritually as well. The people that worked there knew of my story and how I had come to work at that store and after a while, I finally realized the awesomeness of it all myself. Many of the employees had been at that company almost their whole adult lives. Unfortunately, the business succumbed to the economy like so many others and had to close. It was like a death to the employees and the community, but I felt blessed to be part of such a ministry and to be able to minister to the needs of many during the time that I was there.

## I Was on Cloud Nine!

Several years later I found myself in a position at a store where I knew that I wouldn't be staying for long. I just remember *knowing* that it would be a temporary place for me. I was even offered a promotion, of sorts, within the company, but I turned it down because I knew in my spirit that it was only a temporary stop. The funny thing was, people were constantly trying to recruit me and on several occasions they would boldly come into my office to offer me a job, while I was on the clock!

I always knew not to even consider any offers that came my way because I knew that wasn't the plan. I simply trusted that God would tell me when it was time to go. Even though I suffered a bit while in that position as I was not always widely accepted by my peers, I instinctively knew to wait.

After nearly three years, the day came when I was asked to consider a new position and I knew that it was the one that I was to accept. That open position came about because of a very difficult situation and I knew that there would be some challenges, but it was a marvelous opportunity that really spoke to my heart. I also knew that the position would be a huge undertaking and of course, I wanted some type of confirmation that I was making the right decision. A few days after I had accepted the new position I had a wonderful confirmation take place. It was on a Friday, and I will never forget what happened.

I realized that there were only three of us that morning when it came time to open the store. That was not enough people to handle such a busy shopping day but the rest of the staff had things happen to them so they could not be there that morning. The three of us put a plan together so that we could operate the store as best as we could.

We were prepared for the deluge of customers that would be there once our doors were opened, but when I went to open the doors there were no customers. *Huh*? It was Friday! Where was everyone, I thought.

Some time had gone by and finally two men came inside the store. They proceeded to walk up to the counter where I was standing.

"We have a street ministry and we need some Spanish materials," one of them stated.

I had just one person that could assist them with that section of the store so they were led to the items and the materials that they needed.

A few minutes later they came to the register to check out and I had run their credit card without *even asking to see their I.D.*; I always asked for I.D.! When I finished processing their order I told them to have a blessed day, but as they were leaving they stopped right inside of the front doors where I observed them talking between themselves. In the meantime, my assistant had joined me at the register and I was so glad that she did because I would not have believed what was about to happen next, and I needed an eye witness.

Both men decided to come back to the register where my assistant and I were standing.

"We have a message for you," the taller one said to me.

"Okay," I said, very hesitantly. I actually thought that they were going to complain about their shopping experience or something.

"You have been feeling like your ministry has been dry and that it is not going anywhere," he stated.

All I could do was stand there and stare at them.

"We want you to know that God is giving you a ministry that will fill up your sails and will take you to your destination," he stated. "We need to pray for you, and we need to pray for you right now."

I went numb! I thought to myself, *how did they know*? They continued by holding my hand and praying over me. A prayer like I have never heard before in my life. It was totally awesome!

When they finished praying all I could muster out of my mouth was a "thank you" as they left. I looked over at my assistant in disbelief.

"Wow," she said, "I wish someone would pray over me like that."

I was on cloud nine! That was a joyous confirmation from heaven!

A few minutes after the men had left, the store starting filling up with customers. It had been a perfectly God orchestrated morning in order for that to have happen. The employees who didn't make it in to work that morning caused me to be out on the sales floor that day and the customers who didn't show up during that time allowed the two strangers to deliver the message to me without any interruptions. Awesome!

## Where is God Leading Me to Next?

Recently, I was asked what my career goals are. I just grinned and simply stated that I really have accomplished everything that I ever wanted to do for my career. I have new goals now, meaningful goals that have greater rewards.

My career has taken me many different places and my career has given me many experiences. I have met some strange colorful people and some really cool people who remain friends to this day. I have learned from the best and I have learned from the worst.

I have also grown from my experiences from over the years and have learned how to treat people the very best that I can. My life goal is to mentor people in their careers and their lives and help them to be the best that they can be. I want to lead by example on how to treat others fairly and with respect. You have to be able to see people through Jesus' eyes to really get how to love people unconditionally and to be able to teach others how to do the same.

Finally, I want to have a positive impact on all of those who come across my path. I want to be able to meet people where they are at in their lives and help them to grow both spiritually and physically while expecting a lot from them, but not expecting more than what they really have to give.

I have also learned over the years to only give quality time to those who really want it, those who will cherish what they have been given. Jesus speaks about throwing pearls before swine. Unfortunately, it really is a waste of time for some if things of worth are given to them before they are ready. (Matthew 7:6)

Yep, bringing home the bacon is something I plan to be doing for as long as I am able to do so. Working is a mission and I enjoy it, and I also enjoy the people that I meet along the way.

My life and my career has always been an adventure, and I can hardly wait to see where God is leading me next!

### EIGHTEEN

# Family Homecomings

*"His master replied, 'Well done good and faithful servant!*
*You have been faithful with a few things; I will put you*
*in charge of many things. Come and share your master's*
*happiness!'*
Matthew 25:21

### Grandfather Fought a Good Fight

As early as in my twenties I started taking care of the elderly and the ill in my family. Sometimes my helping others came at a great cost, but I would have chosen to have it no other way.

I would take my grandparents to their doctor appointments or help them with different items around their house. The death of my mother's father, my grandfather, really taught me some valuable lessons. He was a quiet man who didn't like going to the doctor, no way, no how! We almost lost him once during my childhood years. He had let a ruptured appendix go unattended for far too long. His life was on the line during a very dangerous surgery which led to a difficult recovery.

It was no surprise to us that many years later we discovered that he was hiding a few health issues from everyone. His hiding included some blood that he had spit up on a couple of occasions. It was grandmother who discovered that by digging through the trash can one day and finding the blood soiled tissues. We would soon find out what the cause was.

One day I took him to see a doctor about a particular health issue that he was having, and it was determined that he needed surgery. The surgery was a very basic simple procedure that would correct the problem that he was having. Grandfather was not happy at all about needing to have surgery, and I could tell that he was uneasy. After all, his last stay in a hospital was a bit rocky!

The day before his surgery I took him and grandmother to the hospital so that he could be admitted. I left the hospital that evening knowing how frightened he was about having the routine surgery that was scheduled for the next morning. I couldn't get off work to be with him for the surgery but my wonderful cousin, who was another caregiver for my grandparents, was able to be with him.

The morning of the surgery I remember arriving at work early, and before I got through the door I was being flagged down by one of my co-workers. She had fear in her voice as she raced towards me.

"Debra, come quickly, your cousin is on the phone and something has happened at the hospital!" she exclaimed.

I quickly ran to the phone to hear that my grandfather had had a heart attack and was in intensive care.

"What, a *heart attack*?" I questioned.

"Yes, they found him early this morning in his hospital room, but they were able to bring him back to life," my cousin stated. "Come quickly!"

I drove to the hospital as fast as I could. I had no idea what I would find when I got there, and I surely was not prepared for what I saw.

Before I could go in to see him I was stopped by the nurses and the doctor on duty. The doctor explained to me what they had found and wanted to prepare me for what I would be witnessing.

Apparently they had done some tests to figure out why he had had the heart attack. They found something that was totally unrelated to the heart attack and was totally unrelated to the surgery that he had been originally admitted for. They had found an inoperable tumor about the lungs and it was cancer.

"If we had only known about the tumor, we probably would have chosen not to bring him back to life again," the doctor stated.

I was then led into grandfather's room. He was intubated and fighting it all the way. His eyes were fiercely wild, almost like that of a wild horse that had been roped and tied. His body was thrashing about even though he was tied down. I had to leave the room because I couldn't stand to see what was happening to him.

That new revelation totally knocked my grandmother off of her rocker. We had some very hard days with her after hearing the news. I remember her calling me at work several times in a panic over menial things. One day she even called to tell me that grandfather wasn't making any sense. She put him on the phone so I could talk with him. He made sense to me, so I told her to please take a few deep breaths and calm down. It was nonetheless very upsetting to me to receive those calls from her.

After receiving one of these calls at work one afternoon, I was pretty distraught. After I had hung up the phone one of my bosses started yelling at me (he often did that to anyone, it was kind of his nature). He usually would try to get a fight out of me which was what he was really looking for. (I know…it was a strange working relationship but we really *did* like each other!) I fell apart after hearing his rampage and started crying so I left his presence quite quickly. Later, someone had filled him in about the upsetting phone call that I had received; he did apologize to me and felt terrible for yelling at me.

My grandfather fought a good brave fight. He lasted about six months, and it was a *long* six months! Watching him whittle away to nothing like he did was a hard process for me and others to handle. The horrible challenges that the lung cancer had brought him was agonizing to witness.

We had relatives staying around the clock with my grandfather the entire time he was in the hospital. My employer would not let me take any time off to help with his care, so I would often go and see grandfather after work and sometimes that wasn't until two a.m. in the morning!

During the early morning hours he was usually asleep and didn't even know that I was there. I hated not being able to be there more often, so thank goodness for the loving extended family members who were able to help with his care.

The disease took him on a roller coaster ride. His vitals were up one day and down the next. We would receive calls to come quickly to the hospital only to have him rally back. That went on for weeks until he slipped into a coma.

I remember the day that he died. He had been in a coma for a couple of weeks and I had called the hospital to talk with my mother who was in town that day sitting with him. I wanted to know how he was doing, and I told her that I was on my way and would be there shortly. There was a strange pause.

"Hold on a minute," she said.

I could hear her place the phone down and there was silence for a while.

She picked up the phone and said, "Debra, I need to go, your grandfather has just sat straight up in bed." She continued, "I need to go get a nurse, I think he's gone!" She then hung up.

I was only a few blocks away and I knew I could not get there in time to say goodbye. It was too late!

His death haunted me for a long time. I felt such guilt for not being able to be there for him towards the end. I found it strange that my employer allowed me to take a week off when he died but wouldn't allow me to have some time with him while he was still alive and going through such a horrible struggle. I didn't want that to ever happen again. If given another chance, I would do much better the next time.

Grandfather was finally at peace and I'm sure that he had a wonderful homecoming party in heaven!

## Father Waved Goodbye

My father had been a hard worker all of his life. He spent many hours working around the clock during his law enforcement career and didn't always eat correctly or at regular normal times, so good eating habits usually took a back seat. For years he wouldn't put down his work until it was completed. I believe that I might have picked up that trait from him as well.

In his early sixties he started developing a bad case of acid indigestion, or so he thought. When he visited the doctor they ran many tests but found nothing. They were treating him for acid indigestion until one day additional tests showed that he had lesions on his liver. Further testing showed that he had esophageal cancer. The acid erosion had turned into cancer.

Father lived for only two months after his final diagnosis, but those two months were the most meaningful to me. He was such a great man of honor and fought a good fight to the end. He was as brave as he had always been known to be even when the chemo treatments brought his body down. He lost a lot of weight as we struggled to find something that he could eat and keep down. His pain was so immense.

I often took father to his doctor appointments and to his chemo treatments. We had wonderful chats about things that mattered and things that didn't. I loved those talks that we had; he always stayed pretty optimistic throughout the whole ordeal.

About the time that father's cancer was discovered he had just paid off the business that he had owned. He had built his business and had worked hard at it. It just didn't seem fair. The upside of having it paid off was that mother wouldn't have to worry about any debt left over from his business affairs.

I went to work getting his accounting ledgers together as he sold off the equipment and took care of other details to shut the business down. He asked me if I had any interest in carrying on his company myself, but I already had a business of my own and I didn't really think his would have been a good fit for me as it had morphed more into an industrial type of service.

While we would wait at the doctor's office we would chat about all kinds of things. He told me how he and mom had worried about me when I was severely ill with mononucleosis and shared how they were scared that I wouldn't make it; it had been a close call. He talked to me about his married life with mom and also wanted to know more about my career and where it was going. Just chatter talks, but very meaningful to me.

One day while driving home after one of father's treatments, we noticed a large area of ground that was being torn up.

"I wonder what is going on over there?" he inquired.

"I don't know," I responded.

I was thinking to myself that he wouldn't live long enough to even get to see what was going to be built there. I often remember that conversation every time I drive by that parking lot. That was what it turned out to be, a parking lot.

My dad was not much of a hugger so I was glad to see him welcome my hugs when I would leave him after my visits. I was also glad to hear "I love you" being exchanged between the two of us because basically it was the first time that we did that.

One day he was in such pain and it was so horrible so we decided to go visit his doctor. The doctor wanted to send him home but dad insisted that he be admitted to the hospital and so he was! After the doctor ran some tests he called for a family meeting.

"He doesn't have much time," the doctor stated, "the cancer has quickly progressed." He continued, "I am not God, so I cannot tell you when; it could be in a couple of weeks or even a couple of months."

It was actually only a few days.

The news was very grim and Hospice visited us at the hospital to make arrangements for father to go home. Plans were made to have equipment delivered to my parent's home as well as nursing care. By all appearances it looked as though everything was in place, but not really.

Mother was not happy about having father come home to die. She simply did not want to remember him being at home and dying there. I personally could see her point but that's not the way it is done anymore.

It had only been a few days after his admission to the hospital that things progressed faster. He started to cough up dark black stuff and it had such an odor to it. My nursing skills hit a brick wall with that one every time I emptied his tray. I just about didn't make it and I hate to admit it, but I am such a *wussy* when it comes to some medical things!

Saturday came and he knew that arrangements had been made for him to go home on Monday. I was getting ready to leave for the evening when he made his last statement to me.

"Girl, you make sure that I get home all right, okay?" he said with a smile.

I responded that I would. But, getting *home* had a double meaning for me, as I think it did for him as well.

When I arrived at the hospital the next morning he was already unconscious. The nurse informed me that he had been in that state all morning. As the day progressed and evening came I decided to go home and change into some other clothes and come back so I could spend the night with him at the hospital. Yes, I *knew* like I always *knew*, once again.

I spent the night and was awakened early Monday morning by a nurse.

"His vitals are coming up again," she said encouragingly.

I sat up on my cot and thought to myself, oh no, we cannot do a roller coaster ride nor do I want him to do the roller coaster ride like my grandfather did. It is just so hard on their bodies.

After I had gotten refreshed, I stood beside him and touched his arm. His kidneys had started shutting down a few days before so his body was terribly swollen and when I touched him, his skin felt like a wet sponge oozing with water. This has got to stop, I thought to myself. A couple of nurses came in to check on him again and I asked them to please disconnect him from the I.V. They first looked at each other and seemed amazed at my request I suppose, but they talked it over and decided that it would be alright to disconnect it.

I sat down beside my father's bed and began to pray through my tears, "Father God, I know you are a merciful God. Dad has been a good and faithful servant. He loves you and I know he will spend eternity with you. Please take him quickly. Do not let him suffer any longer. Please take him before my mother arrives this morning. She needs to be spared from this painful moment. Amen."

As I sat beside his bed, I started to read the Bible. It is so hard to pray a prayer like that. In all of our selfishness we want to keep our loved ones with us longer but I felt that it was time for him to move on to heaven. His mission here on earth was accomplished and what a mission it had been! Besides his being a great husband and father as well as our family spiritual leader, he had touched so many, many lives throughout his lifetime.

Just a few minutes later a couple of nurses came back in to the room to check on him. They were spirited and laughing pretty loudly. All of a sudden, dad rose up his right arm and waved to us! It stopped us all in our tracks as we couldn't believe our eyes. He was still in a coma and waving to us! Was it a wave *goodbye*?

One nurse stayed in the room with me to visit, but a little while later she stopped in mid-sentence because she noticed that father was taking his last breaths. Those last breaths had come about twenty minutes after I had prayed.

"Thank you, Jesus, for answering my prayer so quickly!" I said as I praised him.

The room became very peaceful and calm. I could almost feel the angels hovering over and around him to take him home. The feeling in that room was and still is to this day totally indescribable! That was certainly a moment that strengthened my faith; it was a moment that helped to define my faith, and a moment that I wish everyone could experience who may have any doubts. Yes people, there *is* a heaven!

Father's nurse was a Christian herself and asked me if I was alright, and I told her that I was. She left me alone to be with him for a while. When she returned, she brought a pastor who ministered to my needs and then we were asked to leave the room to allow the staff to prepare father for mother's visit.

Plans had already been made to have my brother bring mom to the hospital that morning. I called him with the news so he could relay the message in the most humanely way possible to her. My aunt, dad's sister, called a few minutes after his passing to inquire about her brother.

"We are getting ready to leave town in a little bit and just wanted to check in and see how he was doing today," she said with hope in her voice.

I had to break the news to her over the phone. The news quickly dashed her spirits.

"He just…passed…away," she said, as she slowly and sadly repeated my words.

### Grandmother's Fighting Spirit

While we were still dealing with dad's illness, we were also dealing with some issues that my grandmother, my mom's mother, was having. Something just wasn't right with her. She was beginning to forget things and one time she almost caught the house on fire when she had forgotten that she was cooking on the stove. She also started to see dark shadows that would creep up all around her and she would occasionally see *little people*. We were really becoming concerned because what was happening to her was worsening while we were dealing with father's failing condition.

When father was in the hospital during his last few days we had taken grandmother to a specialist who determined that she had Alzheimer's and dementia. The diagnosis was a blow to grandmother and to us.

Basically when dad died, we hit the ground running trying to deal with grandmother's diagnosis. Grandmother was in no shape to attend father's funeral as his death had pushed her over the edge; you see he was like a son to her. Fortunately, we had relatives that were willing to stay with her while we attended father's homecoming service.

One day I had taken grandmother some lunch. Her disease had progressed a bit further. I asked her if she was afraid of dying.

"Afraid of dying, no I am not afraid," she calmly answered. "Afraid of what this disease is going to do to me, yes, I am afraid," she continued, "it's a terrible thing to lose one's mind."

Grandmother got to the point where she was seeing little people quite frequently. She even saw chickens running across the room. The black shadow was always coming towards her and most of the time I just went along with her imaginations.

"Grandma, you know that there aren't *really* any little people, don't you?" I asked her one day.

"I know," she said, as she chuckled and then sheepishly grinned.

Her greatest fear was being sent to a nursing home. She stated very plainly and many times throughout her life that she had enough money to stay at home to be cared for. We tried to help her live that way. We disconnected her stove, took her car keys, and made sure that the house was as safe as it could be for her. We employed daytime nurses and helpers, but since grandmother never wandered around at night like so many Alzheimer patients do, we didn't have to have night help. Mom lived next door to her and kept a close watch on things.

I enjoyed taking grandmother her meals every so often and we would spend time chatting with one another. She would reminisce about her childhood and other events from her past and she could remember every detail absolutely perfectly. It was fun watching her tell the stories almost as if she was back in time reliving it all again. She was a sweet soul especially towards the end of her life. The one thing that the disease did not take away from her was her kindness and her love for her family. While the Alzheimer's disease was slowly taking her mind she still had that fighting spirit like she always had, and she knew who we were up until the very end.

Every morning mother would fix grandmother her breakfast but one morning was to be different. Mother was in the kitchen and slowly realized that she didn't hear grandmother stirring. She was not in her bed so mother continued searching the house until she got to the bathroom where she found grandmother lying sideways over the top of the toilet face down. Her lips were blue, and she was motionless. The weight of her body was crushing the air out of her lungs.

I will never forget the phone call that I received from mother that morning.

"Debra, your grandmother is dead, your grandmother is dead!" she exclaimed while trying to catch her breath.

"Mom, hang up and call 911, I will be there shortly," I firmly stated.

I quickly ran my then five-year-old son to the next door neighbor's house and asked them to please make sure that he got on the school bus, and away I flew.

When I walked into grandmother's house I saw her nearly naked body lying on the living room floor with an oxygen mask on. We had a "Do Not Resuscitate" order in place for her and I think the paramedics read my face and mind.

"We did not resuscitate her," one of them quickly stated, "we only gave her oxygen and she regained consciousness on her own."

We watched as they prepared to take her away to the hospital. Her injuries were severe, but she had survived. She was in intensive care for quite a while, and it was there that we saw more of a decline with her mind.

In good conscience the doctor would not let her return to her home. He felt that it would be too dangerous for her to be on her own so we were on the lookout for a nursing facility to place her in.

By that time, our family had been through a lot. Several weeks before that incident had happened with grandmother my mother had decided that we all needed a vacation. She had made plans for us to travel to San Diego and visit my father's brother and his family. We had already made plans to have relatives stay with or check in on grandmother at her home during the time that we were gone.

We then found ourselves in a time crunch trying to locate a facility that would take grandmother so we could get her settled in and adjusted before we were to leave on our trip. Everything did work out. We were able to move her to a facility that could help with her convalescing from her fall and we were able to make her room homey as well. We also arranged to have a cousin check in on her daily to keep us updated while we were gone. It seemed like all the details were covered, but ironically, they weren't.

For the first few days that we were in San Diego, our cousin called us frequently to give us updates on grandmother and we would at that time answer any questions that the nurses had as well. During the latter part of our vacation we never heard from our cousin again so we just assumed that things were going smoothly and that nothing was wrong. We had called the nursing facility and were told that everything was going well so we didn't have any reason to think that anything was wrong. They told us that grandmother was doing just fine but when we inquired about our cousin, they hadn't seen her.

Our cousin was a wonderful generous person. She loved helping others and she loved helping us care for my grandmother as well as my grandfather when he was still living. She was a dear person that had a big caring heart. She often helped her own neighbors when they needed help and she would come to help at a moment's notice. With mother being an only child we knew we could not have cared for my grandparents without our cousin's help. Imagine our shock when we returned home and found that things had gone awry!

While we were gone, our cousin was to look after my mother's house as well by feeding the animals and picking up the mail. But when we returned home from the trip and I had dropped mother off at her house it was obvious that these things had not been taken care of. We wondered what had happened. She was so reliable, something *must* have happened!

We called her home, and her adult daughter answered the phone.

"Momma died," she said tearfully. "She tripped over her dog and hit her head."

Halfway through our vacation, our cousin had died. It was such a shock and we were devastated. Her poor family! We discovered later that she had lived through the emergency room examination but when they were about ready to release her, they decided to do a M.R.I. On the way to do the test she bled out from her head and became brain dead.

We never told grandmother that her niece, who she had loved and who had helped her for years, had died. We wanted to spare her the grief.

As it was, grandmother only lived a few more weeks afterwards. In her fighting spirit she willed herself to die, and she did. She didn't want to be in a home and was not going to cooperate or accept it. Mother and I were with her when she died.

We were called to the nursing home as grandmother had spiked a very high fever from the pneumonia that she had contracted. The nurses tried everything they could to get the fever to come down, and nothing worked. They told us they had never witnessed anyone with that high of a fever live for as long as she did.

Towards the end, her breathing became labored and she was very pale and unconscious. My mother and I decided to call grandmother's pastor late that evening and he came. He read scriptures from the Bible to my grandmother as mother and I listened, and he stayed with us until the end. Her sweet spirit came to rest later that night. I stood beside her and felt of her face, she looked so peaceful, and yes she was gone.

She had breathed her last breath and was going home to be with Jesus. The room was very calm as we prayed together.

With the lives that my loved ones had lived and the examples that they had set, I know in my heart that they were received by Jesus in heaven with his words:

*"Well done good and faithful servant!"*

# NINETEEN

# Children Are A Gift From Above!

*Sons are a heritage from the Lord, children a reward from him.*
**Psalm 127:3**

### Was I to Give My Heart Again?

My parents were quite concerned that I would never marry again, but kept their thoughts to themselves, as I found out later. I was a divorced and bereaved woman in my mid-thirties. It wasn't easy giving my heart again. It had been trampled upon so much, so it was no surprise to me that I bailed on my new beau when he started mentioning marriage and children.

Many years earlier I was quite miffed at two of my girlfriends when they wanted to introduce me to a friend of theirs, especially when I was already involved with my fireman and our relationship was becoming quite serious. I wasn't interested in dating anyone else and they knew that. One evening they pleaded with me to go out with them to a restaurant. I went, and I had been tricked!

When I met him for the first time through those good friends of mine, I was not impressed at all. First of all, my friends had failed to tell him that I was dating someone else, and I didn't know that he didn't know. Apparently, they had not been totally convinced that my fireman deserved me.

Okay! I caved in, and did go out with him once. I recall the first time that he called me and invited me to go with him to a Dog N' Shake. I thought to myself, he wants to take me to a *Dog N' Shake, really, for a first date*?? I knew I was going to be *too busy* to go! I called my mother and told her where my new male friend wanted to take me.

"Who does he think I am *anywho*?" I expressed to her.

Now remember, I was accustomed to being treated like a spoiled princess and I had always been taken to fine dining places.

"Where does he get off thinking...," I ranted on. But mother stopped me in mid-sentence, and told *me* to get off of my high horse!

I did finally go out to dinner with him and he took me to a Chinese restaurant. I was still not impressed and I found him to be a very boring person. He kept talking about his fancy watch that he had on and how it could tell him what the date was, then and way into the future, along with some other impressive features that impressed him, but him only!

After the date was over, I didn't give him another thought and life went on.

Right after I heard that the company I was working for wanted me to move to another state, he had called me again. I didn't have anything to lose, my fireman wasn't stopping me from moving away so when my new friend asked me out on another date, I accepted.

Just after my date had arrived at my apartment, my fireman called me. I felt that I was in just a bit of a pickle here, so I took my phone to my bedroom where I could talk privately. My fireman drilled me on where I was going and with whom I was going with. Of course I lied about *who* I was going to dinner with and then my fireman told me that he was headed out to the grocery store. The plot thickens here!

When I hung up the phone and returned to my dinner date, I asked him where we were going to go for dinner.

When he told me, I was kind of quiet. The restaurant that we were going to was a restaurant that was right across the street from where my fireman was going to do his grocery shopping! I was a complete basket case the whole evening. If my fireman had seen me with that man all war would have broken out! It was funny, but my date was also exceptionally nervous that evening for some reason. I, being the calmer of the two of us, asked him why he was shaking so badly. Apparently I was the one making *him* nervous. Okay, I was still not impressed.

## The Sun Was Soothing to My Soul

After returning to the Wichita area I eventually became engaged to my fireman, but let me digress here and tell you about a vision that I had had.

One of the things I liked doing was to lie out in the sun until my skin turned as dark as it could get. Yes, I was a sun worshiper. I would turn over like a pancake on a griddle trying to get both sides of my body well-done! Several times when I wanted to wear my teeny-tiny string bikini I would go to my parent's house and lay out in their private backyard. Believe it or not, at one time I had a skinny body that would fit into such a small suit!

Lying out in the sun was very soothing to my soul. It was peaceful and quiet and the sun just simply felt good on my body. I would slather on the oil and usually fall asleep, and it was during one of those bake fests that I had a vision. That vision was as plain as day!

I saw myself being married, but not to my fireman, it was to the man that I was not impressed with! I saw myself standing at the altar with him and he was dressed in a light blue tux. The vision was so disturbing to me that I sat straight up. It wasn't just the *light blue tux* that was so disturbing it was the fact that I saw myself marrying *him*!

Five or six years had gone by since that vision, and my fireman had already passed. It was a year after his death before I would even consider dating again. There were several men waiting including the one that I was not impressed with.

I finally saw *him* in a new light that had been hidden from me all those years earlier. I then saw him as an interesting man and he finally had won my heart, but our relationship was getting scary for me, so I broke it off with him.

I recall sitting at a restaurant with him one evening and the conversation turned towards marriage and children. It was then that I froze. My heart started pounding profusely and not because I was happy. We had been dating for about a year or so, but I was frozen at the thought of marriage and children, especially the thought of having children. I had lived most of my life knowing that I did not care to have children. What am I going to do? What else, I bailed and started dating someone from my church who I considered to be a safe bet, you know, with absolutely no intentions in sight.

Several months later I had received a call from a friend of mine who was letting me know that the sister of the man that I had broken up with had died in a tragic automobile accident. I had gotten to know his family quite well through our dating and thought that I should at least check in with him and offer my condolences.

It was an awkward phone call, since I was the one who broke up with him, but I called anyway. I could tell by his voice that he was deeply distraught by the death of his sister as he explained to me what had happened to her. It was extremely difficult for his parents as well, losing their youngest daughter. I thought that I could offer some support to him and his family and asked if he would like for me to attend the services with him.

"Yes, please," he said.

The rest is history and we were married six months later.

## The Proposal

His proposal to me just about didn't happen. We were to have a late date one summer evening, so after work I had gone to the gym for my workout and then made it to his house just in time for our date. When I arrived, he was nowhere to be found. I waited and waited for nearly an hour in his driveway, and no one came. Okay, I let my temper get the best of me. *How dare he keep me waiting like this after I had been rushing around trying to get here on time?*

I was just about ready to leave when he finally pulled up in the driveway. Anybody who knows me knows that I cannot keep quiet when someone is late.

The minute we were inside his front door, I unleashed all of my fire upon that poor man! He never said a word. He disappeared for a while and when he came back into the room, he had something in his hand.

"You have been waiting long enough for this," he stated as he held up a black felt box and opened it. "Will you marry me?" he asked.

I found out the reason the poor guy was so late was because he was trying to pick out a ring for me! He had purchased the ring but felt it just wasn't good enough so he went back to the store to re-think his decision on the carat size. I really ate crow that evening!

He originally wanted to propose to me at the Kansas State Fair on top of the Ferris wheel, but with my tantrum about him being so late and him feeling so bad for how long he had kept me waiting, he decided to go ahead with the proposal.

We did attend the fair a few weeks later with both sets of parents so we could make our announcement to them. In fact, we were going to have a redo with the proposal while atop the Ferris wheel, but it had been shut down, so we used the Scrambler ride instead!

## Our Wedding

The Wedding was absolutely beautiful! It was Christmas time so our colors where black velvet and white satin with red roses. I had designed and made all of the dresses myself.

The hotel that we chose for the wedding and reception was elegantly decorated for Christmas. We had everything that we wanted and thanks to my father-in-law, we had a bit more than we had planned.

Imagine our surprise when we started to walk in to the reception room and saw a huge fountain of Champaign flowing, a dance floor, and a few other things that we did not order! We both looked at each other and wanted to know which one of us had done all of that! We slowly put it together who the real culprit was!

Yes, it was a beautiful enchanted evening and it hardly seems possible that we have been married for over twenty one years as of this writing!

## A Gift from Heaven

I obviously had worked out my issues of having children. For so many years I just didn't want to have them. My husband came from a large family of five children and he loved and wanted children. We were older adults and we knew that we needed to plan right away if we were going to have any. Six months after we were married, I was pregnant!

We were both excited, but I was so ill and was considered a high risk pregnancy from the get-go. My blood pressure had become dangerously high right from the very beginning. Every month I experienced some snag in the pregnancy that had to be dealt with. One time my jaw mysteriously swelled shut, a rib got injured, a cyst had burst inside of me and it had to be cauterized, a tumor inside of me appeared to be growing with my baby, I was RH negative and had to have shots, I was nauseated for seven months, and I was dizzy from the high blood pressure. There were so many weird things happening to me. It just wasn't fun at all and I spent a lot of time on my sofa due to the problems. The only food I could eat was peanut butter sandwiches for the most part. I had always avoided milk but I had to learn to like it for my baby's sake.

The responsibility of raising a child weighed heavily upon me. I just didn't want to screw it up. I was being given a gift from heaven and I didn't take the gift lightly. I gave up drinking, forever. My baby was doing well even though the pregnancy was rather difficult. For someone who is as active as I am, it was hard to slow down and be still, but I didn't have a choice. I was very sick most of the time.

My husband and I enjoyed our birth classes that we took together. I remember our teacher telling the class that there would probably be at least two couples in the class that would end up with a caesarian section. I looked around the room and I thought that I had pegged the two who she was referring to. There were two very small-framed moms in the class and I figured they were the ones that would have caesarian sections. After all, *they were so tiny*, right?

The first sonogram went well. It was fun being able to see our baby for the first time and we were told that it was a girl! I was so excited to be having a girl, and she would be a girly-girl too! She would be my baby-doll to dress up in fancy dresses and wear fancy bows in her hair. But, something inside of me had me thinking that I should not trust that sonogram!

I planned a nursery that would be painted in pastel colors with bunnies. After all, our baby was going to be born around Easter time and bunnies were appropriate and not specifically gender oriented. My nesting instinct took over as I started cleaning, and then cleaning again. I even moved the furniture around. I finally had started feeling better physically towards the last two months of the pregnancy.

Easter came and went, and so did our original due date! I was forty two weeks along, and still no baby. My blood pressure was becoming more and more dangerous and instructions were being given to me as to how to handle a stroke if I had one. It was a bit scary.

At my last doctor visit, there was still nothing happening. The doctor took me into his office and told me that we could just wait. I looked at him with glaring eyes.

"I want this baby out, and I want it out now!" I firmly exclaimed.

The poor doctor didn't skip a beat as he leaned over and picked up the phone. He immediately called the hospital.

"We need a room for Mrs. Lee...today!" he stated.

After eighteen hours of induced labor, we still didn't have a baby! Things took a turn for the worse and then I was placed on oxygen. I heard bells and whistles going off on all of the equipment that was attached to me. My veins were collapsing and causing problems and there was blood shooting out everywhere from any poke that they gave me. The spinal block failed, so another one was being performed. The poor male nurse who had been assigned to me couldn't take notes fast enough. I really think he earned his pay that day, because I took him for a ride!

After a while the doctor cleared the room of all people except for my husband.

"If you want to see your child born, get into your scrubs *now!*" he said as he looked at my husband.

Then he looked at me and said, "Mrs. Lee, we have to perform an emergency caesarian section right now!" *So much for the tiny women theory that I had!*

The next thing I knew, I was being wheeled very quickly into surgery. As I was being taken away I could feel my hair flying with the breeze from the rush down the hallway and I whizzed right past my parents. They had tried to get back to the hospital in time to see me before surgery; I didn't have a chance to say anything to them.

A sonogram had been done an hour before the caesarian section was performed just to make sure that the baby was still alright. The nurse told me that my little girl was starting to stress, but that everything looked good. The surgery was performed very quickly because they were running out of time to deliver safely. Imagine our surprise when they told us what we had.

"Congratulations, you have a baby *boy*!" they exclaimed.

My husband and I looked at each other and said, "*Huh*?"

We both had to look at the baby to make sure that they were right that time!

## I Needed an Instruction Book!

Our new baby boy brought such joy into our family! I do remember calling one of my friends and complaining that the hospital had forgotten to send home an instruction book with us. I was a little bit overwhelmed by it all, and wondered when the bonding thing would happen. I knew that bonding with my baby would work out over time because we were seeing each other for the first time and we needed time to get to know one another; the bonding silently happened, and it was great!

The best thing that could have happened to me was to have a baby boy! It sure grounded me and caused me to see things differently than I had ever experienced before. Every day was a new experience for me and for him. I was experiencing things through his eyes, and how amazing it was! I discovered a new patience and love that I had never experienced before. He was wonderful, and he became the apple of my eye.

The birth of our son also helped to set me back on the faith track and I finally started attending church on a regular basis. I wanted our son to have the same chance that we did, to grow up in the church so that he would be able to make an informed faith decision on his own.

As of this writing our son is twenty. He has brought such great joy to us through the years. We have many childhood stories that we share with him. Most of them he doesn't remember, and some of the stories are really quite funny. He is still a comedian to this day. It has been fun watching him grow up into the man that he has become. He is such a good person with a good heart.

I remember looking into his newborn eyes wondering to myself what he would look like, what he would be like, and what his personality type would be as he grew up. I have to say, that I am so very proud of our son.

The following prayer is one that I compiled for our son's high school graduation. I placed it in a frame and gave it to him as a graduation gift. It is a prayer that describes what my hopes and dreams are for him, and for his life to come.

### A Graduation Prayer for Miles

I pray that you will have a great determination and zeal for life.
That you will see your glass half full and not empty.
That you will dance at every chance you get.
That you will be able to laugh at yourself,
And do something silly every day.
That on your path you will make a positive difference
for all that you meet.
That you will go out into the world and do well for mankind.
That your heart will be full of compassion for the less fortunate.
That you will treat everyone with respect, whether deserving or not.
May you always find the best in others, looking into their hearts and
souls;
Looking beyond what is seen on the outside.
That you will love the Lord your God with all your heart, mind, and
soul.
That you will seek Him in everything that you do.
That you will live a life full and pleasing to the Lord,
And that He will grant you the wisdom to do so.

That God will bless you with a Godly wife and beautiful children.
That you will use the gifts that God has given you and be thankful
every day.
I pray for you to have enough sun to keep your attitude bright,
No matter how grey the day may appear.
That you will have enough rain to appreciate the sun even more.
That you will have enough happiness to keep your spirit alive and
everlasting.
That you will have enough pain so that even the smallest of joys in life
may appear bigger.
That you will have enough gain to satisfy your wanting,
That you will have enough loss to appreciate all that you possess.
I pray for you, my son, the best life ever!
Happy Graduation!


Psalm 84:11
**"No good thing will He withhold from those who walk uprightly."**


**Taylor Marie**

We tried to have another child, but it just wasn't meant to be. I did get pregnant but the medical problems started all over again and I knew it would be very difficult to carry another child, but I was willing to give it a try.

I went for a sonogram so we could tell what was going on because things were not right. The sonographer sat me down after the test and explained that no heartbeat was found and that I would be losing the baby. I took the bad news like I always did with a realistic matter-of-fact way. I accepted the news knowing that it was simply not to be.

I had kept the pregnancy test stick for many years afterwards but had forgotten about it. I ran across it several years ago and allowed myself to grieve the loss for the first time. When I lost the baby it was too early to know the sex, but I still had named my baby Taylor Marie. I kept the fact that I named the baby a secret and didn't tell anyone. I had decided upon the name when I was pregnant with my son, in case he had been a girl. It was a name that honored my grandmother Marie.

Even though it was not meant for her to be here on this earth, I know that one day I will see my baby girl in heaven.

# TWENTY

# An Attitude of Gratitude

*Delight yourself in the Lord and he will give you the desires of your heart.*

**Psalms 37:4**

### Spoken

Let me ask you a question! What is the difference between major surgery and minor surgery? Well, minor surgery is when *you* are having the surgery and major surgery is when *I* am having the surgery!!

A dear coworker of mine told me that after I had announced that I would be gone from work for about eight weeks to recover from a surgery that I was about to undergo. I really got a good laugh out of that one but deep down inside of me, yep, I knew that he was right.

### Faith Gave Me Strength

When it came time for me to prepare for my third major surgery and with a lot of prayer I might add, I had been greatly anticipating the procedure with excitement because I had waited so long for it to be done. That procedure was going to fix a lot of physical problems that I had been having.

The night before the surgery my husband had expressed to me that he knew how excited I was to be having the surgery, but then he asked me if I was scared, because I didn't seem nervous at all to him! I smiled at him and stated that I wasn't scared and that I knew everything would be all right.

The surgery had many risks but I was at peace. I had an overwhelming peace because I knew that God would bring me through it and bring me back to my family. Of course at the hospital my blood pressure was a tad bit high, probably because there was some internal anxiety.

I remembered back to my C-section recalling that I felt pain differently than I thought that I should. I remembered asking the doctor after the C-section if something was wrong with me because I wasn't feeling much pain.

"When you get up and about, you will feel it," he stated.

To be quite honest with you, I really didn't feel as bad as I thought I would.

I remember when a group of my lady friends came to the hospital for a visit to see our new baby just about the time that I was getting out of bed to take a walk. They started laughing at me when I told them that I hadn't taken any pain meds. Their laughing turned to snickering as I slowly moved across the floor.

"*What?*" I questioned, with a little sarcasm in my voice.

"You silly girl, if you take your pain meds you can actually *stand up straight!*" they said as they continued to laugh uncontrollably.

All in all, I was anticipating that the surgery that I was about to undergo would be about the same, and I would *have* to take my pain meds even if I didn't want to. I also had some troubles with anesthesia so I definitely made sure that the surgery team had a heads-up on how I reacted to it.

During my stay in pre-op I had overheard a few conversations from the staff about how some patients were being told that their surgeries were being cancelled. My heart sunk. *Please do not let them tell me that my surgery has been cancelled.* I had come so far with being in that silly gown, IV, and all, but my surgery was one that started on time. Phew!

During the surgery things went awry and I had turned into a bleeder, so the surgery ended up lasting several hours longer than anticipated. But all went well. I had a wonderful surgeon who had saved my life while I was having surgery on other occasions. All in all I have had thirteen surgeries or procedures at the time of this writing, but because of my faith I have no fear. I know that God is with me. I have no doubt about it.

I have often thought about how many times that I could have died if I hadn't had the use of modern medicine and the tests that we have available for us today. Do I believe that God can heal? Most definitely! Do I believe that God can use anything or anyone to help heal? Most definitely! After all, I feel that I am still alive because His mission for me is still not completed here on this earth!

### Bless and Be Blessed

As far as my health issues go, I have never liked to be a burden to anyone. It is just a part of my personality *and* also my inability to ask for help. I am learning to do better at this.

My Sunday school class has always been wonderful in providing meals for my family when I was laid up but I don't think that I had always informed them about every surgery that I was having. I just didn't want to become a burden for them. I felt that it would be, well, *too much.*

I did learn a valuable lesson from this, however. I was keeping people from receiving a blessing! I know how good I feel when I am able to help someone, so why should I deny others the same feeling and a blessing by not allowing them the opportunity to serve? Obviously, I am still a work in progress.

I also know that nurses don't always receive thanks for what they do and I can only imagine how difficult their workday can be sometimes. They picked their careers because they love serving others! But they often deal with out-of-control, ungrateful, mean, and angry people. Some of their patient's attitudes are driven by awful pain while others are driven by pain that had been inflicted upon them years ago. Nonetheless, I'm sure that it is not always an easy job most days for a nurse.

I have always tried to bless the nurses who took care of me by giving them a lighter day. There were times when I felt totally incapacitated and it was then that I had to ask for help. Regardless of how I was feeling I asked nicely and with a smile. There were times when I joked around with them, especially if they were watching me bumble around the room trying to get a grip on whatever it was that they needed me to do. I would make light of the situation and soldier on.

During one of my stays at a hospital one of the nurses brought a nun in to meet me. The nun wanted to meet-the-one-patient-that-they-wished-all-other-patients-could-be-like. I found it so sad that I was an exception to their daily grind.

I even had a few nurses tell me that they really hated their jobs and subsequently, they treated their patients with the same kind of attitude. Those nurses became challenges for me, and I loved it. Before long, I had them laughing too.

## My Joy Comes From the Lord

There is one statement that I have always heard people say about me over the years and that is, regardless of what I am going through, I do it with a smile. This is not to say that I don't often get sad, lonely, mad, and indifferent at times, I do! I am real and I do have feelings.

When my fiancé died many years ago I went through a pretty rough time. A friend of mine basically told me that she thought that I was a hypocrite for smiling and appearing to be going on with life as though nothing had happened. Her comment simply floored me.

"Why would I want to ruin someone else's day just because I am not having a good one myself?" was my response to her.

She never really got my point.

You may be wondering, "How do you do *that;* go through *stuff* and do it with a smile?"

Simply put, I have discovered a true joy and delight in the Lord. The Bible speaks about joy, a lot. We are to pursue joy over and over and the desire to be happy is God-given and should never be denied or resisted. One of my goals in life is to aim at displaying the glory of the Lord by expanding my own joy to others.

C.S. Lewis wrote – "It is a Christian duty for everyone to be as happy as he can."

I'm not saying that we should seek self-fulfillment for ourselves and be lovers of pleasure. We are to be lovers of God and when we practice looking for joy in the Lord, and not looking for it in the world, well, simply put you have an internal joy like none other. You will have an internal peaceful joy that you will want to share with others, regardless of your current situation.

Jesus tells us that there are more blessings, more joy, and more fulfillments in a life devoted to helping others than there is in a life constantly devoted to meeting our material comforts. (Matthew 6:19, 20)

It most certainly does go against our nature to be joyful and happy all the time, right? One of my rules is that I will allow myself to have a one-minute pity party if I need one, and then I need to get over it! Self-pity is nothing but foolish pride. Get it, woe is *me*!

I have a lot to be happy about and I choose to live my life with an attitude of gratitude. I am so very thankful for all that I have. I am not always thinking about what I don't have because I have plenty and I am satisfied. God has promised me a wonderful future with rewards, and I look forward to it, with joy!

I simply cannot complain about my life! Visit a third world country and then tell me that you have something to complain about! I dare you!

If you are a Christian it is your duty to be joyful. How can we win others to Christ if we go around with a frown and our lips turned down? Why have frumpy attitudes? I wouldn't want to join that club myself!

If you are not a Christian, I hope that one day you will experience an internal peace and joy that is like none other; a peace and a joy that can only be achieved by knowing Jesus Christ.

It's so easy to serve others and to do so with joy. When you do, your own problems become very insignificant. Practice serving others by simply offering them a smile; it may be the only smile they receive that day. Practice by complimenting someone on their outfit, their smile, their beauty; it may be the only compliment they receive that week. Practice serving a child by acknowledging them and show them that you *know* that they exist; at home they may not exist!

Serving others may be as simple as offering a smile to someone or as great as offering someone a meal. Maybe you can offer someone a hands-up, giving them a chance at something far greater than even you can imagine for their lives. Regardless of how you serve others, serve with joy and with an attitude of gratitude.

*"What we do for ourselves dies with us.*
*What we do for others and the world*
*remains and is immortal"*
*-Laura Moncur-*

# TWENTY ONE

# Lessons Learned

*Let the wise listen and add to their learning,*
*And let the discerning get guidance –*
**Proverbs 1:5**

### In a Nutshell

I have recorded, for the most part, the earlier accountings of my life so you basically have my life story in a nutshell. There is still a lot of learning for me to do yet, so maybe I will get the opportunity to share more lessons learned in another book!

One of the reasons I even considered sharing my life publicly in a book or with speaking engagements is to help others. A good part of what I have shared with you could be embarrassing, shameful, and in some cases, plain old jaw dropping, but I have a forgiving God who daily offers me the gift of grace and mercy. Somehow with my sharing, I want others to know that they too can have these same gifts of grace and mercy, regardless of where they are at in their lives.

I have often been asked as to why my life took so many wrong turns. To tell you the truth, I just don't know. I am sure that there is some psychiatrist out there who would love to rattle around in my brain to figure it all out, but that doesn't really seem that important to me. All I know is that I am truly grateful for how God protected me through the bad times. And boy, did I give my guardian angels a run for their money!

What is most important to me is the fact that I truly appreciate my salvation, probably a lot more than I would have if I had stayed on the straight and narrow. I have learned what it's like to live without Jesus so I am more compassionate and less judgmental towards those who don't know Him. I truly understand the cost of my salvation. There is hope, and yes, there is help. You can overcome any area in your life that you feel is unhealthy. You too can have a relationship with Jesus and partake of the gifts that he so freely gives. All you need to do is ask. (Luke 11:9-13).

I am glad that I am not who I was. I have been healed and no longer carry the images, the thoughts, and the desires that I had at one time. Nor do I have any temptations to return to such a life. I do not have to carry around the weight of all of the baggage from my past life either because of God's mercy and grace, and that includes being able to forgive all of those who had *done me wrong*. I too have learned how to offer others forgiveness, mercy, and grace.

You see I could have chosen to become very bitter about my childhood, my first marriage, the loss of my fiancé, and many other things that have happened in my life, but I didn't. Yes folks, it is a *choice*.

As you read this last chapter I will cover some of the many lessons that I've learned over the years, but don't expect anything too deep! Hopefully the lessons I have learned will help you see how I was able to make the choice of happiness, overcome the bad stuff, and weather the storms, whether they happened because of my choices or because they just simply happened. Hopefully the lessons that I have learned will help someone else come out on the other side of the darkness with the same hope that I have. Some of these lessons may sound a bit cliché, but, after all, *it is what it is*!

## Live life!

You were given the gift of life, so live it! You have to show up! I choose to live life, but there was a time when I was so painfully shy and such an introvert to the point that it could have hindered me from doing so. I am so grateful for parents who noticed that trait early on and worked with me to overcome it. Yes, there were those *certain years* that I may have gone a bit overboard, but living life to the fullest with God on your side can be very rewarding.

I have watched a few people over the years become stymied or stagnant in their lives because of certain fears that they had. They wanted to live their lives all contained in a bubble so that their lives would be perfect. They wanted a life without challenges and dysfunctions and tried to keep up a perfect reputation, thus letting the world only see what they wanted the world to see. Some became judgmental and pious while their façade screamed look at me and my perfect life! But they were not living; they just thought that they were.

These same people may only have Christian friends and run in Christian circles and go to church to only warm a pew. They never step outside of their comfort zone because it's all about their safety and not getting hurt.

As you take a look at my life, you can see that I am a risk-taker. Some of these risks were obviously plain stupid risks, but I must admit that most of my risks have been well played out. I have learned that when you take risks you sometimes get your heart stomped on and the air kicked out of you. You will have some successes and some failures and yes, when you take risks every part of your being will be affected. You will have ups and down, struggles and challenges, and simply put if you are not experiencing any of these things, then you are not living! So, live life and take a risk.

Just remember that if you think that you are living in a bubble, God won't be asking you about the clothes you had in your closet but instead he will be asking you how many you have helped to clothe. He won't be asking you what kind of a car you drove but will ask you about how many people you helped with their transportation. He won't be asking you how many friends you had but will ask you how many people to whom you were a friend. God won't ask how many blings, things, and diamond rings you owned, but instead, he will ask you how many people in need you helped.

To live life requires that you take action and risks. Discover what your potential is; you have everything that you *need* to do everything that God requires of you. I too am guilty of trying to stay within a comfort zone. It's only natural not to want to engage in other's lives and only natural to want to keep up a façade. I have been a perfect example of this and have felt that for most of my life that I have been the most misunderstood person on this earth! I recognized this dilemma when I was in my early twenties. I had asked a dear friend why it seemed that some people were afraid of me, or standoffish from me.

"Well, you *are* a bit intimidating," she said as she chuckled.

I was floored by that statement and in puzzlement wondered how?

Since the intimidation-air-about-me was finally brought to my attention I have made intentional attempts to break down the façade and make people feel more comfortable when they are around me. And yet people still form first opinions of me, but I too am guilty of making first opinions of them as well. After I get to know someone for a while, they usually come clean and tell me what they thought I was about and then they tell me what they actually found me out to be. Sometimes their comments and thoughts about who they originally thought I was have been quite comical. Other comments, well, not so funny.

I have discovered that being a Christian has made it easy for me to share about the blessings in my life, and of course we want to share those things, but it is not always so easy to share the not-so-flattering things in our lives that could break down our façade.

Sometimes after my speaking engagements people will come up to me and offer their support or opinions and ask some questions. After one such event, someone approached me who had obviously determined in her mind who I was before I had spoken.

"So, you really are a *real* person!" she exclaimed.

ZAP! OUCH! I felt that comment to the bottom of my soul. It is so important for us to share the blessings, the shortfalls, and the troubles that come our way so that we are perceived as *real* people. We need to allow God's glory and strength to be shown to others, not only during the good times, but even while we are in the midst of our own trials of everyday life.

Take risks, and let others see who you really are. Step out of your comfort zone and help others. Don't let those around you who are searching for the truth feel inadequate, and definitely don't make them feel left out because they may not have the perfect life like your façade may be screaming. You see, living life is not just about jet-setting around the world, climbing mountains, setting new records, or sipping a wine cooler while lying on a beach somewhere. These things are all good things and are gifts from above if you have been given the means to do so, but living life is about living the life that God has given to you and living it with the purpose for which He has given it to you for.

Getting out of *you* is living! Getting out of your shell, your bubble, and your fears, is living! Getting your hands dirty once in a while by helping others is living!

Most every family I know is dysfunctional in some way. Most everyone has fears and everyone has sinned, so there are no big surprises here! People who need Christ have messy lives and even those who have Christ in their lives have messy lives. So get over it and start living!

Discover and learn what your self-worth really is. Peel back your façade and know that you are loved by the one who made you! He made you perfectly, so you don't need a façade! By peeling it all back, you will be able to love others better and live your life to the fullest.

One of the biggest regrets you could have at the end of your life is when you look back at it and realize that you tried to live your life the way others thought you should have lived it, instead of living the life that you were intended to live! You find that basically you lived your life based upon someone else's approval thinking that you would not be loved enough or good enough to meet their ideals for your life. Just know that God has a plan for your life. He loves and knows you and has made you for his purpose. God doesn't make junk! Live your life for God's purpose and not for another person or persons controlling ideas.

Live in the moment, the here and now, because every day is a gift. Make good use of the gift!

After all, you are on a journey with Jesus, so don't miss out on the adventure!

## The Instinct of Fear

Fear, in and of itself, is a good thing. It is an instinct given to us to help us to use good judgment and to protect ourselves from danger. For instance, we know that if we were to stick our hand into a poisonous viper's nest we most likely will get bit and die. It's our natural instinct that tells us not to walk down that dark alley by ourselves or not to confront a bear lurking around our camp site. Fear teaches us not to go where the angels won't go!

On the other hand, there is a fear that is not healthy. Fear of failure, fear of what others may think of us, fear of being alone, fear of being left desolate, and fear of fear itself! The list could go on and on and it can be crippling. Just know that Jesus came to help make us brave.

"I'm afraid," you may say.

But God says, "I have not given you the spirit of fear." (II Timothy 1:7)

I have observed over the years that the most consuming fear that a person has will often become a reality for them. Here are a few examples:

One person I knew had a great fear of losing their mind for all of their life, and I watched as Alzheimer's eventually took their mind away from them. Another person had a great fear of being left desolate and I watched as money slipped through their fingers. Another person had the fear of not being healthy as they took very extreme measures in what proved to be an unhealthy lifestyle that worked in the opposite direction, leaving their body in a very fragile state.

There are some that I have watched self-destruct as they worked very hard at protecting their reputations. Their fear was that people would finally discover who they really were and they would tell lies, cheat, and involve others in their cover up. They demanded respect without ever earning it and become angry when people defied them. Eventually they would be found out and eventually they imploded upon themselves and became broken.

Basically, the fears and threats that we have created all on our own and the ones that we tell ourselves to believe make us act, well, senselessly.

I have chosen to live a fearless life. As a child I learned that our lives were often threatened and on a consistent basis because of my father's career, but one thing that my father taught me was that most threats are just that, threats, and that you cannot walk around being scared all of the time. My father was a fearless man.

On several occasions as an adult my life had been threatened or danger had lurked just around the corner, but I chose not to cave in to the fear. I went with my natural instincts of being cautious and not let the fear control me. Because of my faith in God, I have chosen to live a fearless life. After all, He is the One who gave me my life and for his purpose. And I must admit, for a purpose that is far greater than any fear that I may have had. But don't get me wrong because I still deal with fearful situations. One experience that I had several years ago shows just how easy it is to let fear take over.

I was asked to speak at a program during the holiday season and the venue was quite large. I had spoken at large venues before but for some reason fear started to take over.

While at dress rehearsal I was trying to work out all the kinks with the various speakers and performers. When it was finally my turn to go up on stage and practice my speech in conjunction with a video that went along with that speech, fear set in. I had lost my focus and lost my nerve. I started shaking and couldn't stay on cue. I was almost riddled with fear and almost to tears! What was this *thing* that was happening to me? How strange, after all I was the only one in the room except for the technical team and a few performers.

After I had finished the rehearsal I sat down in the first row of chairs so I could try and gather my thoughts, and I was still shaking. Because of the bright lights that had been in my eyes I hadn't seen that one of my friends had snuck into the back of the venue. She worked her way to the front and sat down next to me.

"What is wrong with you, are you all right?" she asked. "You were not yourself up there."

I assured her that even thought I didn't know what went wrong I would be okay. Then it dawned on me as I thought to myself, ah ha, *fear*. I had believed the devil's lies that I was not worthy to speak, the lies that I was a fearful person and that I was not good enough. Lies that I was weak and all the lies that we believe of ourselves that are not true. I had let that deception distract me and I allowed it to set fear in me all the way to my bones.

You may think that this is weird, but I knew that I was under some kind of a spiritual attack. As I drove home that afternoon after the rehearsal I was still shaken up. After arriving at home I went to my bedroom to change into the clothes that I would be wearing for that evening's event. In the silence of my room I spoke out loud and with much determination.

"Devil, get behind me, I am a child of God and you will *not* prevent me from speaking!" I declared.

It was then that the shaking stopped and all my fears and doubts stopped as well. My body and mind were once again at peace and the speech that I had prepared for that evening was not impeded in any way.

If you find yourself consumed by daily fears, just know that God does not give us a spirit of fear. (11 Timothy 1:7)

"I'm always worried and frustrated," you may say.

God says, "Cast all your cares on me." (1 Peter 5:7)

### Love Your Neighbor as Yourself

When Jesus was asked what the greatest commandment was, he answered with, "Love the Lord your God with all your heart with all your soul and with all your mind. This is the first and greatest commandment. And the second is like it: Love your neighbor as yourself. All the Law and the Prophets hang on these two commandments." (Matthew 22:36-40)

Yes folks, we are to love God with everything that we have and we are to love everyone else as much as we love ourselves. Impossible you say? Well it's not impossible, but it can be a struggle. You will find that sometimes people are just not that lovable and sometimes to be quite honest, I'm not that loveable either.

My pastor uses the term "EGR" (Extra Grace Required) for people who are a little bit harder to deal with. I have picked up on that term and have used it quite often when I have had to deal with some very difficult people. It helps to keep my temper in check as I offer extra grace when trying to smooth out a difficult situation with someone.

As we learn to love others as God has commanded us to do we start to realize that it comes with costs and some hurts. To love deeply means that sometimes the hurt will go as deep too. I learned that after my fireman died. I had put up some walls around me not allowing myself to love as deep as I once had. Those walls eventually came down, but with some work. It is still sometimes a struggle for me.

I pray to learn how to love others and pray to see others as Jesus loves and sees them. Sometimes it hurts and it brings me to tears but it also helps me to see the bigger picture. We develop a love for mankind that grieves and aches with compassion. If you have never grieved then you have never loved. When we allow our hearts to know deep grief and pain we are then able to see the depths of God's love. Once you have arrived at that point then it is easier to love, to forgive, and to offer help to all of those in need.

Sometimes I do believe that we Christians have a tendency to practice more religion than we do Christianity.

In my earlier years of attending church, and some more recent, I have noticed that Christians seem to have some hypocritical attitudes when it comes to *loving all people.* If a person you attend church with looks like you and is in the same social status as you all is well with the world, right? But, what happens if someone wanders into your church and they are, well, *different?* What if they are not as sophisticated as others or maybe not as educated as some and maybe they don't know how to act in church? Or maybe there is some inappropriate language or maybe they haven't taken a bath in a while or there is alcohol or cigarette smoke on their breath? Heavens forbid! Run, because we might get the cooties!!! AHHHHH~!!

I remember a story that was told to me about a church group that was bringing a few homeless people into their church each Sunday morning to have breakfast and listen to a sermon. Doesn't that sound great? The only problem was that some of the congregation didn't want *that kind* sitting in their sanctuary with them. They wanted *those* homeless people serviced in the kitchen area. *Seriously,* I ask?

I read another story some time ago that was probably fictitious, but it describes pretty much the same hypocritical thing. The story went something like this...

As a young man was driving up to an intersection the light turned yellow. He stopped even though he could have made it through the intersection. The tailgating woman behind him was furious. She was in such a hurry and he had caused her to miss her chance to get through the intersection. She slammed on her brakes which caused her to drop her cell phone, coffee and lipstick. She proceeded to honk and scream at the young man who was stopped in front of her.

While in the midst of her ranting and raving she heard a tap on her window. It was a police officer with a serious look on his face. He ordered her to step out of her car and then proceeded to handcuff her and took her off to jail. She was faced with all kinds of embarrassments by being booked into jail.

The arresting officer met with her after a few hours had passed, and just before she was being released.

"I am so sorry," the officer stated. "You see, I had pulled up behind you while you were honking, flipping off, and cursing at the young man in front of you," he continued. "I saw the stickers on your bumper which read, "What Would Jesus Do?", "Choose Life", "Follow Me To Church", and the fish emblem on your trunk, so I had assumed that you had stolen the car!"

Another story about Christians behaving badly was told to me many years ago.

An older couple needed to sell their home because they were at a point in their lives that they had to move to an assisted living facility. They only had a certain amount of time to sell their home in and they listed their home for the amount of money that was needed for their care. It was very important for them to get the most of what they could for their home.

Then here comes Mr. and Mrs. Christian who were interested in purchasing the home. They knew of the situation that the older couple was in and knew the reason why they needed to sell their home. Mr. and Mrs. Christian decided to wait it out until the price of the house dropped.

As time grew closer and closer to when the older couple would have to move Mr. and Mrs. Christian kept haggling with them over the price until the older couple was out of time and the house ended up being sold well below the price that they needed to sell it for. They had no choice but to sell. The next thing that happened was that Mr. and Mrs. Christian was bragging about the great deal that they had gotten on a house and were telling others how they went about doing it.

*Really*??? When you cause harm to another person with your *good deals* is it really a good deal? And by the way, as a side note, the Bible tells us to be honest in our dealings and to not brag about our good deals.

We are all guilty of behaving badly and unfairly towards each other. It just happens, but we are commanded to love one another, so we must try. We need to get along, resolve our problems with grace and mercy, ask for forgiveness, and learn to forgive.

We need to learn how to love others where they are at in their faith journey because they may have no faith at all, or have very little of it. Do you expect a two-year-old child to behave like an adult? No! It's the same with faith. Don't expect others to be at the same point that you are in your faith walk.

And by the way, don't make it your life's mission to try to change others. First, work on changing yourself. If you wish to see the best in others, show the best of yourself. If you are always in strife with others or there seems to always be ruffled feathers all around you, you might want to rethink what is really going on! *Ya' think*?

The Bible is very direct when it speaks of how we are to treat others. If we want our prayers to be answered, then we have to treat people right. (1 Peter 3:7)

Another important point I need to make is that to love others we must first learn to love ourselves. You cannot love others until you have worked that out with yourself. A lot of people get hung up on that one thing because they cannot forgive themselves for something that happened in their past. And while they are all consumed with not being able to love themselves, they also buy into the lies that no one else can love them either. This can be very destructive. If you are struggling in this area you might want to start by writing down some positive affirmations about yourself.

First, list out things that you are good at, and things that are good about you. What positive things do you want to be able to say about yourself in the future? Make a list of *"I am's"* and *"I want to be's"* and repeat each item out loud, and regularly. Write them on post-it-notes and place them all around your mirror or refrigerator so that you see them every day. Get to the point to where you can learn to love yourself so that you can forgive yourself. In the next section of this chapter I will talk more about forgiveness.

How do you want to be remembered? Will it be for what you did for a living, or for the life that you lived? How will you be remembered, for the way you made people *feel*? Love costs, but it is well worth the risk.

### Forgiveness is Essential

Forgiveness is another main theme in the Bible and is mentioned many times. Forgiveness is essential and because God has forgiven us, he expects us to forgive others. And if you want to be forgiven, you must first learn to forgive others. (Mark 11:25). To this day I still have to say that I am living proof that God does miracles on this earth. The greatest sovereign miracle of all is a hard heart that has been transformed by God. You see, my heart had hardened against His ways but he forgave me when I returned to the faith.

As I mentioned earlier in this chapter, I do not have to carry around the weight of past sins, because of His forgiveness, grace, and mercy. (Isaiah 41:20).

"If we confess ours sins, he is faithful and just and will forgive us our sins and to purify us from all unrighteousness." (I John 1:9)

Did you get that? He cleanses us, and our past sins are all wiped away!

He not only forgives us, but he restores us. (Psalm 23)

"Therefore, if anyone is in Christ, he is a new creation; the old has gone, the new has come!" (II Corinthians 5:17)

Wow! He forgives us, cleanses us, restores us, and makes us a new and different person!

God forgives us, but I also know that it isn't always enough to be forgiven by Him or by others, you have to learn to forgive yourself too.

"But, I cannot forgive myself," you may say.

But God says, "I forgive you." (1 John 1:9, and Romans 8:1)

If you are the kind of person that struggles with your past, don't carry it around with you like old worn out luggage. If you have confessed your sins, and have asked for forgiveness, move on! *Celebrate the new you!* Remember that your past is not as important as your future.

Forgiveness usually involves someone who doesn't deserve it. When we have been wounded or wronged our greatest temptation is to develop resentment. It takes a lot of energy to carry around an unforgiving spirit.

I have always said, "Don't let someone else's sin become yours."

If you are harboring resentment because of how you felt you were wronged or badly treated, that then becomes your sin. Not forgiving someone grows into darkness like a mold in your soul. It will grow and grow until it eventually takes over. Your soul becomes bitter and sour as you become cynical and hateful towards others. The person, against whom you harbor ill feelings, has gone about their merry way and hasn't given their actions towards you another thought! They are totally clueless about the darkness that you let grow inside of you; the kind of darkness that rots away at your insides.

I have felt that a lot of people have wronged me over the years, but I chose to forgive. If someone has wronged me, and I can truly say that I didn't play any part in what happened, they own that baggage and it is not mine to carry around.

When we forgive, it doesn't mean that we will necessarily forget what was done and it doesn't mean that we won't have to work hard at being able to forgive someone. We learn from these experiences and move on. Maybe we are more cautious when dealing with that specific person or persons in the future.

On the flip side, do not use a person's former sins against them. It is between them and God. If they have asked the Lord and he has forgiven them, he can use them for his purpose regardless of their past transgressions. Of course Satan is just waiting to add an element of truth to the lies that he tells in any situation to try to hinder God's work, so remain blameless in this area and do not allow yourself to be used in this way.

Pray for help if you struggle in the forgiveness area. Remember that God can turn things around for you.

There is an old saying, "To forgive is the best revenge". Think about it. Revenge or not, there is one thing that I do know for sure, it is very, very *freeing* when you can forgive yourself and others.

## Create Opportunities Out of Challenges

"You have to accept whatever comes, and the only important thing is that you meet it with the best you have to give." ~Eleanor Roosevelt, First Lady 1884-1962

I do believe that the First Lady had it right. How do you respond to challenges? Do you act or react? Do you often react and fly off the handle when something breaks, twists or bends? Or do you accept what happens with little surprise and take the proper action to repair the problem?

Sometimes bad things happen because we have made poor decisions and sometimes bad things happen because they just do. Know that God does not tempt us and does not cause us to make bad decisions. Nor does He bring forth the bad things into our lives, but He does bring forth every good and perfect gift, and it is important to love Him through our trials. (James 1:12-18)

I have often been amused when I have watched some people fly off of the handle spewing their ugliness and ruining everyone else's day, all because something fell apart. That's just life, things happen! Am I unveiling some sort of surprise here?

If you have ever owned a car or a home you know that they are not going to stay pristine forever. They will eventually be in need of repair. So why not mentally prepare yourselves for these possible situations ahead of time? Instead of reacting, simply act. The same goes for the way we handle people. In some situations, there's going to be a bit of repair work that needs to be done.

When you act instead of react you will not ruin someone's day and you will find yourself being nice to the store clerk or the repairman who is trying to help you with your problem. You can face the challenge head-on, meeting it with the best that you have to give. Remember that our perception and attitude toward any situation will determine the outcome.

The Bible does not promise us a rose garden but quite the opposite, actually. So be prepared. Jesus said that we will face opposition and challenges on this earth. There will always be problems in our lives; sickness and death, poor and widowed. Always!

John 15:18-25 speaks of how the world will hate us but to remember that the world hated Jesus first. In other words, there is going to be trouble. So how do we deal with all of this? I suggest that you turn these problems into opportunities. How can you turn something negative into a positive? Or even more, how can you see the positive in the negative? It's not always easy.

Sometimes we need quite a bit of distance and time away from a situation before we can ever see the silver lining, and sometimes during our lifetime, we will never see the positive outcomes from a certain experience. The positive may only be seen later by the future generations to come.

I eventually saw the silver lining which came from my fireman's death. It took that tragedy to get my attention and I returned to God. I think a few more people did as well.

I saw the silver lining in losing my father way too early to cancer. He was our family's spiritual leader and our go-to person with any spiritual questions. We didn't need to read or study the Bible, we let him do that. When he died my immediate family and I had to grow up and learn how to nurture ourselves and grow in the Lord's word, which we did.

There will always be plenty of storms to deal with during our lifetime. So be prepared. Sometimes things just happen to us that are out of our control. In the passages from Mark 4:35 through 5:43 there are four stories about circumstances that happened to some people. What happened to them was totally out of their control and when we read these stories we also get to see what happened when Jesus intervened. The first story shows how Jesus calmed a great windstorm that suddenly came upon a crew while they were in a boat out on the water. In the second story Jesus healed a man who was being tormented by demons. In the third story we see a little girl who dies and was restored to life. And a forth story tells of a woman who had suffered for twelve years with bleeding and was healed. Please take time to read these stories yourself. These are great faith stories that can leave you with a lot to ponder.

All of these people had things happen to them that were out of their control. They could not have stopped what happened to them, even if they had tried. Stuff happens. In these stories you can see the different personality traits of each and how they acted or reacted to their situations. Some initially reacted with little faith while others acted with great faith.

So what happened? Jesus happened!

Through all of life's storms, big or small, you can always call upon Jesus to get you through them. When the demons attack you with alcoholism, anger, or lusts, Jesus can get you through it; when you need healing, turn to Jesus.

There will also be times when opportunities will arise and we will be expected to take care of them ourselves. God has given us the tools to do so. We need to pray and ask Him for help, wisdom, and guidance in any given situation, but you need to realize that there are times when God has faith in your abilities and he expects you to use them. Be prepared.

I remember one time when there was a tornado headed towards my grandmother's house. Everyone headed for the shelter as grandma stood outside and watched the sky.

"God will protect me," she stated.

Uh, hellloooo~! God also gave us a brain to use and I think that we are to use it. There's an old cliché that says, "It's hard to help someone who won't help themselves". So even though we have all the faith in the world for God's ability to solve our problems, he will sometimes require us to help ourselves.

As Christians we need to know that we will always be under attack, physically, spiritually, financially, and in so many other ways. Pray for protection daily. That's just the way it is. You never know when the opposition will try to hinder us and our work for God.

I remember attending a Bible Study group and when they were training new leaders they would always tell them to be prepared for possible bad things to happen to them that would keep them from being able to lead their classes. A flat tire, sick kids, waking up late, or whatever, would always happen to new leaders.

Have you often wondered why so many non-Christians become wealthy, healthy, and happy, with apparently no problems? And then you wonder why as a Christian, you keep having all kinds of difficulties? I heard a story that simplifies the answers to these two questions.

A hunter and his dog went duck hunting. The hunter quickly shot two ducks and one fell dead to the ground. The other duck was still alive and floundering around on the ground. The hunting dog did not go to the dead duck but instead went after the one that was still flapping around. The devil is like that as well. He doesn't go after and cause problems to the non-believer because he already has that one. He goes after the one that's still flapping around and creating waves.

There will always be hard days in our lives and everyone will at some time or another experience a hard day or two. Sometimes the hard days last an unseemly long time but just remember that you are not a failure. Keep trying, keep going and find the positive in the situation if you can.

"I can't go on," you may say.

God says, "My grace is sufficient". (II Corinthians 12:9 and Psalms 91:15)

Know that you are more than the hard days that you are facing and that God's love, grace, and mercy, is sufficient.

After all, you have an opportunity to meet your challenges with the best that you have to give.

### We Are So Blessed

We just cannot have trials without the blessings! We all have asked for blessings, haven't we? And we are in so many ways blessed already. We are blessed with family, friends, and provisions. We are blessed in abundance to the point that unfortunately, we take all of it for granted.

We sometimes forget to look at the beauty of nature all around us such as the blue sky above us with the puffy white clouds and the trees that rustle in the breeze. We overlook the beauty and warmth of the sunrise and the wonderful colors of the sunset. We are so blessed.

We don't take the time to walk barefoot through the grass because mowing it has become such a dreaded chore. We are blessed with beautiful homes but focus on our frustrations with the maintenance. We are blessed with family but quickly our daily grind becomes a list of things to do and places to go leaving us without the energy to even enjoy our families. We are blessed with food and don't even take the time to sit down and enjoy it, let alone smell it. And when we do sit down, we say a quick grace with a thank-you-very-much, maybe. We fly through life missing the blessings and taking most everything for granted, especially when life is going well.

Here's a thought, some of our most core-to-the-soul meaningful blessings come from out of our own trials, through our tears, our struggles, and our anguish. However, during the storm we can't even imagine that a blessing could ever appear out of such a horrible event.

You see, while things are going well we have a tendency to live our lives independent from God. We forget his blessings and we forget his gifts. We even forget to pray and to read His word, until one day we find ourselves backed into a corner. And only until we are in a jam and our arm is being twisted do we cry "uncle" as a response. We find that we don't have the strength to go on and it's almost impossible to manage the situation on our own.

*"Why is this happening to me?"* you question.

Things seem to be getting worse and the weight is more than you can handle and you finally say, "I am all alone."

Only then can you hear God's gentle reminder, "I will never leave you or forsake you". (Hebrews 13:5)

Oh yes, God, what a concept! You then, and only then, realize that you had forgotten to include God! You need his power and strength. You need his love, his protection, and at that point, you need *his mercy.* Simply put, our trial brings us back to God and places us squarely in front of him.

When we are weakened by trials, they do become the blessings in disguise. We will be strengthened after being weakened and our faith will stand after the storm has passed. Our relationship with God becomes closer and greatly confirmed. Our faith is renewed and our prayer life is active once again. We begin to see blessings everywhere. You then have a story to tell that's near and dear to your heart, one that you can share with others. You came out of the storm and your faith still firmly stands!

I have received many blessings after coming through the storms. But the two blessings that always prevail in all cases are the blessings of renewed strength with a renewed and stronger faith. You've heard it said before, "What doesn't kill ya' makes ya' stronger". Read the story of Job in the Bible and you will see what I mean. It's a *real* trial and you can draw strength from his story. You will see how he was eventually blessed beyond measure!

## My Road to Recovery

Take a look at Luke 15:11-32. Jesus told the parable of the prodigal son. The son had asked his father early for his inheritance. Early, meaning that he didn't want to wait for the order of things to take place. His father agreed and the son moved away. The son ended up squandering all of his money on his wild living, and soon found himself starving.

v20 So he got up and went to his father. But while he was still a long way off, his father saw him and was filled with compassion for him; he ran to his son, threw his arms around him and kissed him. v21 The son told him, "Father, I have sinned against heaven and against you. I am no longer worthy to be called your son." v22 But the father said to his servants, "Quick! Bring the best robe and put it on him. Put a ring on his finger and sandals on his feet. v23 Bring the fattened calf and kill it. Let's have a feast and celebrate. v24 For this son of mine was dead and is alive again; he was lost and is found." So they began to celebrate.

Take time to read the whole story. There are a lot of layers to this story to unpeel. That was where I found myself when I had returned to God. I did not consider myself worthy but my Heavenly Father was standing there when I returned and welcomed me back with a hug and a kiss.

So how did I get on the road to recovery? How did I overcome all of the different issues in my life? How did I heal from all the different areas in my life that I knew were broken?

The first thing I did after asking God for forgiveness was to rededicate my life to follow Him and I made a personal commitment to obey

His commands the best that I could. Because I had lost so many years of doing my own thing, I had forgotten a lot of what was in the Bible. What *are* all of the commands and what exactly *were* all of my issues? You see, my moral compass had shifted a bit, *me thinks*! I started taking a good look at myself.

I remembered back to a time in my youth when I was told by others how sweet, thoughtful, and helpful I was. I hadn't heard those things about myself in a long while. I wanted that Debra back, the good one, the one that loved and served the Lord with all of her heart, mind, and soul. That was what I wanted more than ever. I prayed to God for help.

I prayed for God to show me my sins because I was so blinded to them. I was so very grateful that he didn't reveal all of them to me all at once! He is good that way. I started out working on one issue at a time, and believe me, there were many!

The changes in my life did not happen overnight. It was a lot of hard work and it took several years to accomplish, but the changes came. My heart, mind, and soul were rescued from the darkness that was within me. Here are the steps that I went through:

**Step One** – I recognized that I needed God.

**Step Two** – I confessed my sins to Him. I John 1:9 states, "If we confess our sins, he is faithful and just to forgive us our sins and to purify us from all unrighteousness."

**Step Three** – I allowed God to teach me. Psalm 25:5 says, "Guide me in your truth and teach me, for you are God my savior..."

**Step Four** – I allowed God to direct my steps. Proverbs 3:5-6 says, "Trust in the Lord with all your heart and lean not on your own understanding; in all your ways acknowledge him, and he will make your paths straight."

**Step Five** – Repeat steps one through four, for the rest of your life!

One of the many things that I have learned is that our background and circumstances may have influenced who we are but we are responsible for who we become. Our bad experiences absolutely *do not* have to determine who we become. We can spend our lives saying woe is me because of our circumstances, playing the martyr or the victim, or we can pick ourselves up and gather strength from the Lord and change who we are.

No matter how old we get, we will always be a work in progress. Keep learning and know that good can always come out of the darkness. No one can go back and create a new beginning but everyone can start now and write a different ending. Whether you are fighting addictions, obsessions, or old bad habits, it is simply hard to do it on your own.

"It's impossible," you may say.

God says, "All things are possible..." (Luke 18:27) Gather your strength from the Lord, and you can do it!

### The Importance of Church and God's Word

For a long time I was a *ChrEaster* Christian. I didn't see the need for church. I attended church on Christmas and Easter and that was good enough for me. I knew what I believed so I didn't need someone telling me what to believe. I didn't need the church to judge me. I can pray on my own. You know, the give me, give me, give me type of prayers! I'm doing just peachy without church, thank you very much!

Simply put, it is imperative that we have a church family. God thought so or he wouldn't have established one in the first place. He knows how weak we are and how much trouble we can get ourselves into on our own. He knows that he has built into us the need for companionship. In other words, our church family provides a great support system on so many levels and *that* family also provides the help that we need to stay accountable.

This is where I may lose some of you. You are probably thinking, oh the rules. I don't need to be a part of something that requires me to follow rules. I don't need people judging me for how I live my life because I can't or won't follow the rules. And that Bible is so *huge*! How would I ever be able to live up to what that book requires of me?

Here are a couple of items that I have learned from my own life. The first thing is, without a good support system it is extremely easy to fall into the wrong lifestyle. It's so very, very easy. The second thing is that the Ten Commandments, if followed, make our lives so much easier to endure! I repeat, the Bible commandments are not intended to make our lives harder but to make our lives easier to live. (Exodus 20:1-17)

If you don't steal or murder you don't have to worry about doing any jail time. You won't have to spend time on the run trying to elude the authorities.

If you don't commit adultery you don't have to face the ramifications of getting caught or the embarrassment of having it go public, or face your family as they deal with the disappointment and disgrace.

If you don't lie you don't have to worry about what lie you told, when, and to whom, and how to keep the lie from getting bigger, and then end up telling more lies to cover up the previous lies, and the cycle continues until you get lost in your own lies!

If you don't covet your neighbor's belongings you live a healthier life of gratitude, and not a life filled with the disease of *Iwantitis*.

Even in the Garden of Eden, God's *permissions* for Adam and Eve to enjoy the garden were much broader than the one *restriction* that they were given. There was only *one* restriction and that was from one tree in the midst of the garden that they were not to eat from. Everything else was permissible.

You see God isn't trying to make it harder on us by giving us a bunch of rules, he is providing a way to make it easier for us to live our lives. He wants us to have a good, moral, healthy, spiritual life. One that is not full of regrets or I should haves. One that does not keep us looking over our shoulders wondering when things are going to blow up or implode on us because of our poor decisions. It is really a life of freedoms that God wants us to have.

So why is it so important to know what the Bible says? Why study? You may have grown up in the church and heard all of the sermons and say that you know what you believe, so you don't need to study the Bible. But how do you know what you *really* believe if you have never read or studied the Bible *yourself?* Aren't you just taking the word of someone else in which to base your belief system upon?

"It is too complicated and I cannot understand what the Bible is saying," you may argue.

I think that it is very important to pray before you read or study your Bible. Ask God to help make the passages clear to you and to give you understanding. Ask for God's insight on how the particular reading applies to you.

From studying the Bible you will gain wisdom, clear direction, and nourishment for your soul. And when you start studying you will soon find that you crave to spend more time reading the Bible because you hunger to know more. Through the Word, God will teach you about life lessons for living so that you can stay the course. You will learn obedience, self-control, and how to love and forgive.

You will also discover God's promises for you and those promises will be affirmed. You will learn of God's unfailing love, grace, and mercy. You will learn about all of God's characteristics and how he really works.

Do not rely on the guesses or opinions of others. Reading the Bible is like receiving daily bread. It is ranked up there with our need for air. It is part of your survival kit and another part of that survival kit is having a good church family to love on you and to support you all along the way.

## Waiting on His Timing

One of the things I've learned to do is to listen to God's voice. This is not an audible voice. I am speaking about but an inner voice that is very different from the psyche voice. I have found that the closer we are to God the more we are apt to be in tune to hear his voice.

I have prayed over the years for God to use me however he wanted to and for whatever purpose to help further His Kingdom. In order to do that, I have had to give control of my life over to God so that I could gain his perspective for my life. Many times I have thrown myself before God asking Him to bring it on! And He has. He has trusted me with much sometimes.

In so many ways God has used my gifts to start ministries, to work in some, and even lead others. I have considered it an honor to be able to do so. He has also called me and provided me with different opportunities so that I could be His light throughout my career. I had to wait for his timing, obey, and follow his directives. And that hasn't always been easy for me to do. I am sometimes impatient, and I like to argue a bit.

I remember many years ago when I was asked to take over a ministry in a church and I was telling them, no, no, no! The person whose task it was to recruit me asked me why I was giving her such an answer. I simply told her that the position required that I speak publicly.

"What are you so afraid of, you have been speaking publicly for years!" she exclaimed.

Oh yes, of course she was right. You see, God equips you with everything you need when he has called you to a position and he will not give you more than you can handle. The will of God will never take you where the grace of God will not protect you. He is not going to hang you out to dry!

Another lesson that I've learned is that when you are given a ministry to lead or to start up, or whatever role you are to play in it, you should give it your best. You should be honored to hold such a roll. Take ownership of your duties, and perform your duties with a servant's heart. *But do not be so foolish as to think that you and only you can hold that position.* There is always someone out there that can do it better, quicker, and in a smarter way than you can. There is always a time and a season for you to be there and in that position. A smart person will listen to God and know when it is time to move on.

I have always taken the stance that the ministry work that I do is God's ministry, not mine. I may be used to get a ministry off the ground and running but it may not be God's intent for me to stay forever in that position. At my church home I do not want to hoard a position and not allow others the ability to serve, others who may be better talented and gifted for the position than myself.

My advice to you is to simply be open to His call and trust His leading. Serve in your church and serve in your community. Answer God's call to duty. God never asks about our ability or our inability, just our availability. He may entrust you with much and it may sometimes be challenging, hard, and worrisome. You may even get tired, but after all, if we are performing our call to duty correctly we *should* leave this world exhausted!

## Showing Our Happiness and Joy

In the last chapter I spoke about happiness and joy. Because I think so many folks are going through life without the internal joy that I was talking about, I want to talk a little bit more about it.

True happiness can only come from the inside. It cannot be found in money, cars, diamonds, or from living a life like the lifestyles of the rich and famous. I remember back to all those many years ago when I stood in my dining room and looked at all of my pretty fineries while I tried to make the decision as to whether or not to leave my first husband. Were all of the things that I owned worth it, was my lifestyle worth it? Were all of the worldly treasures that I thought were treasures, worth losing my soul for? No! Worldly *"things"* do not make one happy.

There are a lot of Bible verses that talk about joy. We know that God is infinitely happy and I am glad for that. I don't worship a God who is unhappy, grumpy, or pouts, and because he is happy, his happiness spills over into the mercy that he shows to me daily! What better way to glorify God then by showing *our* happiness and joy to others!

It kind of goes against our nature to be happy all of the time. Excluding our bad days, *that will happen*, we sometimes become enslaved to the things that rob us of our joy. Have yourself a one-minute-pity-party if you need, then get on with it! After all, we Christians have a lot to be happy about.

Becoming a Christian is like being raised from the dead. We have a new life in Christ; we are changed, and changed for the better. We have a promise and a future that we can hold onto. Being thankful for *everything* should result in joy.

Just take a look at all of your surroundings. What do you see? Have you spent the most part of your life trying to find joy in *"things"* or the worldly treasures around you? Have you been looking for joy and happiness in all the wrong places? Are you depending upon another person to make you happy as you try to fulfill the joy that you are seeking?

Seek and find joy and happiness in the right places then share your joy and happiness with others. Glorify God with your testimony of living a joyful and happy life.

And finally, keep smiling…always!

## Don't Take Yourself So Seriously!

"Laughter is the brush that sweeps away the cobwebs of the heart." – Mort Walker.

Life can be hard and trying sometimes and it is so easy to get, well, serious. Your mind is somewhere else all the time and your lips are turned down. Your jaw becomes clinched and your body gets rigid and stiff. Don't take yourself so seriously! After all as the saying goes, "No one gets out alive!" Sometimes you have just gotta' cut loose and laugh. Laugh hard and laugh out loud! I have a wood cutout sign on my desk that simply says "LAUGH".

Most people who know me know that I do smile and laugh a lot. But most are not aware of my crazy side. Here I am rushing towards the age of sixty and I still like to put on socks and slide across the kitchen floor! I randomly start dancing around the house and if any single word spoken by someone else in the house reminds me of a song, I might just bust out singing! Yes, I am a bit crazy at times.

My random act of weird nesses totally drives my twenty year old son insane! His has a famous statement of shame.

"I have no mother," he says as he hangs his head and shakes it back and forth.

My husband is not exempt from my craziness either and he is as insane as I am. Needless to say you never know what is going to happen around our house. When the two boys (and I'm talking about my husband and son) get together with their orneriness I am totally out numbered.

One day I came home from work and discovered that the two boys had bought a radio control helicopter. You know the kind that is made for the *outdoors*? Well, unbeknownst to me it became an *indoors* helicopter that day. My eagle eyes quickly noticed white litter on the carpet in the family room.

"What on earth is this white stuff all over the floor?" I asked.

Then there came the new helicopter buzzing my head and scraping off the white ceiling bumps.

"*Seriously*?" I asked with a smirked grin. "I am *not* going to clean this mess up!"

I left the room to get a snack for myself and when I came back to the family room, my hopes of putting my feet up and enjoying my little snack and some TV was quickly dashed. All of a sudden I had a helicopter hovering in a fixed position over my head!

Another lesson learned. You just gotta' bust out and have some fun!

### As I've aged…

I have become much kinder and less critical of myself. I like who I have become. I am not constantly worried about what other people think of me, and their opinion that they may have of me is really *none of my business.*

I have collected a few *Debraisms* over the years. They are not typos and you won't find them in any dictionary, so I do hope that when you read this book, you have enjoyed a few of them.

I have learned to embrace my grey hair and my newfound laugh lines that are engraved on my face. I've earned them, and I am glad to wear them. You see, I've had several friends who left this world way too early and they didn't get to enjoy their grey hair and facial lines.

I have learned that life isn't always fair but it is still good. Life may be short but it is definitely worth living. So live!

I've learned to make peace with my past. I now run less of a risk of screwing up my present.

I've learned to pick my battles. Some battles are just not worth it. If no one is going to die it is sometimes just best to leave some things alone.

I've learned that every so called *disaster* isn't really going to matter in a few years.

I've learned to be a good listener which means that *I don't get to talk.* It's not always about me and I have often regretted that I have spoken, but never when I have remained quiet.

I've learned that I don't have to tell everything that I know. I know what I know, it's not important to me that everyone else knows what I know. Gossip is a sin anyways. Sometimes it's best to just sit on it. What I do know may come in handy one day.

I've learned not to compare myself with others. I enjoy and relish in other people's gifts, and I am content with my own.

I've learned that respect is earned and not demanded. Speak softly, love generously, and treat others as you would want to be treated. Keep your moral compass and your anger in check. Your integrity will be remembered longer than anything else you do.

I've learned that the most important thing that you can teach your child is how to make wise decisions.

I've learned that no one is in charge of my happiness but me. It is never too late to be happy. So get crackin'…that smile of yours I mean!

I've learned to believe in miracles. I am one as far as I am concerned. Look around you, there are miracles happening everywhere.

I've learned that it is okay to cry and that it's also okay that others witness you crying. I am still not good at it yet, so I will keep practicing.

I've learned to get rid of clutter; those things that clutter my life, my mind, and weigh me down, the things that aren't useful. You too can lighten the load!

I've learned that life is much easier with God in my life. God loves us because of who he is and not for what we have done or haven't done. And it is okay to be mad at God every once in a while. He can take it. Develop a relationship with Him and he will be your BFF!

I've learned that a day all wrapped up in prayer is less likely to come all undone.

And finally, as I've aged, I've learned that chocolate *is* a major food group and that it should be a part of our life's survival kits! Mmmmmmmmmmmm…

**Live your life the best that you can.**
**Have faith and leave the rest to God!**

**May God bless you and be with you**
**on your journey through life!**

# Amusing Bonus Stories

My career of working with the public has always lent to some very interesting experiences. The following stories made the editor's cut so I have included them in this bonus section for your amusement. I hope that you will find some of them as interesting, strange, and as funny as I have. Enjoy!

### My Part-Time Interests

I always seemed to have had part-time interests that I really enjoyed doing but I knew that I didn't want to make a career out of any of them because that could ruin the simple pleasure that I received from each one.

For example I have always loved drawing, and during my high school years I was recruited on several occasions to design program covers, props, and various other items. After college I was recruited to design logos for several different companies. My first job was working at an exclusive department store in ladies fashions and it was there in my spare time that I would sketch the fashions in the store depicting what that fashion item would look like on a person's body. My sketches caught my boss's eye one day and she told me that she knew of a store that was looking for a fashion sketch artist for their newspaper ads. I was hired and immediately started working for the store and for one of their sister stores drawing fashion sketches.

From a very young age I discovered that I enjoyed marketing. One of my friends was a manager of a well-known hamburger chain and she told me that her company was looking for new blood, you might say, for their marketing department. My friend asked me to create a marketing idea that she could submit to the home office. They were having a contest of sorts to see who could submit the best ideas. I went to work and sketched out several pages of art that had one consistent theme in mind and gave it to my friend to submit. I then totally forgot about it, after all it was a mid-western chain and I didn't really think that my ideas had a chance of winning any recognition. I received a call from my friend about a month later.

"Debra, they *loved* what you did and they want you to come to the home office to visit with them," she sated. "It sounds like they might want to offer you a position."

I could hardly believe what I was hearing but I did decline the offer and opportunity because I was so young and I didn't want to travel by myself or move to another state. So I simply put the idea out of my mind.

Interestingly enough though, about a year later I was standing in line at one of those hamburger shops and I started noticing the marketing pieces that were hanging on the walls and ceiling and quickly realized that I was looking at my own work! I stood there grinning from ear to ear and found it quite amusing.

Another example of my part-time interests was my love for modeling but I didn't care to sign with an agency like a lot of the local girls did. I wanted to be able to have more control over for whom and what I modeled so I started free-lancing. Part of my college education included modeling classes and the school offered some connections that helped to get me started. The gigs never paid any money but I was paid with many free outfits! That was sufficient for me!

Some of my gigs were not very appropriate, such as modeling lingerie in nightclubs! Over the years I have known a lot of young ladies who would do just about anything to rise to the top of the modeling world, but it can be a very dangerous career if a person is not grounded. You cannot be too thin-skinned or the profession will eat you up alive. You will be scrutinized over your weight, looks, hair, and posture. I have witnessed many girls crying over being told that they just didn't have the *look* for a particular project. To this day I caution any young lady who is headed in the modeling direction to not always buy into what the agencies are telling them, as they could take all of their money and then chew them up. It's a brutal career and quite challenging if you are not realistic.

I especially remember participating in a modeling job that caught me off guard. There were several well-known hair dressers, mostly from New York, that came from all over the country to show off their new hair fashion ideas. Not knowing the full details of what the show was about, I signed up. I signed documents that gave the professionals permission to do whatever they wanted to do with my hair. In my thinking I thought that they would do a color treatment or maybe style my hair a bit differently. What else could they possibly do to my hair?

The next thing I knew I was up on stage and in front of a few hundred people and I was meeting my stylist for the first time. I was seated in the styling chair and then it happened. My long hair was falling to the floor all around me. Yes, the stylist was cutting off my long hair! I knew that I had to remain professional and not shed any tears, even though I couldn't believe what was happening! To make matters worse the hair design that he did on my head drew rave reviews. I was asked to come back that evening and join him on stage at the evening dinner gala so he could show off my new do. I was not a happy camper. Needless to say, I never signed up for any more of those kinds of shows again!

## It Was Still a Man's World

When I first started out in my career it was so hard to break into some of the positions that I wanted. It was still a man's world and most of the upper management positions were held by men only. It was not until a few years after I had been working that I started seeing women holding upper management positions. They held the positions but not with equal pay! A lot of demands were placed upon women during that time just so they would have to work harder to prove themselves. Sometimes the demands went far beyond what any man would ever have had to prove. Needless to say, I had a few run-ins with some of the men who demanded so much, most of which were quite amusing. Let me share with you just a few of those stories.

### "THE UNWARRENTED GESTURES"

One of the early positions that I held was a clerk at the courthouse in a public office. It was one of the most sought after positions ever on the earth, the auto license department! (Do you sense my sarcasm here?) I held that position long before computers were introduced. If you think the lines are long now, you should have seen the lines back then!

My first year there was really great and I had a wonderful boss. He knew my father and he had such a gentle spirit about him. He was so kind and fair and I was really sad when he had lost the next election.

Then *he* came in as the new boss! *He* turned out to be quite the charmer, or so he thought. It didn't take long before the sexual harassments started. Everyone complained about his wandering eyes, his unprovoked touches, and his dirty mind. Just spending one day with him at work, you wanted to go take a shower! Please!!

I had had enough of his activity so before I left my employ, I had a meeting in his office and visited with him about his unwarranted gestures and I pretty much told him what I thought about his foolishness. I also mentioned some of the illegal *"things"* that I had noticed going on around the office, but when I left his office he patted me on the bottom right in front of his secretary! That dirty old man was lucky that I didn't lose it and put him on the ground. When I walked by his secretary she quickly hung her head down pretending that she didn't see a thing.

About a year later I saw him on television during a live interview. He was sitting with his wife in their living room.

"Why would I have hamburger at work, when I can have steak at home?" he stated.

Yep, some brave ladies had turned him in for sexual harassment and they had come forward to testify at a hearing. I didn't find out until later that some of the ladies were trying to find me to ask if I would testify but they had lost a way to contact me. After all of the testimonies were heard and the hearing was over, he was found guilty and would no longer be allowed to hold a public office.

### "GET RID OF HER!"

At one time I was a personnel manager of a large store. The manager told me that he had hired me because he liked that I was spunky. He was one of those egotistical men who really thought a lot about himself!

I was responsible for about seventy-five employees and I would hire people on the spot as I needed them. I remember that there was one young lady who kept bugging me for months to hire her. She would frequently stop in to check on her application, and in her persistence, she started to become a nuisance. One day I decided to give her a chance and hired her for the jewelry department. It turned out to be a great decision on my part because she was wonderful!

A few days after I had hired her, Mr. Boss man called me into his office.

"I was walking by the jewelry counter and something *barked* at me this morning," he stated.

It took me awhile to figure out what he meant but I finally caught on to what he was implying.

"Get rid of her!" he shouted.

I remained as calm as I could under such circumstances and told him that if he wanted to fire her he would have to be the one to do it himself. I then stood up and walked out of his office. He never did fire her!

## "HE REFUSED TO SHAKE MY HAND"

I was a soft-lines manager at a large department store and I really did like my position, however the hours were quite brutal. One day we were told that the big bosses were coming in to take a tour of the store. We spent several days getting everything ready so that the store looked perfect. Our boss had us all stay until four a.m. the night before the visit just to make sure that the store was perfect, then we had to be back to work at six a.m.! That was barely two hours of sleep! Needless to say, I was tired.

The day of the tour was the longest day ever and it seemed like it was taking forever for the big bosses to start the tour for my area of the store. By midafternoon, I had fallen asleep on a ladder in the back room while I was waiting. Finally, late afternoon, it was my turn! I had never met any of the big bosses before so I was kind of anxious. When my boss introduced me to the big boss I offered to shake his hand, but he refused to accept the gesture. Even though he had never met me before I could tell that he didn't like me *at all*.

As the tour progressed through all of my departments I could tell that the big boss was trying to trip me up with his snide remarks. At one point he pointed out a pink men's dress shirt that I had on display and snidely asked me what I thought about the color. All right, I was tired and getting very lippy and my attitude was disintegrating fast.

"*It's a pink shirt,*" I answered sarcastically.

When we moved on to another department he asked another annoying question, but that time my boss stepped in and started answering the questions. My boss was a smart man! He knew me well enough to know that I was about to lose it with that person.

That big boss couldn't find anything wrong with my half of the store, so I felt that the tour went well. My boss however, was sweating bullets when he saw my attitude starting to go awry. As for me, I was a little bit perplexed by that man's attitude towards me. I went home that evening totally worn out and beat down, so I cried.

The next day I called the soft-lines manager at our other store across town just to see how her encounter with him went. Mainly I wanted to find out what I had done to set him off. She started laughing!

"Debra, you don't *know*?" she said. "I should have filled you in!"

I did not see what was so funny at the time but I found out from her that that big boss did not like tall women! She, being over six foot herself had already experienced that and just hadn't let me in on the secret! His whole attitude towards me boiled down to that! He was only about five-foot four inches tall, and had issues with tall women. *Really*?!

### "ANOTHER SHORT MAN"

At one store I was actually fired because I was too tall! I had been hired as an assistant manager for a store and a year later the store manager had to move from the area because her husband had been transferred. I had an excellent work record at that store and thought that I would be promoted into the store manager position. The district manager who had originally hired me was moved to another district leaving us with a new district manager who did not like me from the get-go! Again, another short man!

When the time drew closer for the store manager to leave her position she called me in to have a meeting with her. She was in tears. She had been told by the district manager to fire me but she told him that she had no reason to let me go and said that if he wanted me fired, he would have to do it himself. He in turn told her that he would not write her a letter of recommendation unless she fired me. That left her in a spot.

During the firing she cried the whole time. When she was done, she stopped and looked at me.

"Say something, cry, or do something," she said.

Of course I didn't cry and I didn't even ask any questions. I knew what it was all about so I quietly handed her my keys and left. Of course I didn't take it lying down! Being spunky, I decided to consult with a lawyer. I contacted the home office and discussed with them what had happened as well. The home office did their investigation and offered to hire me back, but I refused. I had actually found another job and a better job at that. The district manager, well, he was let go and ended up working for his mother...in her *flower shop*!

## "MADDER THAN A JUNK YARD DOG"

The better job that I had found had its challenges as well, especially when I found out that all of the male managers had a bet going on that I wouldn't last very long as one of the assistant managers.

"Once she breaks a fingernail, or ruins one of her pretty blouses, she will be out of here!" one of them had stated.

Boy, were they so wrong about me! All they saw on the outside was a la-tee-da woman. They didn't know what I was really made of!

One day, while I was still pretty new at my job, the male managers all hid when the buzzer rang at the dock. I was on the sales floor moving shelves around and realized that no one was answering the dock door. I immediately put everything down and headed for the back not realizing that the male managers were hiding on the dock setting me up. They already knew about the temperament of that particular truck driver who was coming that day. The truck driver didn't like it if the dock doors were not opened immediately. These managers were setting me up to see if I would live through the thrashing that the truck driver would certainly give me.

I yanked on the chain to open the overhead door and standing there right in front of me was a very mad truck driver. He was as mad as a junk yard dog and looked and smelled like one as well. That driver went to cursing at me so I slammed the overheard door down between the two of us, barely missing his feet.

"You can't do that!" he yelled through the door. "I am on a schedule!"

I hollered back through the door, "If you start acting like a gentleman then I will open the door."

That was when the test of wills started and needless to say he had to cave if he wanted his truck unloaded! I never had any more problems with him after that. Imagine that! Of course the men that had hid and had watched the whole ordeal all came out of hiding laughing their fool heads off.

"Wow, you really showed him!" they exclaimed.

Within a month I was promoted to store manager. I was also given a store that needed a lot of work, but I was up for the challenge. One of the big bosses who had been hearing about my accomplishments decided to fly in on his private jet to give me a visit. I had never met him before and had only talked with him on the phone a few times so I really did not know what to expect.

He arrived a bit early at the store and obviously was eager to get the visit over with. I introduced myself to him as he shook my hand. He then walked with me through the entire store and didn't say a word, not one single word. I almost felt like I was having a military inspection! When we found ourselves back at the front door, he finally spoke.

"Pretty good looking store, for a X&@#* woman!!" he exclaimed.

And that was all that he said, and then he left. He hopped on his jet and away he flew. A few months later I was promoted to area manager.

Those early years were full of many learning experiences; I call them bumps in the road of opportunities. Don't get me wrong, I have had many good men that I have worked for, it was just that era in time and my stories are far too familiar for the many women who had tried to break into the man's world back in those days.

## "THEY SET HER UP TO FAIL"

My husband Mr. X and I at one time had friends that insisted that I give their daughter a job. It would only be a part-time job because she was still in high school. My hiring her was definitely going against my personal rules to never hire friends or relatives, but I ended up giving her a try anyway.

She did catch on pretty quickly and I never saw any problems. She was getting along with everyone and was very dependable. I didn't think too much more about that hiring except that I had broken my own rules.

Many months later after a heavy sales day our whole team was working very late one evening trying to put the store back together again. The team started at one end of the store and worked their way through the entire store. When I walked past the girl I knew, I just knew that something wasn't right. *How did I know?* At that moment I had no clue as to how I knew; I just knew that she was getting ready to shop lift. I called the loss prevention team and discussed with them the possibility that something was about to go down. The team had worked with me for quite some time and they didn't question me. They knew that I was probably right. As a team we hatched a plan but because of the nature of my relationship with the girl I asked them to not arrest her in front of the other employees, and they agreed. I dismissed her earlier than the others.

At first I couldn't quite figure out how she was going to pull it off, but lo and behold, I found a stash that she had put together at the fitting room desk and it was quite a nice stash of merchandise. I decided to hide in the fitting room next to the desk while standing on a bench so that she couldn't see my feet. I waited and listened until she came to retrieve her stash tucking the merchandise into her purse. I then alerted the loss prevention team and they made the arrest quietly, but that wasn't the end of it.

When the police arrived, she started singing like a canary. We discovered that over the past few months she had stolen over ten thousand dollars' worth of merchandise! She even mentioned that I had almost caught her in the act one night when she had put on several outfits underneath her own clothes!

With further investigation the police discovered that she had priors for shoplifting and her parents knew about it. I became furious! How dare they set their own daughter up to fail! It was like taking an alcoholic to a bar! Fortunately the courts waived jail time and placed her on probation for several years, with the condition that she was to receive help for her kleptomania diagnosis.

## "DID I REALLY CATCH A MURDERER?"

One evening I was the only manager on duty so I had to be available to take care of *problems*. Oh joy! In other words, it was up to me to take care of angry customers, disgruntled employees, or anything else that might get broken, twisted, or bent.

I was eventually called to the electronics department to approve a check, and when I arrived in the department I was met by a very large mountain type of a man that even I had to look up to; he was huge! He was much taller than me and built like a double wide football player. I don't know why I refused to take his check for the television that he wanted to purchase, but again, I knew that I knew that something was up.

Usually in those cases you could count on having a pretty good fight on your hands when you refused to take a check from someone, but he didn't say a word. He didn't get mad and go all ballistic on me. When I started to walk away something told me to turn around and take a good look at him again. As I turned around I saw him just standing there watching me walk away. It was then that I knew that I had to alert security because I knew that something was up. I asked them to follow the guy out into the parking lot. Security not only followed him to the parking lot, they got in their cars and followed him across the street to another store. Our security men quickly called the store that he was entering into to let them know that the man was probably going to try to purchase a television set and to try and detain him as long as they could until the police could arrive.

When the police arrived, he was arrested without incident. The police had run his tags and found out that he was wanted for *murder*! When they searched his vehicle it was full of electronics, paid with hot checks from all over town. Security couldn't wait to tell me what they had uncovered. I was getting a little nervous as they told me the story.

"Hey, um, he doesn't know, um, that I am the one that got him arrested, *does he*?" I slowly inquired.

### People Behaving Badly

Working with the public renders all kinds of opportunities to watch people behave badly. I have always said that everyone should have to work in the fast-food industry or retail at least once in their lives so that they can witness what really goes on. Maybe then, they themselves might have a little bit more understanding and forgiveness in their hearts before unleashing their fury upon some poor innocent clerk or waitress. Here are just a few stories of people behaving badly.

### "THEY ARE NOT RESTROOMS"

As far as fitting rooms go, you know that they are just really provided for trying on clothes, *right*? You would not believe how many times I discovered that some thought that they were restrooms! Yuckeeeeeee!

## "WE STOOD TOE TO TOE"

One Christmas holiday evening, at a toy store I managed, the check-out lines were very long. To add to the confusion and anxiety the newspaper had printed the wrong price for a very popular toy. They printed a retraction and corrected the error the next day, but one man was not very accepting of the correction story. He wanted the toy at the ridiculous low price of basically almost free. He was drunk and we ended up standing toe to toe with each other as he yelled at me, spraying me with his smelly saliva and vocabulary. His poor embarrassed wife was pulling on his arm trying to get him to back down from me and the next thing I knew, he was going up and down the aisle that we were standing in throwing all of the merchandise on the floor! I firmly asked him to leave the store or I would be calling the police. His wife finally convinced him to leave without further incident and without a purchase! I didn't know it at the time, but my brother was in the store watching the whole incident and he was ready to jump into action to my defense if the drunk had started swinging at me.

## "HILARIOUS CROOKS"

One evening I had two ladies come into a leather store that I was working at and they both were wearing full skirts and leotards. I learned that their goal was to shoplift four leather jackets by placing two each between their legs inside of their leotards. As they exited the store I realized what they had done so I chased them. I knew that I didn't have much of a chance of catching them especially when I ran past mall security and they were *clueless!* (Sometimes you just can't get good help!)

I continued the chase outside in the dark parking lot on my own. As I ran after them, I started laughing as I watched them trying to run with those coats tucked between their legs. Oh my goodness, what a sight! It was actually worth the chase just to see *that*! They finally rounded a dark corner and I stopped my pursuit.

## "DID I INTIMIDATE HIM?"

I do realize that pastors are human too, but, we usually expect them to act, well, kinder!

One day I was sitting in my office and I overheard a bunch of loud yelling going on out on the sales floor. Pretty soon a young clerk who had been working on the sales floor came to my office in tears.

"Would you please come and deal with this person?" she sniffled.

I crossed my arms and hit the sales floor ready to do battle. As I reached the man who I soon recognized as a pastor, I looked down upon him.

"Why are you yelling, and why are you making my poor sales associate cry?" I *loudly* asked.

I must have intimidated him because he suddenly developed a quick attitude adjustment, and for the better!

## "YOU JUST CAN'T FIX STUPID"

A would-be hooded robber in an oversized winter coat, in the middle of summer mind you, truly didn't know what he had just walked into! I was on him in a flash and he didn't even have a chance. Sometimes you just cannot fix stupid!

The man's first mistake was that he parked his running vehicle in front of my store with his car tag facing me, all for his quick get-a-way. Duh! Then, after he entered the store, he realized that my store was full of customers. He had missed checking out the back parking lot, it was full of cars! When the shoppers caught on as to what was taking place they wouldn't leave the store and that was when he started getting very nervous. He then decided to buy some expensive items with a hot check;

all the while he was trying to charm me with his nervous conversation. I in turn was charming him out of all kinds of information as well. I was trying to calm him down with my words by being friendly so that he wouldn't pull a hidden gun out of his coat. When I asked for his I.D. he actually showed it to me. Duh! Again!

My goal was to get him out of the store as quickly as possible so I allowed him to leave with about five hundred dollars' worth of stolen merchandise. I just wanted him out of the store so that no one would get hurt. The police couldn't believe how much information that I had pulled out of him. Yep, I picked him out of one of the mug books as he had prior convictions. By the time we went to court all of his drug arrests took precedence over my case. The court did order him to pay me back but I was wondering how that would be possible since he was going away to prison for a very long time.

My father always said that most criminals are really nice friendly people that just make stupid mistakes! Yep, the world is full of colorful people and you gotta' love 'em…because the Bible says so!

## My Cleaning Business

One of the goals that I had in life was to have my own business before the age of thirty. Of course my dream was to have a dress shop, but, oh well I obtained part of my goal!

At the age of twenty-nine, and being inspired by my father and his new business, I finally decided to start my own business. I was so tired of working a tremendous number of hours for others, so I chose to work for myself. In doing so, I worked more hours…does that make any *sense* to you? My father's original business was carpet cleaning, and he was doing quite well with it. I decided that I would start my own home and office cleaning service.

When I mentioned to a few of my friends what I was going to do, I didn't receive a whole lot of positive support for the idea.

*"A cleaning business,* are you *crazy?"* one friend stated. "You're the type that belongs on a yacht, drinking champagne, and having someone clean *for you!"* he said as he laughed.

My own fiancé, the fireman, had a hard time with it too.

"What am I supposed to tell people that you do, clean *toilets* for a living?" he stated.

I sensed that he was a little embarrassed by my business adventure idea. Yes, people thought that I was crazy, and that was all I needed for me to set out to prove them all wrong!

The early startup of my cleaning business was very humble, to say the least. I only had a few dollars to work with and most days I had to make a decision whether to put five dollars' worth of gas in my car or make more flyers to hand out. Yes, I walked the streets of Wichita, Kansas, handing out flyers in many neighborhoods that I wanted to work in.

As I started adding more clients, I would go clean and then hit the streets again in my spare time, handing out more flyers. Eventually I was able to add a few big business accounts, and before I knew it, I had been in business for six months and needed to hire some help.

My business grew very quickly and I added more services to the menu which became a big hit, and before long I had twenty-five employees and I was working with several contractors as well. My father referred people to me and I in turn referred people to him. Sometimes we ended up on the same job together. It was so much fun working with dad. He would sometimes help me with some of my larger projects especially if I would be working late into the night.

Cleaning homes can have some interesting challenges. Trust me, not everyone lives the same way you do. Some folks have some strange habits and issues. I mean that in a funny, weird, ha-ha, and sometimes scary way. Don't worry, this is not a tell-all book because there will be no names mentioned. Here are just a few of my stories.

## "HER DOG HAD SECRETS!"

Some of the strangest most interesting stories I have to tell all come from the house pets that we had to deal with.

I was cleaning a shower stall and had set everything that was in the shower out on the floor behind me. When I was ready to put the items back in the shower I turned around and noticed that the bar of soap was missing! I was the only one in the house except for the dog. The dog had a habit of giving me a hard time and would drag the trash bags all around the house and dump them. The dog would try to eat my sweeper attachments and be rather ornery, as I was apparently the highlight of that dog's day. Surely the dog did not take the bar of soap, or so I thought. I went on a hunt for the dog and sure enough, she was eating the bar of soap and wouldn't give it back to me. I was still pretty new at the cleaning business and all kinds of thoughts were going through my head. Great, the homeowner will think that I stole the soap or worse yet, the dog is going to die or be terribly sick and in a *really bad way*. Can you get my drift here?

It took a while for me to gather my thoughts but I knew that I had to call the homeowner. As scared as I was, I made the call. The lady of the house started laughing so hard when I told her what happened with the dog.

"Don't worry about it!" she stated. "She does that all the time."

I wish she would have let me in on the dog's secrets!

## "AN UNSEALED URN"

One of the ladies on my cleaning staff was cleaning an upscale home when she called me in a panic one day.

"Debra, there is something wrong with the dog, she is acting weird!" she exclaimed.

I told her that I would try to get a hold of the homeowner to let them know that their dog could be sick, but I couldn't reach anyone at all. The next thing I knew, my employee called me back.

"Debra, I was running the sweeper and the dog died on the floor!" she shouted.

Great! We killed a dog with a heart-attack! The dog must have gotten scared because of the sweeper. Great! Just great! I still couldn't reach anyone to warn them that they could be walking into a C.S.I scene that evening when they returned home from work!

The next day I was finally able to reach the homeowners.

"Ah, she was old anyways, so don't worry about it," the homeowner stated.

The homeowners had their dog cremated and decided to place the urn on their fireplace mantel but they didn't seal the urn...and you guessed it, the next week my employee had a bit of an accident and some of the dog's ashes were in the sweeper. I didn't bother to tell the home-owner about that one because I was experiencing a bit of shock myself!

## "A CAT WITH AN INFERIORITY COMPLEX"

One of my homeowners had a very beautiful white Persian cat. I don't care much for cats and basically I am allergic to them. I don't know too much about cats but it just seemed like that cat was very persnickety. I was told that the cat would probably hide from me and there wouldn't be any problems with her. At least there weren't any problems on my end, but I ended up giving the poor thing an inferiority complex!

One day I was coming up the basement stairs and I met the cat straight on, face to face. She stood on the landing at the top of the stairs. Seeing the cat in her *condition* simply made me bust out loud and laughing so hard because someone had gone and shaved that poor cat, leaving only the fluffy head unshaven. Yes, you guessed it. The cat got its feelings hurt when I laughed, and I ended up hearing about it from the owner. Oh, *brother*!

## "GLASS BALLS FLYING EVERYWHERE"

I had a few home accounts that became my favorites. The homeowners were very wonderful to work for.

One of the homeowners that I had worked with for some time had asked me to clean their home for a Christmas party. I never really had any problems in that particular home with their cat, at least not until Christmas time. The home was decorated very nicely for the holidays and as I was cleaning, I noticed that a glass ball had fallen off of the Christmas tree and it had broken. I cleaned the mess up and didn't think anything more about it. A little bit later I found two more broken balls on the floor. I left them, but I wondered what was going on. Ah, the cat was hiding in the tree!

When I started the sweeper up, that cat went all *skitzy* on me! Glass balls were flying off of the tree and breaking as they hit the floor. Great! Cat, you are going to get me fired! I very timidly called the homeowner to let her know what had happened with their cat.

"Oh, just leave the mess, the cat does that all the time," she stated.

I don't know, but my thoughts would be to maybe use plastic ornaments next time? Just sayin'!

## "TACKY PAPER AND A MOUSE"

I am not very fond of mice even though they are sort of cute when you really take a close look at them.

I was training a new lady at one of our house accounts. She was someone who I had known for quite some time and she eventually became my office assistant for the business.

We were busy cleaning and all was quiet. I was in the bathroom cleaning and she had taken on the chore of cleaning the kitchen when all of a sudden I heard a blood curdling scream, and the scream didn't stop. I went running to her thinking that she was being attacked, and lo and behold, she had reached under the sink to grab the trash can and her rubber glove had gotten stuck to the tacky paper that was under the sink. Of course, there was a live mouse stuck to that tacky paper!

When I arrived at the kitchen door, I saw that poor woman jumping up and down flapping her hands, with a mouse stuck to her glove! She had a red face, wide open startled eyes, and her mouth was wide open screaming. Her loud screaming was continuous, and boy, did I wish I had had a camera!

I finally was able to calm her down enough to help her out. That poor mouse had taken the ride of its life with her. We eventually got the glove unstuck and I threw the tacky paper with the mouse attached in the dumpster that sat right outside of the kitchen door. I thought quite ill of the homeowners for killing mice that way. It seemed like a cruel way of starving them to death.

After all of the excitement it took my friend a bit of time to finish cleaning the kitchen, so every once in a while I would open the kitchen door where the dumpster was located.

*"Help me! Help me!"* I would quietly say in my little tiny mouse voice.

She didn't see the humor at all with me making fun of her and the incident.

The next day the homeowner called and asked me if we had found the tacky paper under the sink. I informed her that yes we did find it and threw it out because there was a mouse stuck to it.

"Oh, no!" she exclaimed. "We take the mice off of the tacky paper with oil and put them in a cage and then we take them to a field and let them go."

I thought to myself, *you have got to be kidding; I am the mouse killer, not the homeowner*?!

## "THE MOUSE HOUSE"

I have learned that some people live just a little bit differently than most of us do. I was contacted by one such person.

A man wanted to put his house up for sale and needed to have it cleaned. It was usually my custom to meet with the homeowners to quote a price, but because that house was out of town, I shot him an estimate over the phone with the understanding that the price could change, especially if we realized that more was involved. He agreed, so I sent a team out the next day to his house. My team called me and stated that they could not get into the house because there was a very large unhappy dog on the other side of the front door.

The homeowner was not happy when he discovered that his house did not get cleaned that day, but he did agree to pin the dog up so that we could clean the house the next day. That time I decided to go with the team to make sure that there were no further problems. I was concerned that the homeowner was not the least bit worried about my cleaning team being bitten by a Boxer; that kind of bothered me.

When I drove up to the front of his house, it looked to me like the Adam's Family was living there. When my team and I went inside the house, and I kid you not, we held each other's arms as we walked from room to room checking out the mess. I really thought that we might have a chance of finding someone dead in that house.

We found each room to be very filthy with piles of cigarette ashes on the floors almost a foot and a half tall. There were no ashtrays. These piles were found beside the chairs and around the toilet stools. The three leveled home was very dark, dusty, used up, and even looked abandoned. Dog hair was piled up about three inches high all around the queen sized mattress that lay directly on the bedroom floor. The double kitchen sink was loaded all the way to the counter top with a huge mouse nest with dead mice all mixed in it.

We should have known better that to open the cabinets because there were live mice and their nests all mixed in with the food items. That house quickly became known as the *mouse house.* There were dead mice everywhere, and in everything.

It took our team three days to clean up the mess. That was of course before we knew about the toxic danger of working with mice and their droppings. We had to disinfect all of our equipment when the job was done. I had just assumed that it was a house that no one had lived in for a while.

About halfway through the cleaning job, the homeowner called me and was upset that it was taking so long to clean. After all, he wanted to come home to a clean house.

"*What*?" I asked. "You actually *live* in that house?"

"Well, yes," he answered quite seriously.

I then had a feeling that even though he was the mayor of that small town, we were working with someone whose elevator did not go all the way to the top. So, it really wasn't any surprise that he stiffed me for the bill either.

## My Real Challenges Were People

Even though the animals provided some great entertainment the homeowners were sometimes the greater challenges. We worked for some really well known, high profile people in our community as well as some plain old ordinary folk. It didn't matter their status or lifestyle because some just had unusual ways, hang-ups, quirks, and often strange requests. Some places were filled with maggots and feces while other places looked like they had been cleaned before we had arrived. We would sometimes catch many homeowners off guard some days because they had totally forgotten that we were coming!

Walking in on affairs, finding adult items that should have been tucked away, and other strange findings really added to our amusing work days. Here are just a few of my favorite people stories.

## "AFRAID OF OVEN CLEANER"

A dear sweet lady called one day and she wanted me to clean her apartment and her oven. It sounded like a simple job. When I arrived and started cleaning she followed me all around the entire time I was cleaning, just to make sure that I did it correctly. After I finished cleaning out her oven with an oven cleaner, she had me throw out the sponge that I had used but, it had to be wrapped in five layers of newspaper and two layers of brown paper bag. Apparently she was afraid of oven cleaner?

## "SHE HID HERSELF"

One of our clients was a prominent doctor and his wife. They owned a lovely home. After a few months of cleaning their house my crew was not coming back to the office with the payment. So I asked them what was going on and they stated that when they were ready to leave they could never find the lady of the house to get the payment. They told me that they had looked in the garage and her car was still there, but she was nowhere to be found. I thought that sounded kind of strange.

I decided to go with my crew the next time they went to clean to see what was going on. Sure enough, as soon as it was time to go, the lady of the house had disappeared! It occurred to me that she was hiding out somewhere in the house so that she would not have to pay until it was more convenient for her to mail a check in, which of course, was not our terms and agreement for payment.

After the team had finished cleaning I asked them to load up the equipment and I would be with them shortly. I walked all throughout the house hollering out her name. I started on the top floor and then graduated to the middle floor, then onto the sub middle floor, main floor, and then down to the basement. When I got to the basement, and I'm sure that she thought she was well hidden, I found her standing in a dark room behind a door. Yep, it was a little bit embarrassing for her when I called her out of her hiding place.

"It is time for us to leave," I stated. "Is there anything else that we can do for you today?" I continued on, "If not, I need to collect our payment." I said this very cheerfully, hoping to ease her pain of embarrassment. Needless to say, it never happened again.

### "THE BLUE EYES OF DEATH"

I don't normally get scared very easily or that often, but I did get scared when I visited a house to do an estimate one time. I was given an address that was in a trailer park. The park was located in a fairly decent part of town and was somewhat new. It did take me a while to drive around and find the exact lot, and when I finally arrived, I was greeted at the door by a friendly elderly lady. She motioned for me to enter in as she closed the door behind me. It was totally dark inside and it took me a while to adjust to the dim sunlight that filtered in through the dark closed blinds. It was creepy, and little did I know, we were not alone.

As soon as she started taking me through the house, I could see well enough in the dark to know that it was not a job that I would be willing to take on. It was just too nasty.

She eventually led me to a bedroom that was at the front of the house where she positioned herself so that I would have to enter the bedroom before her. She blocked the doorway and I felt trapped as I was standing between her and a very creepy man who was basically naked, very obese, filthy, and had long stringy, oily hair that hung down on his face. He had blue eyes of death that stared at me, surveying me up and down. On the inside I could feel my heart thumping faster and faster. I needed to get out of that situation fast. On the outside, I gave the illusion of being as cool as a cucumber and I acted like the man didn't even exist. My conversation didn't even skip a beat as I bowled my way back through the doorway, causing her to have to move out of my way. I left very quickly and without any conversation.

Even though the quote that I had given her was very high and terribly unreasonable she bugged me for weeks to come clean her house. It was just too highly suspicious as far as I was concerned. Every time she called I would tell her that I didn't have any openings, and I didn't, *for her*.

### "DID I JUST FALL OFF THE TURNIP TRUCK?"

I learned very quickly after hiring a cleaning crew that they had their own ideas of what *clean* was. I eventually had to write a training manual so that everyone I hired would be on the same page. There were times that I had some really good help and then there were other times that I had really bad help. I went through a bunch of people initially, but eventually we ended up with a very good core team that worked really well together.

My ladies came from diversified backgrounds. Some were single moms who were just trying to make life work. Some were stay-at-home moms who needed something to do. Some of my help were well off, while some were extremely poor. Some were abused daily by a husband or a boyfriend, while others led a fairytale life. Some made it as one of the team while others were let go because of their unbelievable actions. There were times that I just had to shake my head at some of the things that these ladies had done, and wondered what on earth were they thinking when they pulled some of the stunts that they had pulled. Maybe they thought that I had just fallen off of the turnip truck as they were sometimes greatly surprised to find out that I knew what they had done.

I always had very strict rules about the use of drugs, alcohol, and smoking while on the job. It was a deal breaker if it ever happened. The same held true with theft.

## "A TWENTY DOLLAR BILL"

One day when it was close to closing time, one of my lady's from the team was hanging around the office a little longer than usual. I could tell that she had something on her mind and she was struggling to talk about it. My secretary was able to get her to open up. Apparently she had a work partner that day who decided to smoke pot between jobs and she was afraid to tell me because she was afraid of what the pot-smoker would do to her for telling.

"You know, Debra is pretty good at this kind of stuff," my secretary told her. "Your co-worker will never know that you were the one who told on her."

After my secretary convinced her that she was protected, she then left the office.

"What are you going to do?" my secretary asked as she turned to me.

I just grinned and said, "If she will smoke pot on the job, she will also steal."

I then created a plan that I was sure would work.

The next day I put that gal in a house that I used to basically spy on my employees if I had any doubts about them. It was my brother's house but no one that I sent there knew it was his house, except for the regular cleaning lady. My brother had a babysitter that was at his house all day so I used her to help with the plan.

I arrived at the house early so I could place a twenty dollar bill on the bedroom floor next to the bed so that it looked as if it had fallen off of the night stand. The babysitter made sure that it was still in place when my unsuspecting worker arrived.

Back at the office I had replaced her sweeper bag with a new bag and when she returned from the job I had slit open her sweeper bag to make sure that the bill did not accidentally get swept up. I then called the babysitter and sure enough, the twenty dollar bill was missing.

The next day I called that employee into my office and I asked her if she had found a twenty dollar bill at the house when she had cleaned the day before, because it was missing. She, of course, denied even seeing it at all. I then asked her a few more questions that allowed her to trap herself. I finally told her that I had set her up. The surprised look on her face was priceless! She was let go and never knew that the other co-worker had ever told on her about the pot smoking incident.

### "A NEVER-ENDING BOYFRIEND"

Some of my ladies weren't fortunate enough to have abandonment in their lives. They often faced brutal abuse every day. One such lady was a dear sweet person who had endured a lot from her ex-boyfriend.

She had dumped her abusive boyfriend a long, long time ago, but he just wouldn't go away. He would often break into her house and wait for her to come home, only to beat, rape, and threaten her with death as he would hold a knife to her throat, or a gun to her head. Countless police calls and restraining orders never seemed to keep him away. It only angered him more, and his violence towards her had been going on for years.

One day when she came into work she was especially nervous. Apparently he had threatened to come into my place of business and shoot her that day. I informed her to just go about her work and I assured her that he was not coming in to shoot her.

When she left my office, I turned and caught my secretary's shocked expression.

"Debra, what if he *does* come in today to kill her?" she asked with eyes wide open and with her jaw dropped.

"Well, it *ain't* going to happen today," I emphatically stated.

Unfortunately about a year after that lady had left my employ, she made headline news. Apparently her boyfriend had done it again but that time when he left, she pulled out a shotgun and shot him right there on her sidewalk! Fortunately, he didn't die. Even though she was the one who had been beaten, raped, and threatened with death, she was the one who was arrested, tried, and sentenced.

Social Services contacted me after her trial was over to ask me some questions about her. I was very relieved to know that they were actually trying to get her help by having her placed in a facility that could help her with her P.T.S.D. (Post Traumatic Stress Disorder) At least she would be receiving mental health care, even if it was still in a prison-like setting. Sometimes it just doesn't seem fair how things work out for some people.

## "ABANDONED"

I had a couple of ladies who worked for me that had been abandoned by their husbands and they were left with a mess. One of these ladies called me one morning and told me that she couldn't come to work. She informed me that she and her baby daughter had been abandoned the night before and were left without heat or electricity; they had no winter coats and no food nor money. I told her to come on into work because she needed the money and I let her know that I would have everything that she needed by the end of her shift.

I called one of my friends who owned a daycare and made arrangements for my employee's daughter to be taken care of, for free. During the work day I continued gathering all the things that she needed, including continuous support from local agencies.

That day a very good friendship was born, and it gave me great joy to be able to help her and to watch her grow from that experience as she continued to get her life put back together.